So Your Teen Knows All the Answers...

So Your Teen Knows All the Answers...

An LDS Parents' Survival Guide

Corrie Lynne Player

Covenant Communications, Inc.

Covenant®

Published by Covenant Communications, Inc.
American Fork, Utah

Printed in the United States of America
First Printing: October 1999

06 05 04 03 02 01 00 99   10 9 8 7 6 5 4 3 2 1

ISBN 1-57734-532-0

CONTENTS

PREFACE

I've Been There and Back

You probably picked up this book for one or more of the following reasons:

- You have a chameleon daughter whose black-rimmed eyes and death-white face powder prompt passersby to ask her why she celebrates Halloween in July.
- You have a changeling son who refuses to occupy his bed at night or climb out of it in the morning.
- You've noticed odd creatures slouching out the back door during sacrament meeting.
- You've looked into the upturned face of your toddler and wondered what's going to happen to that sweet innocence in the next nine or ten years.

Congratulations! You have either a teenager or a potential teenager. I know the realization is upsetting, but don't worry about that weird human being who has invaded or will soon invade your life. Actually, I think teenagers have been given a lot of bad press.

They are kind of nutty and they're capable of driving their parents absolutely bonkers within a short period of time. But they're also idealistic and insightful—capable of great love and earth-changing ideas.

FOR SALE: PARENTING EXPERIENCE
(The Price of This Book)

I've been a foster mother to dozens of kids, some of them disturbed or disabled. In addition, I've taught junior-high, high-school and college English to hundreds of twelve- to twenty-year-olds, and I've served on countless committees for youth in the Church and community. But, like every parent before me, I was almost unhinged by the onslaught of my own children's puberty.

When I first decided to write this book, I had managed to raise six kids beyond the terrible teens and had three stuck between thirteen and nineteen: Dolly, twenty-eight; Sherri, twenty-six; Gary Willis, twenty-three; Roch (pronounced "Rock"), twenty-two; Eric, twenty-one; Linda, twenty; Micah, seventeen; Brian, fourteen; and Nathan, thirteen. Obviously, circumstances have changed in the six years it took to write the book.

You'll note that the middle four kids were all born within four years—that was quite an eventful time in my life. I actually thought years of mothering a bunch of babies and toddlers would shape me up for coping with adolescents. After all, *nothing* could be worse than fifteen consecutive years without sleep!

BOY, WAS I WRONG!

When my oldest child, Dolly, entered adolescence, I thought she'd lost her mind. Although she was only two and a half when we adopted her, Dolly's maturity and sensitivity were those of a sixty-three-year-old. I never hesitated to take her with me to weddings, stores, and restaurants. Still a baby herself, she demonstrated a surprising sense of responsibility for her two-month-old sister (whom we also adopted) and each baby born in the next ten years. My friends asked me to Xerox Dolly; she was the perfect child.

Then Dolly turned thirteen. Her room disappeared under a pile of romance novels, shampoo, and eye shadow. She forgot to change her sheets, iron her clothes, and do her homework.

She nearly burned down the house by leaving her curling iron plugged in against a pile of used tissues. She argued with me about who should fold laundry or sweep the front porch. My taste in sweaters, haircuts, and fingernails was hopelessly senile; shopping trips left her red-eyed and me grim-lipped.

Things Could Be Worse

As unsettling as Dolly's transformation was, my oldest son, Gary Willis, disturbed me more. He changed from a smiling, handsome boy who loved to sing and dance in the spotlight to a snarling young man with tangled hair who threw up beer on the bathroom floor.

He locked himself behind a vibrating door decorated with a picture of a bare-fanged attack dog. "Don't Even Try to Come In" was scrawled below it. He never spoke to me except to ask for the car keys or money. If I hugged him or commented on the weather, he pulled away and glared at me as if I'd tried to smear his teeth with squashed flies.

They Really Do Grow Up

As unlikely as it seemed at the time, both Dolly and Gary Willis survived their teen years and turned into well-adjusted adults.

Dolly finished a degree in child development and has worked in a day-care center for disadvantaged and abused children. She also developed and ran her own preschool and became a licensed foster parent with her husband, Roland A. Roy.

She decorates her neat little house with intricately crafted centerpieces and wreathes, makes meatloaf and homemade bread as good as my mother's, and teaches Primary. Dolly's most outstanding achievement, however, was that she and Roland presented me with my first grandchildren: Cameron, Nicholas, Dakota, and Maddie.

Gary Willis has made changes in his life that I never would have suspected. At one time his room qualified for demolition and his bathroom was declared a National Monument to Filth. He tested us on every gospel principle imaginable, and we felt real despair at times.

However, by the time he was nineteen, he washed his own laundry, whipped up gourmet lasagna and spaghetti, and logged hundreds of chauffeuring miles without complaint. He occasionally swooped me up in a shaving-lotion-scented hug and even waxed my car.

When Gary Willis arrived in the Curitiba Brazil Mission, he wrote home that he wanted to "keep every mission rule possible, because I know those rules are for *my* benefit." He also thanked me for throwing him "out of bed every morning," insisting that he finish his chores, and "loving me through it all."

Gary Willis was named assistant to the president and zone leader over two zones simultaneously during the last six months of his mission. He wrote long letters home every week, with occasional tapes of him singing (something he'd refused to do as a teenager). Today, he has a happy temple marriage with Norine, a lovely returned missionary who served in Chile. He is the father of Dolli Grace and Traci Lynne.

For a long time I didn't know quite what to make of Gary Willis, because his changes were so profound. However, I do know that his personal testimony and recognition of Christ as his "best friend" were chiefly responsible for those changes. Although my husband and I can't take much credit for his reformation, we were heartened by the realization that we provided the structure and support he needed at critical periods in his life.

Gary Willis's maturity gave us courage to confront the challenges we continued to face with the rest of our kids.

Another Teenager at My House

Linda, my youngest daughter and sixth child to travel the teen road, was just as mixed up and illogical as her older siblings, but her thirteen-year-old antics amused rather than horrified or bewildered me.

One minute she stood like a stork by the back fence, grabbed her slender foot in both hands and straightened her leg into a graceful pirouette while she gazed at the sun dipping behind the red hills. The next minute she screamed through the house, chasing a little brother who "messed in my stuff and ate every red jelly bean in the bag."

Sometimes Linda sprawled on her rumpled bed to pen tear-stained journal entries, then giggled as she hung on my shoulders and smooched me like a demented guppy. Other times she surprised her brother Roch (who was just as nuts as she was) by washing his sneakers and scrubbing out his shower.

Most of the time, however, Linda's productive efforts were limited to talking on the phone, writing love letters to her current crush, and deciding which of her big brothers' T-shirts to wear shopping.

This, Too, Shall Pass

Linda's soaring emotions (and the volatile emotions of six adolescent brothers) left me undisturbed; I'd been through the same thing before with all the other roller coaster passengers. I knew her tears would soon be smiles.

When she screamed that everybody hated her and it was Roch's fault she'd become a social outcast (because he wouldn't drive her to the mall), I hugged her and told her I loved her.

When she calmed down, I explained the "hormone attack" that made her feel so weird. The culprit was the chemical stew swirling through her veins—not her brothers, sisters, parents, or friends. Linda weathered her teens and turned into the happy wife of a returned missionary and mother of our eighth grandchild.

You'll meet the rest of my kids, including several foster children, in the following pages. Their stories illustrate the different concepts and ideas I'm trying to explain. My children have given me experience in facing every normal (and some not-so-normal) adolescent situation possible.

After many years as parents and counselors who provided a special needs foster home, my husband and I decided we should share our experiences. Our parenting successes (and failures) have been joint efforts, but to simplify things, I wrote most of the book in the first person. I have also changed the names of foster children to protect their privacy.

This book can't give all the answers; psychotic behavior in teenagers is way beyond the book's scope. But we can show those of you whose children only *seem* psychotic how we've survived, and even enjoyed, parenting adolescent people.

We've dealt with the same arguments, lack of logic, and emotional tirades you face, and our kids turned out okay. Of course, we still have a couple who aren't finished yet. And we have a bounteous crop of grandchildren coming up who will continue to provide ample opportunities to test our theories.

Nothing written in this book comes with a guarantee. **The only guarantee I can offer is that God will never disappoint you. Turn to Him and let His love operate in your family, and everything will turn out.**

WHAT'S YOUR PARENTING "STYLE"?

Application of parenting skills differs in almost as many ways as teens differ.

Three general parenting styles are recognized by psychologists:

1.　Autocratic: This kind of parent says things like, "Because I'm the parent—that's why!" "I know best," and "Shut up."

2.　Permissive: This kind of parent says things like, "Do your own thing," "Whatever," and "Don't bother me."

3.　Authoritative: This kind of parent says things like, "Let's figure it out together," "You're important to me," and "I'd like to help you."

Autocratic and permissive parenting styles are opposite extremes—and, as in life, extremes rarely work very well. The authoritative approach is more balanced. Most of us should try to be authoritative with autocratic or permissive tendencies (whichever style suits us best).

HOW THIS BOOK IS ORGANIZED

I've divided this book into fourteen chapters that attempt to answer the six basic questions I hear most often about teenagers.

QUESTION 1. WHAT IS A TEENAGER, ANYWAY?

Their Physical and Mental Changes

Chapter 1, "Defining Adolescence," provides an overview of typical adolescent behavior. It also talks about why "teenagers" are a modern phenomenon and discusses some of the idiosyncracies that crop up. However, this book isn't an adolescent psychology text.

The chapter divides adolescence into phases that correspond to the Young Men/Young Women classes (Beehive/Deacon, MIA Maid/Teacher, Laurel/Priest). I've included a brief discussion of the physical changes that occur during adolescence to help you learn, in general, what to expect from various ages.

Their Health Needs

Chapter 2, "Healthy Teens—Putting Food into Perspective," covers three aspects of the care and feeding of teenagers: (1) what, where, and when food is consumed; (2) rapid growth and special needs of young athletes; and (3) avoidance of eating disorders.

Teenagers' diets require almost as much attention from parents as do the diets of small children. While catering to a teen isn't required, you have to provide well-balanced nutrition and teach cooking skills.

The Word of Wisdom can be a big help in maintaining balance and sanity. I've also given clear guidelines about when you should seek professional or medical help instead of trying to handle a situation alone.

Chapter 3, "Healthy Teens—Establishing Good Sleep Habits," deals with the difficulties of convincing adolescents to turn out the lights before 2:00 a.m. This chapter also refers to the Word of Wisdom while it gives practical tips on maintaining the delicate balance between a kid's independence and his or her need for sufficient sleep: teenagers don't understand that over-sleeping and under-sleeping harm their bodies in ways similar to over-eating and starving.

QUESTION 2. HOW CAN I TEACH SELF-CONTROL?

Chapter 4, "Learning to Talk to Each Other," discusses *communication*, the most important step in developing healthy family relationships. I give specific activities that promote effective listening and focus on communication skills.

Building communication skills requires parents to model the behavior they want their kids to have. Basically, parents need to open the channels of communication, use "I feel" statements (rather than "you"-centered statements), listen effectively, and use appropriate body language and tone of voice.

The rest of the chapter describes how to make the abstract concrete through "The Point System," a method I have developed over the past twenty-five years (and that I have adapted from behavioral modification strategies originally used by group homes). The Point System clarifies parental expectations and eliminates nagging.

Chapter 5, "Developing Self-Esteem and Self-Control," is organized around the "three-legged stool" metaphor for developing self-esteem: (1) feeling appreciated, (2) feeling skillful, and (3) taking responsibility. I give specific ideas and activities that will enhance your child's success in these three areas.

Chapter 6, "Discipline Strategies That Really Work," deals with the necessity of establishing consistent, simple discipline that teaches as it designates boundaries. Disciplining teenagers involves under-standing teen logic, handling anger appropriately (and avoiding con-tention whenever possible), and maintaining consistency.

This chapter also discusses three areas that cause a lot of con-tention: curfews, dress standards, and the telephone.

QUESTION 3. HOW CAN I PREPARE TEENAGERS FOR LIFE AND TEACH THEM TO WORK?

Chapter 7, "Getting the Most Out of School," discusses the great-est influence on maturing teens outside their homes. Although school is primarily the child's responsibility, you can help your children suc-ceed. My experience as a teacher gives insights into the balance between home and school.

This chapter also discusses simple techniques for organizing the school day and effective ways of resolving homework issues and study problems.

Chapter 8, "Raising Responsible Drivers," talks about a main source of family conflict and poverty: a sixteen-year-old with a driver's license. The basic concept, which should be repeated continually as a kid grows up, is that *driving is a privilege, not a right.*

My experience comes from dealing with my nine who have reached driving age. My way to enlightened teen drivers is littered with blown engines, speeding tickets, mangled fenders, and gnawed fingernails. But the same discipline system that brought family har-mony and shaped successful students has produced young drivers who contradict insurance statistics.

Chapter 9, "Convincing Kids to Help Out," gives handy hints designed to help parents convince their capable, but lazy, offspring to do more than indent his pillow or organize her eye makeup by color. Motivated teens can accomplish as much as any adult—but the key word here is *motivated.*

This chapter and the accompanying Appendices contain examples of chore charts and other devices that I've used to effectively teach a work ethic.

QUESTION 4. HOW CAN I STOP THE FIGHTING AND MAKE MY HOME A REFUGE?

Chapter 10, "Diffusing Sibling Rivalry," deals with quarreling siblings and focuses on building family harmony as defined in King Benjamin's address. This chapter is built around correcting common mistakes parents make by emphasizing that mortal life requires living under a paradox. Kids must learn the principles of charity. They must know that emotions can be changed, and they must be encouraged to express their emotions in a positive way. The story of the prodigal son contains a powerful message for families and is especially appropriate.

This chapter also gives concrete pointers for reducing contention and developing a sense of service and love between siblings.

Chapter 11, "Encouraging Suitable Friendships," covers ideas about helping your kids develop and maintain friendships. It delves into the touchy subjects of what to do when a destructive friendship leads to conflicts with family and society. It addresses the equally important concern over what to do when a young person seems to be rejected by peers or has trouble maintaining a friendship.

QUESTION 5. HOW CAN I TEACH ETERNAL VALUES AND TESTIMONY IN AN IMMORAL WORLD?

Chapter 12, "Talking Straight About Morality," discusses developing and maintaining morality in an immoral society. Violent and depraved videos, explicit television programs, and X-rated magazines and books illustrate the overwhelming obstacles for families who want to be "in the world, but not of the world." It teaches ways parents can guide their teenagers through the dangers of premature sexual activity and give them strength to build healthy, loving relationships.

This chapter also covers sane, sensible advice about relying on gospel standards to eliminate drug use, including alcohol and tobacco. Rejecting behaviors that lead to lung cancer, drunk driving, and AIDS takes standing up to peer pressure and courage—courage that comes when you are firm and clear about your own standards.

Parents who keep their baptismal and temple covenants shine as examples that their children will usually follow. But active, faithful members can't automatically expect their children will never make mistakes. Relying on personal inspiration and the principles of repentance are absolutely necessary if you want to succeed.

And sometimes, no matter how hard you try, you may experience grief and sorrow because of the actions of your children. When such sorrow comes, however, you can be at peace, knowing you did your best and that your children are responsible for exercising their own free agency.

Chapter 13, "Strengthening Testimonies," discusses how parents can help their youth develop strong, personal testimonies. Breaking away, growing up, and cutting ties are all necessary stages of growth, but they don't need to involve breaking a commitment to the gospel.

This chapter discusses sticky issues such as whether or not to force a kid to attend Church meetings or participate in activities. I share the methods Gary and I have successfully used, methods that resulted in the temple marriages of seven of our nine children and the temple worthiness of the two who are not yet married. I also talk about different methods that have worked for other parents. The chapter focuses on the right of all parents to personal inspiration when handling problems in their own homes.

Chapter 14, "Forging Eternal Family Ties," discusses connecting with extended family through organizing successful family reunions and family councils. Teenagers need to understand their place in the eternal scheme of things.

The chapter discusses some of the rewards that come from parenting a large, varied family. The last twenty years of struggling with kids between twelve and twenty finally flipped on a light in my brain. Now I *know* why Heavenly Father suckers people into having babies and keeps secret the bewildering facts about teenagers. I think you'll chuckle and agree with my revelation.

AFTERWORD: "MY NEST RUNNETH OVER"

People ask me how I ever get all my kids out the door in the morning almost as often as they ask, "Are they all yours?" or, referring to our special-needs foster home for troubled teens, "Are you insane? Who in her right mind would *choose* a bunch of teenagers?"

While I can't imagine ever suffering from "empty nest syndrome," I know the time will come when our food budget and car insurance bills no longer resemble the national debt. My shampoo and conditioner will cease evaporating at the speed of light, and I'll be able to fall asleep without setting my curfew alarm.

SMILES ARE THE FLIP SIDE OF TEARS

After a talk I gave on coping with adolescents at a women's conference, one mother approached me. Through clenched teeth she said, "You make it all sound so funny and light-hearted. Have you ever had to face the really awful stuff?"

She went on to tell me that her sixteen-year-old son, an alcoholic, had been kicked out of every school within commuting distance. He now lived with his father, who couldn't control him any more than she could. We talked for a long time.

I told her I'd dealt with foster kids and counseling clients who'd been jailed for burglary and drunk driving, who had molested children, and who'd been suicidal. Obviously, certain things are much less laughable than others.

Sometimes no matter how hard you try, you won't be able to help kids with serious emotional or psychological problems—you must turn to doctors, psychologists, and the law. And sometimes you must separate yourself physically and emotionally from circumstances that could destroy the rest of the family.

When dismal situations developed, I could have become very depressed, but instead I chose not to. I do know the heartbreak that comes from doing my best when my best just wasn't good enough.

Earthquake and hurricane victims use humor to deal with their incomprehensible situations. I think parents of teenagers have an equal need for humor.

Whatever your stage of parenting, I hope this survival guide helps you figure out areas of control and spot problems before they develop. May you delight in the good times and endure the bad times with a bit of laughter.

Most of all, I hope my approach to the whole adventure of parenting teens reassures you that your Heavenly Father is in control; He loves you and He loves your children—and He will always be there for you.

Trust Him, go to Him in prayer frequently; then, act on the gentle promptings you receive. The gospel is true, and clinging to it is the only way to peace and happiness.

Now, relax and read on.

What is a Teenager?

CHAPTER 1

Defining Adolescence

If young couples gazed into each other's eyes and murmured, "Let's have a teenager" instead of "Let's have a baby," very few children would be born. But LDS parents continue to have babies, and those "little blessings" turn into teenagers.

Thousands of couples who "asked for the privilege of bearing children" in the last decade of the twentieth century will be faced with teenagers in the twenty-first. Most of them are terrified of the prospect that their sweet-smelling bundle or charming toddler will turn into a purple-haired creature from another planet.

SOMETHING NEW ON THE SCENE

The main reason teenagers are so puzzling and difficult to handle is because they occupy a ten-year period between childhood and adulthood that didn't exist a hundred years ago. Modern industry, schooling, and antibiotics have combined to produce an extended period of apprenticeship, where children try out various personalities (and where they help their parents test the Lord's principle of "endure to the end").

In the not-too-distant past, kids lucky enough to survive whooping cough and malnutrition quickly established their own families. It wasn't unusual for people to marry at the age of fourteen. Because people entered old age in their forties, nobody had time to worry about adolescence.

Your Worst Nightmare . . .

Over the last thirty-four years, as my kids competed for lap space and lunch money, I've had few moments to wonder why I have nine children. But I have occasionally wondered what I've gotten myself into—and why.

Aside from the fact that we have been told that children are wonderful blessings, why should grown people who finally have it all together want to link their lives with kids? Anyone who gives the matter much thought knows that children come from outer space, and—as comedienne/writer Jean Kerr puts it—"They're all a little bit nuts."

Adolescence is that period of child-rearing that your friends are always warning you to "just wait until." All of us who are mired in arguments over curfew, car insurance rates, deafening rock music, and Church attendance look back on 2:00 a.m. feedings with nostalgia.

New parents of infants are expected to be bewildered, but most parents of a hairy fourteen-year-old are more confused. Just because kids have already cluttered up the house for an extended period of time doesn't mean they are any *easier* to be around.

Teenagers are a paradox—part infant, part child, and part adult. I've watched all three aspects of the adolescent personality flicker through some of my kids in the space of two minutes.

I'm sure those of you with a teenager or two have had the same experience. Just when you're ready to break out the strained carrots and teething bibs, your adolescent stops blowing bubbles in her root beer long enough to wash the living room windows and polish the fireplace screen.

Then she throws her arms around you, declares, "You're the best mom (dad) in the whole world!" and dances out of the room. A minute later she slouches back, frowning and munching on a candy bar. Crumbs of chocolate and bits of wrapper litter the carpet in her wake.

Why Didn't We Just Settle for a Puppy? Or a Guppy?

Why sacrifice the best years of your life and ninety percent of every dollar you will ever earn? Human children hang around longer than any other living creatures. Even elephants manage to leave home by the time they're twelve or thirteen.

Teenagers bring the *empty-headedness, destructiveness,* and *down-right dumbness* of every other childhood stage to new heights:
1. They need archaeological dig directions to find their closets.
2. Their idea of a good time is muttering, "Gross," "Dude!" or "I could just die" into a surgically implanted telephone.
3. Most of them are unable to find dishwasher soap, vacuum cleaners, algebra books, or socks.
4. But their skills at tracking the car keys, Mom's chocolates, and little brother's piggy bank are awesome.

Teenagers have no more sense of their own mortality than toddlers or grade-schoolers. They scale barbed-wire fences marked "Danger" for the sheer joy of penetrating a forbidden zone. The fact that they might be fried by a high-voltage transformer never crosses their minds.

Teenagers would also rather be "cool" than warm. During the winter, teenagers who live in Anchorage, Alaska, do not admit to owning bulky coats or fleece-lined boots. Their counterparts in Tulsa, Oklahoma, or Cedar City, Utah, deny possession of umbrellas, rubber boots, and raincoats.

Male—Female—Finding a Common Ground

My children's adoptions and births spanned the decades from the sixties to the eighties. I also cared for dozens of foster children during that time. As the kids came along, I did my best to follow trendy guidelines for eliminating inequities between the sexes; I tried to treat both boys and girls the same.

But I quickly discovered reality. While boys and girls share many human characteristics and emotions, at no time are their differences more pronounced than in the teenage years. Yet this variety brings richness and delight to family life. I'm glad I didn't miss the fun.

The differences can be hilarious, especially the physical differences. Boys develop large muscle control before girls; they walk earlier and are more likely to break things as they explore. They are also fascinated with the appendage that dangles between their legs.

Little girls are supposed to be easier to potty train, but when my boys discovered the possibilities inherent in their anatomies, they were out of diapers sooner than any of my girls.

All my girls yearned for ruffled underpants, wanted to wear make-up before they could walk, and felt that perfumed bubble baths were necessities rather than luxuries. Although they enjoyed pudding conditioner and creamed carrot mascara as they learned to feed themselves, they developed table manners years before any of their brothers.

How in the World Did That Happen?

Not only are boys more blatantly physical than girls, boys break things. This results from some mysterious energy that radiates from their bodies. At four years of age, Micah broke twelve pairs of glasses in five months. And I never actually saw him intentionally mistreat them.

This tendency to break stuff emerges early and stays around until they leave home. Roch dismantled his baby brother's swing with his bare hands when he was only fifteen months old. He also managed to destroy three kitchen chairs and a set of bunk beds by the time he was fourteen.

The demolition arts continued to improve with age. Every son blew an engine or wrecked a car by his seventeenth birthday. All Dolly and Sherri ever achieved were a couple of scraped fenders and a flat tire.

Linda was the exception that proved the rule. Generally cautious behind the wheel, she never had a speeding or reckless driving ticket. However, shortly after her seventeenth birthday, she panicked when the radiator went dry in our old Chrysler Laser while she was driving. Every time the car stalled, she managed to restart it and drive a few more feet. The three other people with her were just as mystified as to why "the car acted so funny."

When the car gave up and refused to turn over again, Linda called home. Her dad gritted his teeth, but didn't say much, because he'd put off replacing a leaking water hose.

While my boys bullied their way into life at a tender age, my girls learned to express their emotions (and manipulate others) more easily. Linda, like her sisters, used less brute force than her brothers as she grew up. She seldom ripped or crushed things; she was a tool and people user, early on.

She figured out how to shove a chair to the cabinet and climb up to the "goody shelf" while she was still in a walker. She pried the lids off cans, opened packages, and booby trapped the kitchen. She also cajoled Eric, who was only a year older, to assist her with anything she was too little to manage.

When they entered their teens, she pulled the same stunts. Eric invariably ended up covering for her at school and taking the blame for curfew violations.

Boys are big and strong, fascinated by their bodies, and likely to break things as they learn about them. But boys have strong emotions as well as strong bodies, and learn by precept and example to express themselves positively and develop sensitivity.

Girls, on the other hand, make up for their smaller size by developing "people skills" as soon as they can focus their eyes. They are more fastidious and less likely to create havoc; they also have a greater sense of self-preservation and take fewer risks.

Thank Heaven for Big Girls and Boys

The neat thing about raising boys and girls together is that their qualities rub off on each other. Our boys bring a sense of adventure into the family; the girls lend finesse and communication skills.

Both sexes benefit from the give-and-take of living under the same roof. Consequently, by the time they reach their teens, they've developed an understanding of the opposite sex that serves them well in their adult lives.

PHYSICAL SIGNS OF APPROACHING ADOLESCENCE

Kids grow more rapidly between the ages of ten and twenty than at any time other than infancy. Not only do they become bigger and taller, but they turn into men or women (gradually). They may look like adults, but they don't *act* like adults. Because they are changing so fast, they have trouble keeping track of themselves, physically and emotionally.

All this growing can take you, the parent, by surprise. After all, your little angel has been able to wear the same size for months, even years, at a time. Life has loped along at a fairly even pace. Okay, so it's been a bit crazy all along, but let me tell you—early childhood is like a lazy summer afternoon compared to the hurricane-whipped seas of adolescence.

Behavioral psychologists define the end of childhood and the beginning of adolescence as that time when secondary sexual characteristics begin to appear. However, I know my kids are approaching adolescence by the way they erupt with volcanic intensity when I make such weighty statements as "Please shut the door behind you" or "Pick up your towel."

I don't have to peer under arms for sprouting hair to think, "Here we go again, another teenager in the making!"

Just What Is Going on Here?

Anybody with a child rapidly approaching the teen years should read up on the physical changes of puberty and talk to a doctor about any questions. I can't cover everything that happens to young boys' and girls' bodies and minds in this book. But a short summary of typical changes and the average time they appear might help you avoid the panic I suffered when one of my daughters showed strange symptoms at a tender age.

Besides, if you are well-informed, you can help your child understand what's happening. The cyclone of hormones roaring through adolescent systems can terrify kids. They've never endured anything like this before, either!

SUMMARY OF PHYSICAL CHANGES: GIRLS

Body hair appears around age eleven, but can show up as early as nine or as late as fourteen. It becomes noticeable first on legs and arms, then in underarms and the pubic area.

Usually welcomed by boys, the growth of *body hair* can be upsetting for girls. Don't believe the old wives' tale about shaving making hair darker and coarser; a first shaving cuts some baby-fine fuzz that hasn't been replaced yet, but those maturing follicles are going to produce dark, coarse hair regardless of whether she shaves. So go ahead and let your daughter shave her legs and underarms whenever she wants to.

Breasts begin to form about the same time as body hair. A painless, pea-sized lump ("breast bud") forms first under one nipple, then the other. How you react to your girl as her breasts begin developing and her body gets ready for her monthly cycle could profoundly affect your relationship for many years. If you welcome the change from girl to woman, she'll feel positive about her maturity.

As soon as a she begins developing, buy her a comfortable "training bra." These serve no particular physical function, but girls forced to wear undershirts feel "weird" and those who don't wear anything under their clothes look immodest.

Menstruation typically begins by age thirteen, but in normal situations can be as early as ten or as late as sixteen. Flow is usually scanty and irregular for the first year.

A period can be scary when it happens for the first time. One of my foster daughters thought her cramps meant appendicitis. When she started bleeding, she came to me in tears. She was only eleven and had no idea what was going on. She'd only been with us a few days, so I didn't realize how uninformed she was.

Girls should be told how to take care of themselves and their flow. Be sure to supervise disposal and hygiene closely at first; this is a good opportunity to teach discretion and modesty.

SUMMARY OF PHYSICAL CHANGES: BOYS

Age twelve usually brings body hair, but as with girls, it can be as early as ten or as late as fourteen or fifteen. It appears first on legs and arms, then in the underarms and pubic area, and—finally—on that manly chest. The genitals gradually get bigger, beginning to grow about the same time as body hair.

I mentioned earlier that boys tend to welcome the onset of body hair, but when it becomes obvious, some boys are just as concerned/worried as girls are. The hair usually grows slowly, although I've encountered guys who could pass for apes when they were barely out of kindergarten. One of my sons remained smooth and hairless throughout his teens. He rarely used a razor until he left on his mission, but he looked like a fur rug two years later when he returned home.

Either extreme can be embarrassing. Reassure your son that he'll pass through these trying times where people (mainly his peers) make fun of or criticize such physical variations.

Facial hair follows body hair around age thirteen, but it, too, can be as early as eleven or as late as sixteen. Facial hair is one of the most obvious signs your son is growing up. I encourage my boys to start shaving as soon as those first hairs straggle along their upper lips. In my opinion, the scrawny beards on teenagers are best relegated to decorating the bathroom sink.

An adolescent who tries to grow a beard can look positively ridiculous. The hair is too sparse to really qualify as a beard, and it sprouts among all those pimples! Of course, all those pimples are a reason your son avoids shaving in the first place.

The voice usually deepens around age thirteen, though it may be as early as twelve or as late as seventeen. Both facial hair and voice change have been the subject of much merriment in our household. All my boys are singers, so we're tuned in to tonal shifts. A couple of my sons were intrigued by the quavers and cracks that happened whenever they opened their mouths. They recorded and competed with each other to see who could make the weirdest sound.

Embarrassing and confusing, genital growth and the accompanying "wet dreams" must be considered with delicacy by parents. "Wet dreams" are a physical release of semen that occurs during sleep. Dads should have private talks with their sons before those dreams start. Boys who don't realize that the dreams are normal can be consumed by guilt.

I know of one boy who thought for sure he was some kind of pervert. He suffered for weeks before his folks figured out what was the matter with him. He confided to them that he probably couldn't go on a mission because he had no self-control: "No matter how hard I try, I still get those bad dreams."

Dads should also reassure their sons about varieties in genital size. During their first locker room experience, some boys worry about being deformed. Boys need to know that genital size has little bearing on manliness.

Obviously, this brief treatment doesn't begin to cover the physical changes that teenagers and their parents endure. If your child's physical development happens earlier or later than these guidelines, check with your doctor. Deviations usually have a benign explanation, but don't risk overlooking a need to correct something.

As in all aspects of your parenting, you must use judgment and personal inspiration to decide how to handle your own child and his or her behavior. Check confusing or questionable episodes with your doctor, bishop, or mental health worker.

THE THREE PHASES OF TEEN

While everybody talks about "teenagers" as if they were one kind of beast, teenage behavior ranges all the way from a toddler's destructive curiosity to an adult's earning and working capacity.

Adolescent interests and maturity fall into three categories. I call them "The Three Phases of Teen," or the Early, Middle, and Late phases. The Early phase corresponds with the Beehive/Deacon period; the Middle phase corresponds with Mia Maids and Teachers; and the Late phase extends through Laurels and Priests until graduation from high school. The Church was inspired to set up the Young Women and Aaronic Priesthood programs, because they perfectly fit these changing needs.

THE EARLY PHASE
Idealistic and All Mixed Up

Early adolescence can start in the fourth or fifth grade, although full-fledged symptoms usually don't appear until junior high or middle school. The time for "normal" development spans a period almost as broad as adolescence, so don't be taken by surprise.

When Gary and I adopted our eldest daughter as a three-year-old, we were told she had Turner's Syndrome, which meant she would never mature without taking hormones and she wouldn't be able to bear children. When she was about eight, I saw dark hair sprouting under her arms and a lump developing behind one of her nipples. I imagined all kinds of things like cancerous growths and leprosy, so I took her to the doctor who had diagnosed her condition.

He examined her, sat back in his chair, and said, "Well, it's a little early, but she's starting puberty. I guess we don't have to worry about Turner's."

She wore a bra in the fourth grade and started her periods in the fifth. Today she's happily married with four children.

Putting Away Childish Things

Different families celebrate the onset of puberty in different ways. Graduation into the Aaronic Priesthood or Young Women programs serves as a memorable beginning for this transition into adulthood. My family throws a special party for each child's twelfth birthday. We also celebrate our deacons' ordinations with congratulations, gifts, and outings.

What seems appropriate in one part of the country might be considered excessive in another. Keying into regional variations has become necessary as families become more mobile.

Some of my friends spare no expense; their relatives travel from across the country to participate. A big celebration is fine if you can afford it; just be sure you mark *each* child's Primary graduation, ordination, or twelfth birthday in a similar manner.

This milestone gives you an opportunity to talk about and establish rules for the next six years. Twelve-year-olds are so eager to embark on their "teenage-hood" that they readily agree to curfews, personal responsibility, and household chores without much fuss.

If I know I'm dealing with a particularly hard-headed child (or a new foster kid), I write down the basic rules. Sometimes I phrase the family expectations as a contract and have the kid sign. Then we both get copies.

I make a lot of contracts and charts. I also post notes and write letters to my children. Writing things down protects me from a litany of "But I didn't know," "You never told me," and "I forgot."

Each Child—An Individual

I mentioned earlier that kids grow fastest during their teen years. Kids grow faster during the Early phase than during the next two phases. Boys grow at especially astounding rates, although boys in the same family can display very different growth patterns.

My second son, Roch, went from eighteen inches and six pounds twelve ounces at birth to twenty-six inches and twenty-five pounds by the time he was six months old. I figured he'd be a linebacker for the San Francisco 49ers. My pediatrician accused me of "blowing in his big toe."

Shortly after his second birthday, however, his growth slowed. By the time he entered kindergarten, he was one of the smallest kids in his class. I searched catalogs for clothes that would fit him lengthwise without bagging off his non-existent hips.

Roch's seventh-grade picture showed an elfin-faced boy with a mischievous grin. His eighth-grade picture didn't look like the same person. Between September 1983 and September 1984, Roch grew six inches, added fifty-five pounds, and passed through four shoe sizes. His straight brown hair tightened into thick curls and, much to the chagrin of his older brother, he had to shave every day. He was suddenly bigger than most of his classmates.

Roch stopped his growth spurt, however, while his brother, Gary Willis (G.W.), gradually kept on growing. When Roch left for his mission, he was no longer bigger than most of his friends. He stood 5'10" and weighed about 150 pounds.

When G.W. came back from his mission, he stood 6'1" and weighed 179. He wrote me that he was leaving most of his clothes for the Brazilian elders. I thought his actions were due to an exalted frame of mind developed from serving his fellow man. When I saw him step off the plane, I learned that he left his clothes because none of them fit him any more!

So don't fret about a child who seems to lag behind his or her friends. And don't be too sure about any size predictions that may come to mind at any particular stage of your child's development. The fun things about parenthood are the surprises. They help us learn to accept our children as they are rather than as we want them to be.

Boys—Bigger and Bigger . . . and Better

Boys seem to have a harder time coping with rapid growth than do girls. Even the ones who grow more slowly tend to be clumsy. They just don't know quite what to do with all that extra body.

They bump into door jambs and trip over slight ridges on a vinyl floor. And they look like somebody shrunk all their clothes.

It's impossible to fit them properly. You can take a thirteen-year-old boy down to a department store for a sport coat and pants suitable for passing the sacrament. By the time you pay for the purchase and drive home, he'll have outgrown it.

A friend of mine with six sons was the oldest in a large family, so she knew what to expect. Well before her boys hit puberty, she began haunting Deseret Industries and other second-hand stores. She bought two white shirts, two pairs of pants and a coat in every size from a boy's 12 to a men's 16. Since her boys all hit the sizes at different times, none of them looked like Frankenstein, arms and legs hanging two inches beyond shirt and pant hems.

I thought her idea was great, but it never worked for me, because my big boys all wore the same size throughout high school. And the younger boys wanted to wear their brothers' clothes, even when the shirts looked like dresses on them.

My friend's boys were also more amiable to their mother's fashion sense than my boys were. I stopped buying clothes without my boys (or girls) by the time they were in the fourth grade.

I still haven't mastered the art of what's "in" or "out." One fourteen-year-old son loved a shirt his big brother gave him before he left for Brazil. I took careful note of the material, the color, the cut, and sleeve length. Then I bought what I thought was a similar shirt for his birthday.

Early Teen thanked me politely, folded the shirt neatly, and crammed it into his dresser. I found it some six months later in the same drawer with the tags still on it.

When I questioned him, he admitted he didn't like it, because the "collar was too wide." I couldn't see any difference between the collars on the two shirts, but he could. Or maybe the difference was between what an adored brother had worn and what had come from a store.

A Baby Still—and Always

Early Teens are responsible for many of the goofy stories about teenagers. You'll be startled one day to realize you're looking up at your son, but he still wants to be snuggled like a three-year-old. One of the silliest sights I can remember is seeing my sister calmly holding her 6'5", thirteen-year-old on her lap.

One minute your boy wants his back scratched, his feet rubbed, and lots of hugs. The next minute he slams into his room so hard the door splinters the frame. And your "time for dinner" announcement is met with a frosty "I don't feel like eating."

Your daughter will bargain with you to be able to wear makeup to school. She'll give you all kinds of logical reasons why she should cut her hair (or shave one side of her head) and pierce her ears in eighteen places.

Then, without warning, she'll accuse you of plotting her demise for the insurance money or declare her life is over because she can't go to the mall. Unwary parents find such shifts between logic and emotion a bit unsettling.

Helping Early Teens focus the energy of growing and surging hormones can be a challenge. They have a tendency to fly off in all directions at once. A simple but complete schedule keeps things on an even keel.

MIDDLE PHASE

Calmer But More Obnoxious Than Ever

By the time kids become Mia Maid and Teacher age, their growth spurts have reached a lull. They're the oldest in junior high or they've entered high school.

Middle Teens have "been on the scene" for two years; they're no longer awed by it. The next few years stretch beyond their comprehension. They think they'll be young forever.

Kids this age tend to cut classes and ignore homework deadlines. They turn away from the family; friends take on tremendous importance. They can be mouthy and rebellious.

I find that fourteen- and fifteen-year-olds are the most troubled foster kids we've had over the years. Communication breaks down and a variety of emotional illnesses can crop up. These kids react strongly to discipline. "Use kid gloves" is an apt approach. You must balance between letting an inexperienced, hot-headed child do his or her "own thing" and denying this emerging adult opportunities to use free agency and take reasonable chances.

Balancing takes sensitivity and determination. I've found that keeping my own temper helps me stay in control and calms the troubled waters.

But I Thought You Meant . . .

Middle Teens love to test boundaries. Their behavior resembles that of one-year-olds, but they aren't as cute. Your Mia Maid or Teacher is likely to break every rule you devise at least once—if not a dozen times. Dealing with all the rule breaking, testing, and just plain orneriness should qualify you for workman's compensation.

A case in point happened at my house not too long ago. Gary and I had gone out to dinner with Dolly and Roland for Dolly's birthday. Sherri came along, while Linda babysat for Dolly. Gary Willis, recently returned from his mission, had his first genuine date that night. Eric, who had just graduated from high school, stayed home to walk the dog and hang out by the compact disc player.

The rest of the kids were all Middle Teens, with the exception of Nathan, who was only ten at the time but well on his way to Early Teen. Since this was a school night, everybody had homework and

Young Men/Young Women activity night. We didn't leave until quite late, and I didn't expect anything out of the ordinary.

This tale points up another truism: "Never let your guard down."

When Gary, Sherri, Linda, and I opened the front door, I heard the TV snap off and somebody flee down the hall. Cellophane and comic books were scattered all over the living room. John, my sixteen-year-old foster son, scurried around picking up papers and comics, but nobody else was in the room. He looked guilty, so I jumped on him.

I pronounced the television off limits for everybody until further notice. I thought that would be that. I was mad about the TV being on (which is against the rules for school nights), but my reaction was, more or less, instinctive.

Then Mary, my fifteen-year-old foster daughter, called me into her room and started babbling. "This gross, disgusting guy and his friend followed me around WalMart. . . ."

She finally came to the point. "He bumped me and grabbed my butt and said, 'Ooops, my hand slipped,' and I got scared and he started to do it again. . . ."

"What?" I said. "What are you talking about? Weren't you at Young Women?"

Mary fell silent and cast a sideways glance at Linda. Clearly, Mary's attempt to bypass the WalMart setting had failed. I hadn't reacted quite as she'd planned.

Truth Comes in Many Guises

After cornering John, Micah, Nathan, and Eric, I finally put the whole story together. Eric had come back from walking the dog to an empty house, and he righteously absolved himself from all blame with, "I *told* them not to do it. I don't even know when they left."

Micah (who had been too sick to go to school) turned out to be the chief instigator. A gifted artist with a fixation on comic books, he wanted the next installment in the series he collected. In typical Middle Teen fashion, Micah totally ignored every established rule he'd ever been told and focused on the one thing he wanted above all else. He took Mary, John, and Nathan with him to dilute the blast he subconsciously knew would result.

Mary and John were equally culpable, however, because they had in their possession a written list of "house regulations."

They tried to say, "Well, Micah said Gary Willis said it was okay." But they knew that nobody except Gary or me could give them permission to leave. If we weren't home, then they couldn't go, period.

Micah and John then tried to deflect my chastisement with "We didn't go alone," "We were together," and "We took the back roads."

After hearing about Mary's near mugging, on top of the kids being where they weren't supposed to be, my initial reaction was to ground everybody "for the rest of your lives."

A Community's Finest Resource

Then I called the police. A patrolman, in full uniform with a .45 on his hip, came out to take Mary's statement.

He, bless his heart, stood there and repeated my three points:

1. Your first mistake was in breaking the house rules. You went someplace without permission.
2. Your second mistake was not calling the police immediately.
3. Your third mistake was walking home in the dark. If the man had been a bonafide scumbag, he could have hurt you.

He couldn't have made a bigger impression if I'd coached him. Hometown policemen can be a parent's best friend. All teenagers, including Middle Teens, tend to reject authority, but few of them have the courage to dismiss such direct counsel.

Four very subdued kids crept off to bed that night. Not once did I have to say, "Finish your homework," "Fix your lunch," "Find your backpack," or "Stop goofing around and turn out the lights."

LATE TEEN PHASE

Almost Grown, But Not Quite

About now—after four or so years of teenage madness, you're positive your child will not survive until his next birthday (you'll either kill him, or he'll impale himself on one of the fences he keeps climbing over). Then he turns sixteen.

Sixteen is a magic age for both girls and boys, because it means a potential DRIVER'S LICENSE and FREEDOM. Wise parents will capitalize on this situation.

During this phase, the process of relinquishing control accelerates. However, don't let go too suddenly. One of my counseling patients who graduated from high school at fifteen was excommunicated and divorced by his twenty-first birthday.

Hold to the Rod

He voiced what I'm trying to get across when he said, "My folks are the most righteous, loving parents a guy could have. They loved me without condition. But their big mistake was in letting me make decisions I had no business making."

He left home when he graduated from high school and got a job several hundred miles away. He wasn't ready to have his own apartment or establish his own curfew. In short order, he lost his job, maxed out his credit card, and had his car repossessed.

I know of other children who have skidded off the "straight and narrow" for the same reason. One girl, who convinced her mom to let her date at thirteen because she was "more mature than the rest of the kids," was pregnant and married at fourteen and a half.

Another teenager lived with an older man and got pregnant before she married a nonmember. These kids brought grief and heartache to their parents, who had tried very hard to raise them to live gospel standards.

While all of these kids turned their lives around through repentance, their struggles didn't need to be so disruptive. These families' experiences illustrate that the Church advice about dating and other standards is based on reality.

Although each of us should take counsel and apply it in the best way for our own situations, none of us knows enough to dispense with rules.

Truth and Consequences

I've heard the statement "I should be able to . . . ; I'm more mature than . . ." thousands of times. I even remember using that line of reasoning myself.

Several of my children are brilliant and talented; it's tempting to translate a genius I.Q. in math to a genius social and spiritual I.Q. But don't be deceived.

Sixteen- and seventeen-year-olds still need parenting. They are upper-classmen in high school (or maybe they've already graduated), yet they are not ready to take on complete responsibility for their own lives. They chaff and complain and say, "I can't wait until I'm eighteen and out of this house."

But they haven't had enough experience to understand all the ramifications of their choices. As I've seen repeatedly, they often make poor choices about their health, their relationships, and their eternal salvation. They haven't learned to "take an eternal perspective."

These two or three years in the Late Teen phase are your last opportunity to influence the direction your child's life will take. On the other hand, you can't make every decision for eighteen years and suddenly turn your kid loose on his or her birthday. Growing up and accepting responsibility are gradual processes. This Late Teen phase can be a time of joy for you and your child. It doesn't have to be filled with fights and contention.

The adage "Sweet Sixteen" is apt. Heavenly Father gave us sixteen-year-olds to compensate us for the headaches of the previous four years—and to prepare us for the next year or two.

Reasons for the Calm

Late Teens are no longer at the mercy of raging hormones. Although the hormones still rage, they're more familiar and they don't cause such panic. Your daughter will be more apt to believe the comfort you offer. Your words, "Relax; you're furious right now, but it won't bother you in the morning" won't seem like a put-down.

Late Teens are more comfortable with their bodies. Boys have learned to walk across a room without tripping. They don't smack their heads on doorways; they duck. Girls have learned to use eye shadow and blush and to stand up straight. They won't tease or laugh so often at other people; they've learned some empathy.

Don't be lulled into complacency, however. These kids will still test the boundaries. But they don't kick as hard and they don't react as vehemently to restrictions. They're more open to discussion and will even cooperate around the house—occasionally.

SUMMARY

The three phases don't always correlate completely with the age groups I've described in this chapter, but the stages do follow each other in order. Early Teen might last almost through Middle Teen. Middle Teen might be very brief, turning almost immediately into Late Teen.

Just as you know that the "terrible twos" can arrive by a child's first birthday or be delayed until her fourth, be assured that your child will eventually go through the confusion and clumsiness of Early Teen, the headstrong and willful behavior of Middle Teen, and the almost grown-up but vulnerable Late Teen years.

CHAPTER 2

Healthy Teens—
Putting Food into Perspective

"There's nothing to eat around here!" is one of the more irritating comments my kids can make. The sight of my 150-pound, six-foot-tall son gazing mournfully into the depths of the refrigerator drives me crazy.

"Something to eat" usually translates into anything that doesn't need more preparation than unwrapping. That mournful son ignores the hamburger he could fry, the carrots he could peel, or the eggs he could scramble. Prepared foods are expensive, and I've never been able to afford to indulge my kids that way. If I did, my food budget would have outpaced my mortgage payment, which it did when I was in the midst of feeding five teenage boys.

How, when, what, and how much your teenager eats is loaded with social and emotional issues. The care and feeding of your teenager, therefore, can become a huge, complex dilemma.

You probably paid a lot of attention to your kids' diets when they were young, but you should remember that teenagers' diets require almost as much interest and attention as those of babies and small children. Somebody once told me that small children and babies instinctively eat what they need in the quantities they need. This expert assured me that I didn't have to stress over my kids' diets. "Let them eat whatever they want to," I was told.

The assumption was that if I started them out right, they'd be paragons of healthful living by the time they were teenagers. I tried. I really did. But somewhere along the line I failed. While many of my grown kids watch their fat and salt intake and avoid too much refined sugar, the kids at home continue to outwit my every attempt to feed them nutritiously.

My best advice is to set a good example and follow the spirit (as well as the letter) of the Word of Wisdom. Setting an example and following the Word of Wisdom will sustain you when your teenager dashes for the door in too much of a hurry for breakfast, leaves his lunch sack on the stairs (after stuffing the can of juice and bag of corn chips in his pocket), or glares at the tuna noodle casserole in the middle of the dinner table.

My experience with the Care and Feeding of Teens falls into three general categories: what, where and when food is consumed; special nutritional needs; and avoidance of eating disorders.

THE WHAT, WHERE, AND WHENS OF FOOD
The Spirit of the Word of Wisdom

Did you ever wonder how little Eskimo kids manage to develop a yen for whale blubber and raw fish? Or how other cultures learn to like such things as dried ants or squid?

Kids develop tastes for the foods their parents eat. Foods you and I might think are disgusting are considered delicacies by somebody else. Don't worry—if your diet is balanced, your kids will follow your example (eventually).

And remember—your teenager will notice (and resist) your hypocrisy if you indulge in popcorn dripping with butter, cream-filled doughnuts, and peanut butter fudge while admonishing him to "eat right." Your virtuous "eat your spinach and broccoli" won't carry much weight if your plate never holds anything green or leafy. Kids have a disconcerting way of aping our worst characteristics.

Section 89 of the Doctrine and Covenants provides a vitality law that, when observed, will bring "health in their navel and marrow to their bones." And isn't that what you want for your teenager? And yourself?

The Word of Wisdom is much more than a list of prohibitions. It contains a simple description of the four food groups and an admonition to exercise—couched in terms the average nineteenth-century person could *understand*.

. . . the will of God in the temporal salvation of all saints in the last days—

Given for a principle with promise, adapted to the capacity of the weak and the weakest of all saints, who are or can be called saints.

. . . thus saith the Lord . . . I have warned you . . . by giving unto you this word of wisdom by revelation—

. . . all wholesome herbs God hath ordained for the constitution, nature, and use of man—

Every herb in the season thereof, and every fruit in the season thereof . . .

. . . flesh also of beasts and of the fowls of the air, I . . . have ordained for the use of man with thanksgiving; nevertheless they are to be used sparingly;

. . . only in times of winter, or of cold, or famine.

All grain is ordained for the use of man and of beasts, to be the staff of life. . . .

All grain is good for the food of man; as also the fruit of the vine; that which yieldeth fruit, whether in the ground or above the ground. . . .

All saints who remember to keep and do these sayings, walking in obedience to the commandments, shall receive health in their navel and marrow to their bones;

And shall find wisdom and great treasures of knowledge, even hidden treasures;

And shall run and not be weary, and shall walk and not faint.

Nutritional research was unheard of in the mid-1800s. Nobody really knew why or what they should eat, but the Saints understood that God spoke through prophets. They were willing to accept their leaders' directions. Like the children of Israel who spread lamb's blood on their door posts, they did as they were told—although they had no idea why.

A hundred years later, science caught up with our religion. Today, we know that bodies and spirits are inexorably intertwined. Following the Word of Wisdom is necessary for a healthy life now, as well as exaltation in the life to come.

In a 1988 *Message From the First Presidency* about the Word of Wisdom, President Ezra Taft Benson said, "There is no question that the health of the body affects the spirit. . . . Disease, fevers, and unexpected deaths are some (of the) consequences directly related to disobedience. . . . What needs additional emphasis are the positive aspects of this law."

WHAT/WHICH FOODS TO EAT—A BRIEF REVIEW OF NUTRITION

If you've been reading magazines and newspapers, you've probably noticed that controversies are developing about the role of animal products in modern diets. Also, many LDS nutrition writers advocate strict vegetarian diets.

I take the easy way out; I don't recommend any extreme diets. My recommendations are based on optimum health for minimum fuss. Reducing "fuss" in homes containing teenagers should always be a priority—a priority that, to me, overrides optimum nutrition.

Besides, the Word of Wisdom doesn't mandate a wholly vegetarian diet. Verses 12, 13, and 15 place restrictions on their use but clearly state that man may use animals (their flesh as well as their hides). Animal products are high in fat and calories—both of which are required in cold climates. Examples can be found in the diets of peoples like Eskimos, Swedes, and Norwegians.

Therefore, my recommended meals for finicky palates include:

1. A complex carbohydrate,
2. A dairy product (or dairy substitute),
3. A complete protein source, and
4. Two servings of fruits or vegetables.

Complex carbohydrates are found in grains and legumes (wheat is for man); the most common food sources are breads and cereals. Grains can completely sustain human growth and health if they're unprocessed. Life with teenagers being what it is, however, you'd better include additional foods in the family diet or face mutiny.

Dairy products contribute calcium, protein, and minerals. They also taste good and provide the high calories needed for growth spurts and sports. Cheese cubes, pudding, and yogurt are favorites. If your child is allergic to milk, find substitutes; soy products are the most common. Milk-intolerant kids can use dairy products if you provide the missing lactase. Several companies manufacture a lactose-digesting enzyme; ask your pharmacist or nutritionist.

It's easy to distinguish whether your kid is milk intolerant rather than allergic to milk. If he breaks out in a rash or gets headaches when he drinks milk, he's allergic. If her stomach hurts or she feels nauseated and/or gassy, she's milk intolerant. Unfortunately, some kids have both conditions; they suffer from rashes, headaches, *and* nausea. For a certain diagnosis, see your doctor.

Complete protein foods like chicken, fish, beef, and eggs provide iron and other minerals along with the protein. But meat, especially beef and pork, should be "used sparingly . . . and only in times of cold or famine." Sparingly means mostly as a flavoring and in small quantities—especially when the meat is high in saturated fats.

Some nutritionists say that unsaturated fats (such as those in fish products) are just as bad as saturated fats—and I'm not going to get into that debate. In food matters, as well as every other instance, use inspiration. Most of my children have extremely high metabolisms that require plenty of calories. A large portion of those calories came from fats—especially when we lived in Alaska.

Fresh or frozen fruits and vegetables are "in their season" all year-around today and should be a substantial a part of your teenager's diet. They provide fiber and water, as well as vitamins and minerals.

Most young people like fruits because they're sweet. Dried apples and apricots, seedless grapes, cherries, and other easy-to-eat fruits are favorites. Avoid commercially prepared dried fruits, however, if anyone in your family suffers from allergies; the sulfides used to maintain color and freshness can cause life-threatening reactions. Home-dried fruits are much cheaper, anyway.

Vegetables are another matter. Certain kids take vows at birth not to let anything green pass their lips. If your pride and joy is such a person, try raw vegetables with dip. Celery stuffed with soft cheese or with peanut butter and raisins (for "ants on a log") always goes over well. Salads made from grated carrots, sprouts, and zucchini sticks are interesting enough that your kids might not notice they're eating vegetables.

Another way to coax greens into your teens is to cook vegetables properly. Mushy veggies, besides being pretty disgusting, don't have enough nutrition left to make it worth the energy involved in eating them.

Steaming or baking vegetables is the best way to preserve vitamins and minerals. However, my kids like their squash, onions, and carrots fried in Japanese tempura batters. Tempura is lighter and crunchier than breading, and I prefer it. But I use both; I use *any* way I can to get vegetables into my offspring.

When/Where Food Is Consumed

Now that we've run through types of foods to feed your teenagers (at least the types I feed mine), let's talk about the next important consideration: when those foods are eaten.

Teenagers (especially boys) need little encouragement to eat—they'll eat constantly, but they do need some kind of schedule. Breakfasts, lunches, and dinners are more than "feeding" times; they bring families together. But sitting down to a meal at a table seems to be becoming obsolete, even among LDS families.

I think it's worth the effort to have as many meals together as possible. Three meals a day supplemented by two or three nutritious snacks will provide optimum energy for activities and growth. Breakfast, lunch, and dinner can also be opportunities to build family unity.

BREAKFAST

By any definition, breakfast is the most important meal of the day. It's also the hardest meal for my family to eat together. I suspect that most of you have the same problem.

At my house it's "every man for himself." Our schedule runs something like this:

5:30 a.m.   Early-morning seminary and swim team eaters
6:00 a.m.   Mom's early breakfast (I have a metabolic condition that requires multiple meals at frequent intervals)
6:30 a.m.   Middle-school and "A"-period eaters
7:00 a.m.   High-school eaters and Dad
8:00 a.m.   Grade-school eaters and Mom's second breakfast

As you can see, there's NO WAY we could ever sit down to one breakfast together. Therefore, I work at ensuring adequate nutrition rather than family togetherness for this meal.

Our refrigerator is loaded with convenient, simple foods that won't break the budget but that my fussy children will eat. I keep things like powdered breakfast mixes, boiled eggs, muffins, granola bars, and dried or fresh fruit on hand. We don't buy sugared cereals very often; when we do, it's only as "topping" for plain cold cereals.

I spike hot cereal with wheat germ and powdered milk, along with a dollop of brown sugar and vanilla. I keep a big batch in the refrigerator that can be microwaved in individual portions. Cereal cooked Monday morning lasts several days.

I don't consider only "breakfast foods" at breakfast time, either. Chicken noodle soup, toast, and fruit slices with cheese provide a lot more nutrition than a bowl of cold cereal with milk.

LUNCH

Body-satisfying lunches provide approximately thirty-five percent of a teenager's daily requirements. Convincing a kid to eat the wide variety of foods necessary to meet those requirements can be tricky and exasperating, though.

During the school year, I like to "send a bit of home" with my kids. "Brown bag" lunches are loving reminders that warm them throughout the day. That's not all: well-prepared sack lunches are more nutritious than school meals, if only because the home lunches are more likely to be eaten. Over a twenty-three-year period, I packed twenty million (only a slight exaggeration) lunches. Believe me, I'd much rather have bought lunch tickets. However, even when I could afford eight lunches a day, some of my children wanted a "Mom's lunch."

Lunch time at school is as much a social event for teens as a meal—probably more so. What you send to school (or allow your kid to buy) becomes a status symbol. Fortunately, teenagers pick nourishing foods if nutrition is their only alternative; no kid ever succumbed to starvation because he or she couldn't eat junk food. But the choices had better be attractive, or the lunches will be tossed after your child eats barely enough to stave off hunger pangs.

Mom, Get Real . . . I Mean, Gross!

As a Middle Teen, Micah continually "forgot" his lunch until I was ready to tie it around his neck. I finally figured out that he'd rather go hungry than carry a lunch, because nobody in his crowd "brown bagged"; they bought lunch. We're talking the local convenience store and hamburger joints—not the school cafeteria.

I gave up trying to figure out how to convince this particular group to carry a lunch or eat at school, because of the "open" campus. I liked things better when my high school kids attended a "closed" campus; they stayed at school during their thirty-five-minute lunch periods.

Around Cedar High at the time, the big deal was to leave—there wasn't enough time, but they left anyway and racked up tardies. The administration adopted a punitive attendance policy (including tardies) that made everybody mad, but they still let the kids leave during lunch. I'd have worked to change the policy if I hadn't been so busy writing this book. . . .

Remember: The most captivating ideas are no good unless they fit what's "in" or "out" at your kid's school. For example, when we lived in San Luis Obispo, California, *nobody* over ten carried a lunch box. Paper bags (except grocery bags) were the unanimous choice. Anything that looked "babyish" was also out, unless the carrier was a girl who happened to like "cute."

Definitions may be difficult to establish, however. About the time you figure out what will make your kid happy, the fad changes. As in Micah's example, some kids would rather starve during the school day and then run home to demolish the refrigerator.

DINNER

Because of work and school day realities, dinner is the only meal we have any hope of sharing. Like many other families "on the go," our table sometimes turns into a feeding trough. People scrounge through the refrigerator and jostle each other at the stove as they prepare to eat and run.

Our hours were often so out of whack that we had to write each other notes. Our family time was fragmented by two kids with jobs; several kids in band, debate, and drama; and other kids with soccer or baseball practice.

But I try hard to make dinner a family meal, especially on Sunday and Monday evenings. When I taught at night and Gary was frequently out of town, the kids still sat down together—the oldest at any given time made sure meals were balanced and everybody ate together. That person declared a majority so they didn't have to let the pot roast dry out and the gravy congeal, waiting for somebody who never showed.

I use weekends to plan the evening meals with the kids in an effort to ensure that they will eat what they're served. I also put together homemade TV dinners or extra meals that can be stuffed in the oven by a thirteen-year-old on his way to soccer practice.

Crock pots and Dutch ovens are a working mom's salvation. I also believe that since we all have to eat, we should all cook the meals. Luckily for me, Gary enjoys cooking and has always taken an active role—even when I was a stay-at-home mom with a bunch of babies and toddlers. When we began working together in our company, Gary took over the cooking almost exclusively. His example has meant that my boys cook as well as or better than my daughters.

Service, Anyone?

How food is served is important, too. The table should be set attractively with a centerpiece and/or a theme. Just because it's easier, I encourage you not to plunk down the food in pans and cartons.

The more we learn about the relationship between emotions and health the more I understand my grandmother's preoccupation with "setting a nice table." Her dishes and silverware matched and she used cloth napkins and fresh flowers. Dinner at her house was always an event.

Gary's grandmother was the same way, only she used a few tricks suitable for large families. Whoever set the table turned the plates over and the chairs away from the table. The family knelt for the blessing in front of their chairs. Then everyone reversed his or her chair and set the plates right side up. This ploy effectively side-tracked ravenous boys who might load their plates with much more than their share of the food.

Rituals like ringing a dinner bell and asking to be excused seem to have gone the way of high-button shoes and corsets, but I think they should be brought back. When I observe the rituals, mealtimes are peaceful and my household is happier.

SPECIAL NUTRITIONAL NEEDS

As I stated earlier in this chapter, your teenager's diet requires careful monitoring and more attention than at any other time of life, except infancy. But teenagers are much harder to supervise than babies and toddlers. Most teenagers are woefully uninformed about nutrition. Their raging bodies (especially boys') require huge amounts of fuel, so their appetites overrule good sense. As long as they can stop the hunger pangs, they're satisfied. I've found mountains of candy bar and cupcake wrappers under my kids' beds.

Rapid Growth and Huge Appetites

Muscle, blood, and bone don't appear out of thin air. That kid who adds forty pounds and five inches in twelve months will consume his weight in edibles every day (at least you'll think he does). If building blocks for growth are absent, deficiencies and illnesses could result.

Less seriously, woeful diets and rapid growth combine to produce aches and pains and "I don't feel good." If you can convince your teen to balance the four food groups, the "yuckies" should disappear (unless a virus or other outside influence is at work).

Kids tend to want to gulp a pill rather than put up with pain or eat sensibly. "Give me a vitamin; then I won't have to eat (gag) vegetables."

Dialogue and plentiful choices will help you influence this attitude—refer to the Word of Wisdom frequently as you shop and prepare meals. In fact, I've found that a family home evening or two devoted to just what the Word of Wisdom means can be very effective.

Sports to Grow On

Sports allow growing bodies to dissipate built-up energy. I coax my kids into as many hours of intense physical activity as possible. However, the emphasis should be on personal development and team cooperation rather than competition. I don't like the vandalism and other negative results of some kinds of "school spirit."

Young athletes need high-energy foods that are loaded with calories. When fifteen-year-old Eric joined sixteen-year-old Roch on the swim team one year, I was astounded at the amount of food those two put away.

At breakfast after early morning practice, each boy ate a bowl of oat-meal with half-and-half cream and brown sugar, four slices of toast or two biscuits with jam, four to six scrambled eggs, several sausages or bacon strips, a pint of orange juice, and a large glass of instant breakfast.

I packed their lunches in two brown bags or a grocery bag in order to hold the three sandwiches, two pieces of fruit, pie or cake, half-dozen cookies, granola bar, and bundle of cheese and crackers. I also tucked in a thermos of chocolate milk or soup to wash it all down.

When they came home from school they devoured another sandwich or two, milk, and cookies. I was hard-pressed at dinner to prepare enough food to fill them up—and I usually failed. My pans weren't big enough.

What's for Dinner? Lunch? Breakfast?

Cooking for adolescents in the midst of a feeding frenzy takes little talent but great persistence and endurance. I shopped and cooked in bulk.

Three teenage athletes (and sometimes four or five) meant becoming creative about filling them up. Spaghetti, lasagna, and other pastas made up in individual portions and kept in the fridge and/or freezer provided quick snacks. My sister who raised twelve kids, including four football players, usually kept a pot of chili or soup simmering on a back burner.

Lots of whole-wheat bread should be on hand, too; when I'm not working full-time, I make bread, because I can tailor it to family tastes and needs. Pita bread, English muffins, and crackers by the bushel are handy, too. A big basket of fresh fruit, canned fruits packed in juice or light syrup, and dried fruits give athletes quick energy—and vitamins. Homemade cookies with "healthy" ingredients are good, too.

My athletes ate anything (including, on one occasion, a whole batch of cookie dough) to satisfy their pangs. Pasta salads, vegetable soup, boiled eggs, and sliced cheese in the fridge at all times helped curb their demolishing of the food budget—sort of.

Before I had any athletes, I wondered why a friend complained that her food bill resembled the national debt. After all, I had more children than she did. Now I understand: two teenage water polo players can out-eat six or eight little kids plus their mother and father.

This kind of preoccupation with food by young athletes is very different from the obsessions that accompany eating disorders, however.

AVOIDANCE OF EATING DISORDERS

How obsessed teens become determines whether or not they have an eating disorder. For some kids, food is no longer a vehicle for building strength; it turns into a mania.

The two recognized eating ailments are:

- Anorexia—eating too little to sustain growth and bodily functions.
- Bulimia—vomiting or using a purgative to shove food through the digestive system before it can "turn into fat." Bulimic kids will eat huge amounts and then throw up, a process sometimes called the "binge and purge" cycle.

Both boys and girls can suffer from these disorders, although girls are much more likely victims. To deal with these complex ailments, you need all the divine guidance you can get—and, most likely, medical help.

Because I've dealt with several bulimic and/or anoretic girls, including one of my own daughters, I've found that a calm attitude, combined with education and early intervention, is most effective.

Education—Know What You Face

Your daughter must understand biology and nutrition enough to comprehend that anorexia and bulimia can ravage her body. She must also learn to express her emotions through words and to find a sense of control other than through her intake of food.

I've watched *The Karen Carpenter Story* on video and brought home books like *Starving for Attention* by Debbie Boone to discuss with my kids. We've talked about why anyone would starve herself or binge and purge into a bulimic stupor. One of the main reasons is that teenagers, who think that "everybody's looking" at them, are never satisfied with their appearance. They want to be bigger, stronger, and more good-looking or smaller, daintier, and more attractive.

Certain clues (besides a fixation on appearance) can alert you to trouble. Following are the most common danger signals. If you recognize more than one of these signals in your son or daughter, take some sort of action.

ANOREXIA

- You never see her eat much.
- She develops a sudden fascination with diet books.
- She may take a bite or two, but usually says she doesn't "feel well" or "isn't hungry."
- She claims to have eaten at work or at a friend's house or to have made a sandwich earlier.
- She pushes food around on her plate or hides it in a napkin.
- She feeds food to the family dog or puts it down the disposal.
- She exercises excessively—tries to do 500 jumping jacks or run several miles in one session.
- Her period stops.

BULIMIA

- She spends time locked in the bathroom with water running or the toilet flushing.
- She showers right after dinner (running water masks the sounds of throwing up).
- You smell unpleasant odors associated with vomiting or diarrhea.
- She has halitosis and new cavities (stomach acid damages tooth enamel).
- You find packages of over-the-counter laxatives or diuretics.
- Her weight fluctuates more than ten pounds within relatively short periods of time.
- Food mysteriously disappears—especially sweets. The gallon of vanilla ice cream you just bought vanishes, but nobody claims eating it.

Studies indicate that oldest children and those who are too eager to please are most at risk for an eating disorder. Because their yearning for approval prevents them from expressing anger toward parents, siblings, and friends, they turn their anger inward.

If food becomes too important, it looms ever more powerful and becomes the focus of a struggle for control. By denying themselves food, even when they're starving, anoretic people exercise a perverse type of dominion—the benefits of fasting gone haywire.

I can't go into a complete discussion of the causes and treatment of these disorders; in fact, research reveals new information almost daily. Just be aware that these are real illnesses, and not merely "mind over matter." Scolding and nagging won't help, but talking to your family doctor will. A physical examination can rule out diseases and establish a base line for assessing physical health.

Early Intervention

Recognizing warning signals and seeking medical help when those signals persist may save your child's life. Disrupting a pathological behavior early is similar to rooting out a tumor before it grows big enough to cause trouble.

When I suspected one of my girls was throwing up after every meal, I immediately took her aside for a quiet interview. We talked about why she felt better when she threw up and discussed other ways she could deal with her stomachaches. I didn't accuse or say such things as "Why are you throwing up?" because I knew she had no idea.

One talk alone didn't help much, either. I had to persist in those talks and in trying to find out why she was so unhappy. If she hadn't responded positively to my counseling, I would have consulted a therapist or a nutritionist who specializes in eating disorders.

Above all, don't ignore your promptings. If the Spirit tells you to find medical help, don't delay. The longer an eating disorder lasts, the more difficult it is to treat.

Although girls are more likely than boys to develop anorexia or bulimia (or a combination disease called "bulimarexia"), both sexes may become compulsive eaters with the accompanying obesity and low self-esteem. Parents of compulsive eaters face similar challenges to those experienced by parents of children with anorexia or bulimia.

SUMMARY

This chapter cruised through some information about using the Word of Wisdom to teach proper eating habits and to safeguard your teenager's health. We also considered the special dietary needs of rapid growth and young athletes, as well as eating disorders that can arise during this self-absorbed, yet vulnerable, time of life.

As in every aspect of dealing with your adolescent, ignoring eating disorders won't make them go away. Take your concerns to the Lord and follow up by talking to your child. Then, if you feel prompted, consult with your doctor or health-care professional.

CHAPTER 3

Healthy Teens—
Establishing Good Sleep Habits

Why don't teenagers go to bed at night? And why won't they get out of bed in the morning?

I've pondered these two questions forever, it seems, and I haven't come up with any real answers, so (as when I feed my teens) I fall back on the Word of Wisdom—our inspired health law.

We are told to "Retire to thy bed early and sleep no more than is needful." Proper use of sleep is as important to well-being as proper use of food. The pituitary gland releases growth hormones into an adolescent's bloodstream while he or she is asleep. Since teenagers only grow during sleep, they should understand the consequences of sleep habits. But they don't. When it comes to sleep, we're talking about free agency, independence, and personal responsibility.

Like most parents, I'm frazzled by bedtime. All I want is to get those kids to their rooms so I can have some peace and quiet. My children, on the other hand, move into overdrive as soon as I say, "When are you going to turn off that thing (computer game, boom box, video, compact disc player), finish your homework, and go to bed?"

I've discovered an incontrovertible fact about teenagers: they never sleep during the night. They only sleep during the hours of 6 a.m. through 7 p.m. This schedule allows maximum rest during geometry, English, and whatever time may be scheduled for room or garage cleaning. Teens are thus assured of being ready for building campfires on the beach, racing motorcycles across land marked "No Trespassing," and sending Dad into orbit over the phone bill.

Establishing good sleep habits means instituting an appropriate bedtime schedule. In order to do this, you have to deal with biological and environmental factors:

- Allowing the body to set itself in finding the right amount of sleep
- Utilizing stress-beaters and relaxation techniques
- Setting aside a place and finding a time conducive to sleep
- Avoiding distractions like television and video games

Fights about sleeping habits are representative of all the fights we parents have with our children from infancy through young adulthood. Certain aspects are worth fighting over and others aren't.

For some reason, teenagers recognize their need for adequate food, but they think sleep is some kind of option. They don't understand that oversleeping and under-sleeping harm their bodies in ways similar to overeating and starving.

Your teenager cannot be forced to sleep, just as she cannot be forced to eat. In fact, the same kinds of problems involving eating disorders can crop up around sleep. In both these areas, you may need to seek medical intervention. But some basic scientific information should help you deflect most problems before they arise.

BIOLOGICAL/PHYSICAL FACTORS
The Benefits of Sleep—Finding the Right Amount

According to Shakespeare, sleep "knits up the raveled sleeve of care." It allows our bodies to rest and repair. During sleep, we breathe deeply, and increased oxygen in the bloodstream replenishes our cells. Our immune systems are strengthened, helping us more effectively fight disease and heal from injury.

Sleep must be deep and full of dreams to be most beneficial. Some people can recharge their batteries in only a few hours of uninterrupted sleep, but most of us need six to seven hours of deep sleep, plus one or two hours of light sleep where we drift just below consciousness.

Being able to go to sleep is a combination of genes, environment, and luck. We have to shut off disturbing thoughts and drop into the sleep that heals. Some of my kids have their father's talent for shutting down and going to sleep no matter how frazzled they are or how uproarious their problems. Others, sensitive to every noise and movement (like their mother), are quick to wake up.

Either pattern has its good and bad points. Gary can relax when he runs out of energy—even if the job isn't finished. He just goes to sleep and wakes up better able to deal with whatever hassle is in progress. I, on the other hand, am incapable of such stopping. I literally vibrate until I reach some sort of lull or break in the action. And sometimes I suffer the consequences of too much too often.

Sleep Disorders

Too little sleep is against the Word of Wisdom. So is too much sleep. When proper sleep habits are not observed, a young growing body is damaged.

Insomnia or over-sleeping can signal mental and emotional problems. Stress interferes with sleep, which can in turn interfere with physical and mental development. All kinds of things cause stress: procrastinating a report, worrying about algebra finals, breaking up with a girl/boyfriend, worrying about health, and fighting with Mom or Dad. Your teenager may escape such pressures by crawling into bed and going to sleep.

Or she might get "wired" and be unable to relax. Hours can go by while she fidgets, reads, or watches TV. Once she's unwound and able to fall asleep, she may be impossible to drag out of bed in the morning.

You might be tempted to use over-the-counter sleeping aids or antihistamines to help her "settle down," especially if she's worried about a big test or has had a fight with her best friend. But once you use medicine for relaxation, then you'll be tempted to give her caffeine so she can "wake up" when morning comes. A destructive cycle can quickly evolve.

If your teen has persistent difficulty sleeping, he or she needs a medical exam to rule out physiological problems. And you should follow your doctor's advice. If a checkup doesn't reveal a medical problem, try some of the following techniques for dealing with a kid who wanders the house until 3:00 a.m. or whose mattress seems fused to his body.

Provide a Restful Atmosphere

First, check your teen's chocolate and cola intake. Filling up on these favorite flavors can cause restlessness at night and hangovers in the morning. Other things being equal, this step alone may solve the problem.

Second, many teenagers, especially during a growth spurt, need an extra meal at bedtime. Just like growing babies, they can't last twelve or thirteen hours without nourishment. This meal should be high in carbohydrates, B vitamins, Vitamin C, and tryptophan (a protein amino acid). Research indicates that these nutrients ease tension and depression. The meal should not contain caffeine, salt, or large amounts of sugar.

Don't fall into the "supplement trap," however; carbohydrates, vitamins, minerals, and proteins work best in combination with other nutrients as found in food. The following are rich sources of these nutrients:

Carbohydrates—bread, cereal, crackers, potatoes

Vitamin C—oranges, strawberries, tomatoes

B vitamins—bread, bran, turkey, tuna

Tryptophan—almonds, pecans, cheese, shrimp, turkey

For a complete list of foods rich in these nutrients, see your doctor or nutritionist.

Acupressure and Massage

If your kid's sleep problem is due to an inability to relax, try rubbing her feet. This activity involves touching, warmth, and service. Many of my problem teens open up only after a few foot-rubbing sessions. The equipment is minimal: clean feet (the teen's), hands (mine), and lotion. A towel to protect clothing is optional.

Foot rubbing at my house takes place anywhere both parties are comfortable, but most often the insomniac teen stretches out on his bed while I sit at the end with his feet in my lap.

Other types of massage can evoke relaxation. Massage your teen's hands by making circular motions in her palm with your thumb, pressing your fingers against the back of her hand. Work your way across from her thumb to her little finger. Then massage each of her fingers, from the base to tip—gently pulling upward as you go. Repeat the process with her other hand.

Acupressure is a word derived from acupuncture, which involves stimulating curtain points along the nervous system with fine needles.

Acupressure doesn't require needles and is simple for novices to use. Try this acupressure technique to help your child relax: Locate the pressure point in her right hand by placing the ball of your thumb over the web of skin between her thumb and forefinger. Then gently squeeze the web between your thumb and forefinger for several seconds. Release and repeat several times.

I also teach my kids relaxation techniques they can use by themselves. These techniques involve actions that enable kids to exercise control over their situation.

Breathing Exercises and Visualization

Breathing and visualization are forms of self-hypnosis that help you tune into your body and change what's going on inside. Try this simple exercise before you explain it to your teen.

- Sit or lie down in the most comfortable position you can find and clear your mind of every negative thought.
- Take as deep a breath as possible to stretch your lung capacity. Hold your breath for five seconds, then slowly exhale through your nose. Concentrate on your breathing and keep your mind empty.
- Be aware of your spirit inside your body. Feel the mattress or chair under you, the pressure of the cushion or pillow at your back.
- Tighten and relax each muscle group; begin with your toes and work up. Focus on toes, ankles, knees, thighs. Don't allow your mind to conjure up anything else—make it stay on toes, knees, and so on. Keep your thoughts inside your body as you clench and release your muscles.
- When you reach the top of your head, reverse the process or go on to a visualization exercise.

Visualization Exercise

Once you have brought your thoughts and body into conscious control, use your imagination to move away from your worries and take a brief vacation from reality.

Where you go depends on you. I like to send myself back to a meadow where I played as a child in Alaska. My family homesteaded in the Interior about halfway between Fairbanks and Anchorage. My brothers and sister and I called the place behind our cabin "Fairy Meadow."

When I'm stressed, anxious, or just plain burned out, I transport myself to Fairy Meadow. Bright northern sun streams through the aspens that ring the meadow. I sit on a rustling carpet of last year's leaves while the sun warms my face and a breeze quivers the silver-green leaves above and around me. Scents of earth and grass waft on the air; butterflies chase each other on swirling drafts.

I stay in Fairy Meadow for a few minutes, then return, refreshed, to whatever challenges are in progress. You, too, can take yourself away and teach your stressed-out offspring to do the same.

ENVIRONMENTAL FACTORS
A Time Conducive to Sleep

Evenings at our house are times for scriptures and prayers (S&P) as we try to follow the prophet's admonition. These gatherings sometimes last as long as an hour, but usually last closer to ten minutes. Like our morning prayers, this time allows good feelings to flow between family members and brings the Spirit into our home.

This time also allows us to address any problems. In self-defense, we started S&P about twenty years ago when Dolly entered her teens. The nighttime family routine we'd developed for babies and toddlers simply didn't work any longer.

At first, assembling everyone was my biggest problem. I could never seem to corral them all in one place long enough to read one verse of anything, but I persevered. After fits and starts and setbacks that occurred over several years, we gradually developed a habit that is now so strong that the kids remind us when we forget.

I still check the family calendar to find a time when a majority will be in the house. I snag various bodies before they slip off to basketball practice, a night class, concerts, or other activities.

If I can't be sure everyone comes to S&P, I try not to let one person "fall through the cracks" too many times. But I don't wait until I have a full count, because procrastination only weakens the habit. It's too easy to dispense with the activity "just this once."

Besides settling everybody down with scripture reading and prayers, I try to make sure particular tasks are accomplished before bedtime. Otherwise, when I tell certain kids to "head for bed" they counter with, "I have to finish my (book report, lab notes, drill sheet)."

When to Sleep

Bedtimes for teenagers are difficult to define, because teenagers need so much more sleep than their younger siblings. Remember: teenagers grow faster than at any other time in their lives, except during infancy, and growth occurs only during sleep.

If you can figure out a way to convince your fourteen-year-old that she needs an earlier bedtime than your eight-year-old, write me! I haven't a clue on that subject.

I just growl, "I'm going to bed; if I hear one sound out of any of you, I'm nailing your bedroom door closed—with you behind it."

Then I make sure that particular kid gets up without argument the next morning. If he groans, "I'm too sick to get up," I haul him out of bed anyway. The only way I don't is if he's actually running a fever or looks sick. Throwing up doesn't count: a couple of my kids can "hurl" on command. Such gross activity must also be accompanied by some measurable level of genuine illness. Mom's intuition helps make the distinction.

A Place to Sleep

Your teenager's bedroom should be a quiet, distraction-free, clean, and private site—a relaxing place rather than a living place. Most experts tell us not to read in bed, but to reserve beds for sleeping. The idea is to avoid any mentally stimulating activity where you should be reposing. I like to read in bed, because that's the only time I can settle down with a newspaper or magazine. However, I frequently read too long and lose sleep I should be getting. I'm not a very good example to my kids on this subject.

Let teens decorate their own rooms. You may not agree with the decor, but if it's modest and within gospel standards, just shut the door. Linda's walls were covered with posters of every description, and Micah tacked up cartoons he'd drawn. Micah, like G.W., also spray-painted original poems and slogans on his walls. Those kids' rooms gave me a headache—they were too cluttered and "busy," but I didn't live in them.

You can insist on a certain level of cleanliness, however—I certainly do. I demand that my kids take care of their possessions and clothing, and they have to avoid health hazards like baloney sandwiches rotting under their beds or juice glasses growing mold on the windowsill.

The Army manages to convince young people to make their beds and keep the barracks neat; mothers should be able to do the same. Maybe the Army is effective because the sergeant never gives up in despair and cleans the room himself.

Of course, a sergeant has many more options at his disposal for motivating behavior—some of which you could try. Daily inspections with demerits, extra KP duty, and forced marches might encourage your slovenly offspring to change his ways.

The Boob Tube, Spacing Out, and Relaxation

Television watching and bedtimes tend to become intermingled. Nothing else in our society has had quite the impact of television.

I believe television is the single most detrimental influence on modern kids. Most of them spend more time watching television than they do sleeping or in school.

I've read the studies tracking skidding achievement scores and have seen the proof for myself. So, with few exceptions, my children were not allowed to watch television on school nights or Sundays. They watched two hours (about the length of a movie or a couple of sitcoms) on Friday and Saturday nights, but they had to ask permission and I had to approve the programs. At least that was my intention.

My kids were always sure they'd been warped for life because they didn't know the latest adventures of Bart Simpson or who was sleeping with whom on *Beverly Hills 90210*, *Melrose Place*, or *Friends*. Nor could they quote from memory the last eighty reruns of Saturday Night Live and Cheers. But their school records indicated differently.

Even my learning-disabled kids read well above their grade levels and expressed themselves in writing with enviable ease. I've had foster kids who came to us with failing grades, but who soared to Bs and As after being influenced by the restricted television policy.

The kids moan and groan and whine about "being bored," but they eventually wander off to read or play chess with an equally bored sibling. As the kids get older, I drum the uselessness of television time into their heads and encourage them to do "something productive" when they do watch it. Sometimes they fold or iron clothes in order to watch a favorite show. Even here, however, I must be alert. One of my sons folded and refolded the same basket of clothes for six days before I caught on.

Another negative influence closely related to television is video or computer games. A few minutes or an hour spent joggling a joy stick or maneuvering a mouse has little impact and might improve eye-hand coordination, as well as provide fun. But there are so many other games that provide exercise and social interaction as well as fun.

It's impossible to avoid animated games completely. I did put my foot down about the more gruesome ones that spurt technicolor blood and spray body parts accompanied by stereo shrieks.

Monitoring and shutting down the television and/or video games drains my energy. I often feel like giving up, but (so far) I think I'm making some headway. Again, it would help if we could come up with some consistent way of approaching this problem.

Besides "laying down the law" about television, I try to keep board and card games on hand. There are hundreds on the market to choose from. We have Scrabble, Triple Yahtzee, Trivial Pursuit, Monopoly, and UNO, as well as chess and checkers. We also have LDS games like Celestial Pursuit and Seek.

When Kids Won't Sleep

"But I can sleep late tomorrow" is an erroneous statement, but one kids try a lot. Going without adequate sleep, then "resting up" yo-yos the body between inadequate and too much sleep. Although the results are slower to develop and not as dramatic, this pattern of sleep damages the body as much as binge and purge eating.

So, how do you convince your kids to sleep at reasonable hours for reasonable lengths of time? The following description of a typical Player Family Bedtime Battle illustrates that, while I have good ideas, I'm no better than anyone else at putting them into effect!

The incident took place in the fall of 1988; we lived in Shell Beach, California. Bedtime arrived for Nathan at eight. Nathan's behavior at bedtime reflected his eight years of being the baby. Until he was ten years old, he never spent an hour alone in bed (or anywhere else) in his life.

As our age increased and energy decreased, Gary and I retired to bed earlier and earlier. But actually making it to sleep was (and is) still a struggle. Nathan asked every night, "Is Daddy going to play his trumpet?"

Daddy's playing his trumpet meant Nathan could climb into the waterbed to snuggle with me for a while. We read stories, wrote in his journal, and talked. This half hour or so was a special time for me and my "baby."

The other kids gave us a few minutes, then one by one they trooped in for reports on their day's activities. Ten-year-old Micah took a running jump from the doorway, wrapped his blankie around his shoulders and slipped off his glasses in one swift motion, then splooshed down on my other side.

Linda, fourteen, climbed across the foot of the bed to burrow her lanky body beside Nathan. Nathan was almost asleep and easily shifted. I tried to make sure he didn't end up too far onto my side, because he'd sweat all over the sheets. Linda brought forms and brochures about summer camp and volunteering for Special Olympics. We tried to fill them out, but the bed sloshed too much; I told her to give them to me in the morning.

Rock and roll vibrated my bedroom door. "I know a girl named Boney Moroney! She's as skinny as a stick of macaroni!" Eric's gravelly fifteen-year-old baritone drowned out the singer on the tape. Eric was a throwback to the late fifties and early sixties. He wore a black leather jacket, combed his hair into a DA, and memorized every song he could find recorded by Chuck Berry or the Beatles.

Micah and Linda jumped up to run into the living room. Gary Willis, seventeen, lounged in a chair and critiqued Eric's performance. "You need less pelvis and more leg action."

Sherri, twenty-one, bounced in from the kitchen. "Put the couch back; Kelly's coming over to watch a movie." Eric continued gyrating and bellowing, and Micah and Linda began to croon and sway behind him.

Roch (sixteen and an exception to my "teens don't sleep" observation) stormed into the room and growled, "Will you turn that down? I need some sleep!"

Then he saw me standing by the couch, so he peeled off his T-shirt and led me back to my room to scratch his back.

"Rockin' Robin" shook the walls. I could barely hear Gary's trumpet serenading the surf in the back yard. Headlights bounced off the fence and briefly lit the curtains in my bedroom.

Suddenly, Robin stopped rockin', and Linda and Micah joined Roch and me on the waterbed.

"Get off Nathan; he's under the pillows." I shoved them over. Nathan didn't wake up.

"Kelly's here. Sherri made me stop practicing!" Eric plopped down beside Roch. Roch leaned back with his eyes half closed and wiggled closer when I tried to stop scratching.

Gary Willis strolled in, jingling my car keys. "Can I go get Todd? He's got a carburetor for my scooter."

"Todd lives an hour from here. Don't you think 9:30 on a week night is just a tad late to start anything?" I took my keys away from him. He rolled his eyes at me and slouched off.

By now the noise in my room had reached Rockin' Robin level. Gary opened the patio doors and yelled, "Get out of my bed, all of you; I'm tired. And take that sweaty little body with you." He pulled Nathan by the ankles across the bed and handed him to Roch.

When nobody other than Roch—who departed with Nathan lolling against his shoulder— left the room, Gary unbuttoned his shirt and took off his shoes.

Linda continued her saga about the "gross guy" at the bus stop and her English grammar woes. Micah pretended he was asleep. Eric described the computer he wanted us to buy him (fat chance). Gary started to unzip his pants.

"Okay! Okay! If I grow up warped because you wouldn't listen to me, don't blame me!" Linda smooched me, made a face at her dad, and left. Micah still pretended to be asleep, but Gary stood him on his feet and Eric led him away.

We finally dozed off, interrupted shortly after midnight by Sherri when she told us Kelly had left, by Gary Willis who tried one more time to get the keys to my Laser, and by a phone call from married Dolly who was pregnant and bored. I told Dolly to enjoy the boredom; her turn was coming!

SUMMARY

And there you have it: a brief run-down on why teenagers need more sleep than younger kids and how I try to make sure they get it. But I also accept reality—and you should, too.

We can insist on certain types of behavior, watch physical and environmental influences, and teach relaxation techniques, but we can't force sleep. . . .

How Can I Teach Self-Control?

CHAPTER 4

Learning to Talk to Each Other

Sociology and psychology experts all say the same thing: *the most important aspect of health family relationships is communication.*

Relief Society, Priesthood, and Young Women's organizations hold workshops and teach lessons to help members communicate. So why is the Generation Gap more like the Generation Chasm in many of our homes?

I've heard countless kids say, "What? Talk to my folks? I can't. They don't understand me, and they never listen to me, anyway." Many of my foster kids and counselees confide that their parents are "too busy" or "not interested." And the kids themselves have terrible communication skills. Not only do they refuse to turn to their parents, but they have no idea how to let others know what they want or need. The inability to express feelings scars more human beings than all the weapons of war ever invented.

If you and members of your family both talk and listen to each other, your chances of developing positive family dynamics are excellent—and you can learn to communicate. That might seem too simplistic—of course you talk and you listen (unless you have significant speech and hearing handicaps)!

But in many homes, people talk *at* each other, rather than *to* each other. Instead of trying to communicate, all they do is blather. And they don't listen, either.

Does the following exchange sound familiar?

Kid: "Can I have five bucks?"

Parent: "What happened to the five dollars you earned for cleaning out the carport two days ago?"

Kid: "Oh, that. I spent it."

Parent: "On what?"

Kid: "Stuff. Come on, I wanna go with Todd and Matt to the movies."

Parent: "I don't have any cash."

Kid: "You still owe me five dollars."

Parent: "For what? I just paid you for the carport."

Kid: "You said you'd pay me for moving all that stuff around to the side of the house."

Parent: "That was part of cleaning out the carport."

Kid: "No, it wasn't. It wasn't even inside the carport."

And so on . . .

The parent is focused on whether or not certain chores are finished. The teen wants money so he can hang out with his friends; he couldn't care less whether he actually earns the money or whether anything concrete is accomplished.

Communication is more than moving air currents with your vocal cords; it's a two-way street that involves talking and listening—with the emphasis on listening. There are various methods for improving speaking and listening skills. Let me share my method with you.

I break the communication process into four sections. The first three sections require you to model the behavior you want your kid to learn:

1. Set an example by opening the channels of communication.
2. Set an example by using "I Feel" statements rather than "You"-centered statements and by listening effectively.
3. Set an example by teaching about body language and tone of voice.

The fourth section makes the abstract concrete through use of the Point System, my adaptation of a behavioral modification system used in group homes.

By the way, you'll develop fewer gray hairs if you don't take *anything* your teenager says or does personally. Teenagers delight in testing and demonstrating their power. Decide early on that you will keep a sense of humor and you will not be drawn into a fight. Not reacting when your feelings are hurt is difficult, but it's the only way you'll stay sane.

I can't repeat this point enough: Don't debate with your adolescent—it doesn't accomplish a thing. Some of my kids are born debaters. No matter what subject is being discussed, they'll take the opposite point of view. But being drawn into a battle of logic and wills with a teenager is an exercise in futility. In the first place, that teenager will always, and without any shred of evidence, think he's right. It won't matter whether or not he really is. Nothing you say will make an ounce of difference.

POINT 1: OPEN THE CHANNELS OF COMMUNICATION

French babies learn to speak French, Russian babies learn Russian, and English babies learn English. Just as you learned to speak your "primary" language from your parents, you learned how to communicate your needs from your parents. And your children are learning from you. Whether or not you have difficulty relating to your children depends on what you learned from your parents.

Do you listen when your children speak to you? Or do you tune them out? Unfortunately, most of us tend to tune them out—but for good reason.

Little kids yell, "Watch me!" several hundred times a day. They're also adept at tugging on a distracted mother's hand, skirt, or hair while chanting, "Mom? Mom? Mom?"

After a while, Mom just gets kind of numb. Unfortunately, that numbness doesn't wear off as the little kid turns into a big kid. Tuning out becomes a habit.

Parents who didn't listen to a first-grader's blow-by-blow description of "Marcy's barfing during story time" won't be told a few years later about Marcy's beer bash while her folks were out of town.

Conduct an experiment with yourself. Pause right now in your reading and reflect on the last encounter you had with your teenager.

Receiver On . . . or Off?

Can you remember what you said? What she said? Do you know how she felt? Did she say anything that might let you in on her true feelings? If you only remember a few words, you're pretty typical. And if you don't have a clue as to your teen's frame of mind, you're also typical!

You can break the tune-out habit if you're determined. A good way to start is to take your child aside and say something like, "I'm sorry if I've seemed distracted (or haven't paid attention, or haven't been there for you). Please help me improve. You are more important to me than anything else in this world."

For some reason, a lot of parents think admitting error or weakness to a teenager is like letting a growling dog sense fear (I will admit there are certain parallels—especially with the growling dog image). But I've found that telling my kids I've made a mistake or I'm unsure opens avenues of communication that didn't exist before.

At Wit's End—The Channel Finally Opens

One of my fourteen-year-olds had just about defeated me. He failed three-fourths of his classes, he never lifted a finger to help around the house, and he continually wandered off without telling anybody where he was going. I'd exhausted all of my creative coping methods, many of which I've detailed in this book.

I finally said, "Look, I've tried everything I can think of—except a sojourn into child abuse and bodily harm. I admit it—I'm stumped. I have no idea what to do with you. Do you have any suggestions?"

When I first told him to sit down, that I wanted to talk to him, he automatically tensed up and scowled. But as I admitted my frustration and told him how much I loved him, he blinked a couple of times, muttered, "Love you, too," and relaxed.

Then my son said, "Make me a list of what you want, and I'll give you a list of what I want. We can do a contract." Since I'd already tried these things, I guess just the fact that *he* was the one to suggest a contract made the idea more appealing.

This particular fourteen-year-old didn't change overnight, or even over the next month, but his grades gradually improved and he usually told us where he was going. Helping around the house was a different matter, but he did become a little more accountable in that area, too.

POINT 2: USE "I FEEL" STATEMENTS AND LISTEN EFFECTIVELY

Once you've opened the channels of communication, your child will be ready to at least notice the examples you try to set.

1. **EXPLAIN** the difference between "I Feel" statements and "You-centered" statements. "I Feel" lets your listeners know how you feel without forcing them to defend themselves.

2. **HELP** her understand that all organisms fight back when they're attacked.

3. **SHOW** her how to define her emotions, rather than to indulge in name-calling.

Be sure that *you* use "I Feel" words whenever you talk with your teen. For example, consider the totally different atmospheres these statements create:

A. "When you don't tell me where you're going, I feel worried and upset." (**I Feel**)

B. "You are a thoughtless, selfish kid without a shred of sense." (You-centered)

A. "Coming home from work to a horrendous mess gives me a stomachache." (**I Feel**)

B. "You're such a slob; why don't you clean up this pigsty?" (You-centered)

Once you break the "tune-out" habit and consistently use "I Feel" statements, you can try effective listening.

DEVELOP EFFECTIVE LISTENING SKILLS

Mark Twain quipped, "If we were supposed to talk more than we listen, we would have two mouths and one ear." Effective listening requires you to hear and understand what your child says enough to repeat his or her meaning. Psychologists call this "reflective listening."

A family home evening activity called "Are You Really Listening?" helps me teach my kids the value of listening to each other. I first learned about it when my daughter Linda took a course called "Teen Skills," a program for adolescents designed by Quest International and sponsored by the Lions Club. A full description of the activity is found in the Appendices.

Begin the family home evening lesson with an example of poor listening. I usually write something for my children to read when they're younger, but by the time they're thirteen or fourteen they're such hams they have no trouble coming up with something to say.

How Not to Listen to Anybody
Exchange 1: Interrupting
Teen: "I had this weird dream last night; I dreamed we were back in Alaska. . . ."

Parent: "I wish we still lived in Alaska! I read a piece in the paper about Anchorage."

Exchange 2: Me-Tooing
Teen: "I'm so stressed about the auditions coming up. My stomach hurts and I think I might throw up."

Parent: "Work was awful today. Three people wanted their jobs done right now—I didn't even have time for lunch."

Exchange 3: Giving Unsolicited Advice
Teen: "Abby has been so funny lately. She won't talk to me in the halls, and today when she saw me come into the cafeteria, she turned around and walked out."

Parent: "I don't think she's much of a friend. You're better off without her. Just ignore her."

The preceding sets of words (they're *not* conversations) illustrate the three most common listening failures. When somebody else talks, most of us are so hung up on what we want to say that we (1) interrupt, (2) say "me, too," and (3) give advice without being asked.

You should also point out to your children that listening failure can be nonverbal. The following actions indicate lack of attention:
- Looking around the room rather than at the speaker
- Twiddling with hair or fussing with clothes
- Yawning or glancing at the clock

My teenagers have a lot to say about how poor listeners make them feel. This activity promotes some great discussion and always improves communication in our family.

Olympic-Level Listening

Once your kids are aware of the importance of listening, you can then discuss the components of good listening skills: focusing, accepting, and encouraging.

Take a look at the three earlier exchanges, this time with good listening responses:

Conversation 1: Focusing

Teen: "I had this weird dream last night; I dreamed we were back in Alaska. . . ."

Parent: "Really? Tell me about it." (Looks into speaker's eyes and nods slightly.)

Conversation 2: Accepting

Teen: "I'm so stressed about the auditions coming up. My stomach hurts and I think I might throw up."

Parent: "Trying out for something you really want can be awfully stressful. What exactly about the auditions worries you?"

Conversation 3: Encouraging

Teen: "Abby has been so funny lately. She won't talk to me in the halls, and today when she saw me come into the cafeteria, she turned around and walked out."

Parent: "You've been such close friends, I can understand why her behavior would bother you. Do you think you should call her and see if something is wrong?"

POINT 3: UNDERSTAND HIDDEN MESSAGES

You can use the family home evening on listening skills to point out that *how* we say something is as important as *what* we say. Explain body language; don't assume your child understands the messages she sends through her behavior and tone of voice.

I always insist that everyone watch tone of voice. During another family home evening, we practiced changing the meaning of "Hi, it's wonderful to see you" by changing our speaking pitch, volume, and tone. That simple statement could be one of delight ("I'm so glad to see you"), sarcasm ("I'd rather see anyone else"), boredom ("Not you again!"), and surprise ("I never thought you'd actually show up!").

The kids were astounded to realize that the *way* they said something could completely change the meaning. They learned a valuable lesson in human dynamics.

Not only did I show them during the lesson what I meant, I followed up whenever arguments began. I often said, "Repeat that in a softer, nicer voice." See how this technique works in the following incident:

Learning to Understand One Another

Micah wanted a ride to school. He'd been home sick with a cold for a couple of days, so he was kind of crabby. When he grumpily demanded that Sherri drive him to school, she said, "Forget it!"

Sherri's snippy answer infuriated him and they were soon in a shouting match. "You're a selfish nerd!" he screamed. "You're a snotty little brat!" she countered. I finally dragged them both into the living room for a "teaching moment."

First, I told Micah to repeat his request as if he were talking to his best friend. He took a deep breath and said, "Sherri, I feel crummy and it's cold outside. Would you please take me to school on your way to work?"

Sherri rolled her eyes as she said, "I'll be late for work if I go clear over to the high school."

I stopped them. "Obviously, you both want something. Micah wants to avoid walking in the cold, and Sherri wants to avoid being late for her job. Sherri, do you think Micah's request is reasonable? Should he aggravate his cold by walking through the snow?"

Sherri said, "Yeah, I guess he wouldn't want to walk, but I can't take him; I'm late now."

I said, "Then what would have been a more thoughtful answer than 'Forget it'?"

"Ask Gary Willis?" (who was still in bed and didn't have to be at work until 10:00 a.m.).

And so the exchange went. I tried to reinforce the importance of tone of voice and seeing the other guy's point of view. Grabbing these teaching moments as they come along can be very effective.

If your children insist they "didn't say anything nasty," consider carrying a tiny tape recorder and switching it on when you notice trouble brewing. Listening to themselves is a real eye-opener for most kids.

Hugs Communicate Better than Words

As important as communication skills are, I want you to know that loving, physical contact breaks barriers between parent and child and calms as nothing else can. If I feel like smacking my tantrum-torn offspring, I hug them instead.

I've used this technique since my children were babies. It works just as well with a raging fourteen-year-old as it does with a fussing two-year-old. Many times when I've been confronted by furious young men or women, I've realized that they needed hugs more than anything else.

An incident with my son Eric underscored just how effective hugs can be. Eric stood before me, angry at the evaluation of his performance that I'd written on the chore chart. He'd received a "6," which means "you can do better."

Eric recited a litany of everything he'd done that day and ended with his main argument, "I was in bed; you told me to go to bed early, and I did."

I explained that since dishes had been his chore for the day and the dishes weren't finished, it didn't matter what else he'd done—he still could have done a better job on his assignment.

My words fell on deaf ears. Tears filled Eric's eyes as he tried to convince me that I was wrong and he was right. I finally reached up, hugged him, and said, "Eric, *I'm* the one who has to decide whether something is finished or not. *I* decide whether you performed as well as you could. You usually do your chores very conscientiously, but this time you goofed." I hugged him again and said, "I love you, you know."

His shoulders stayed rigid for a few seconds, then he hugged me back. He rested his cheek against the top of my head and sighed, "I love you, too."

When emotions and reasoning collide, emotions usually win. A hug and an "I love you" will dissipate anger more quickly than all the logical arguments ever uttered.

But I Thought You Said . . .

In addition to the communication and listening skills already discussed, you should strive to be as concrete as possible. I'm forever hearing, "You didn't tell me," "But you said," and "Huh?" from my teenagers. So I've come up with a method that clarifies what I want from them and reduces my need to nag.

Households like mine—occupied by three or four adolescents, all of whom vie for attention, discipline, and "a place in the spotlight"—require a lot of creativity to handle the confusion and disorder. I'd have given up at least ten years ago if I hadn't discovered the Point System.

THE POINT SYSTEM

Some of the most asked-for copies of my weekly column were those that addressed my Point System. The Point System wasn't my original idea; I adapted it from programs used in group homes. I started using it when all nine kids were at home and we went on vacation.

Whenever the family climbed into our van for an outing, I gave each child a hundred points, with each point valued from a penny to a nickel (based on available funds). During the trip, the kids collected (or lost) more points, depending on how they acted.

For example:
- Cleaning up apple cores and mashed graham crackers off the floor without being asked was worth ten extra points
- Spitting on or kicking a sibling cost ten points
- Answering a whining little sister with a hug and an offer to read a story was worth five extra points
- Screaming, "Take off my headphones, you little creep!" cost five points—ten if the screamer whacked the little creep

When people began to comment on how well-behaved my herd was in public, I decided to adapt the Point System for daily use at home. It worked wonders in getting the kids to do chores, pick up after themselves, and become more pleasant living companions.

I graded them on a scale of one to ten, with ten meaning "couldn't be better" and one meaning "absolutely worthless." Most of the time the kids scored between five and nine.

Putting a numeric value to types of behavior helped eliminate confusion over what I meant when I said, "Shape up." During family gatherings, we decided exactly what kinds of behavior we wanted to eliminate in our house and what kinds we wanted to encourage.

Physical violence and verbal abuse have always been absolutely forbidden, so they elicited the most negative reactions. If my Early Teen flew into a rage and threatened her brother with the mop, she lost points. She also lost points if she screamed, "I hate you, you B— Hole."

However, if she emptied the dishwasher without being reminded, she gained points—even if she forgot to wipe out the sink. If she gave the last piece of her candy bar to her little brother or rushed to clean up the bathroom, she gained points. The points doubled if the bath mess belonged to someone else.

Understanding the Spirit of the Law

All this giving and taking away of points can become a bookkeeping nightmare. Some of my kids added in their heads faster than I could add with a calculator, so I never even pretended to tally everything. Instead, I set down the basic premises and reminded everybody frequently about the purpose of the Point System. I stressed that the idea wasn't to collect points, it was to improve the peace and harmony in our home. I also stressed that I'm not perfect; I do the best I can, but I have to be the final say on who earned which points for what.

How to Avoid Misunderstandings

Writing things down and discussing the terms guarantees that everybody concerned knows what's going on. I didn't always use contracts, and I continually ran into problems with my kids' memories or mine. Some people might be able to recall vividly what they said a week or two earlier, but I can never remember details much more than three or four minutes after a conversation ends!

The contract in the Appendices represents an example of the kind of behavior modification tools Gary and I used with our hard-headed kids. You'll notice that it includes many severe restrictions. The word *hard-headed* is key: we only used this kind of contract when a child had lost our trust or if a foster child had come from an abusive or permissive environment.

Sometimes, a kid refused to agree to the contract. In that case, we negotiated further—usually, the problem was simply some kind of misunderstanding. If a foster kid still refused to sign after we talked things over, we reluctantly said goodbye. But we did so without guilt, because the contract, after negotiation, represented what we were willing to live with.

So far, we've never faced a situation where our own kids wouldn't give in and follow the rules. We've done a lot of praying, and we try to follow the promptings of the Spirit.

I know effective, loving parents who have allowed their rebellious youths to spend the night in jail, be suspended from school, and in many other ways reap the consequences of their actions. That choice is right, but painful. We love our kids so much that watching them suffer can tear us up like nothing else—even if their suffering results from choices they made in defying us.

Sometimes I think back on an incident and wonder what I could have done differently. Relying on the written word ensures I can be at peace and know I've done my best. I can look at my charts and contracts to reinforce that assurance.

SUMMARY

You can learn to talk to your teenager if you set an example by opening the channels of communication, using "I Feel" instead of "You"-centered statements, cultivating effective listening skills, and teaching about body language and tone of voice. Finally, use some type of concrete tool like the Point System so you won't be at the mercy of an adolescent's version of reality. Then, hang on.

Family communication skills are worth building, but the process isn't easy, short, or sure. Examples of exercises in the Appendices offer suggestions, any of which you are welcome to try or adapt. Use any of my charts or checklists in your home without worrying about copyright, because keeping our youth close to the Iron Rod supersedes all other concerns.

You'll note that I don't say "*holding* onto the Iron Rod," because no one can force good behavior. Our best bet is to hang onto the Rod ourselves, and then keep our arms outstretched, so we can help our kids make the connection between Christ-centered living and happiness.

CHAPTER 5

Developing Self-Esteem and Self-Control

Once you've figured out how to talk to your teenagers (and elicit a response), you'll probably wonder about teaching them self-control. When kids love themselves, and only then, can they love others; self-esteem comes before self-control.

Self-conscious and vulnerable, all teenagers need large doses of unconditional love. Their minds and bodies in turmoil, they think everybody's looking at them. Adolescent psychologists term this attitude "The Imaginary Audience" or the "On Stage" mindset.

Early Teens are the most affected by this phenomenon; they're constantly "on stage." David Elkind, a modern research psychologist, asserts that because young adolescents believe in that imaginary audience, they behave as if the whole world is watching. Fortunately, kids tend to outgrow this preoccupation, but they can be pretty difficult to live with until they do.

You've probably experienced something very similar to what I experienced with one of my twelve-year-olds.

I picked Daniel up after school to take him to the bank to open a savings account with his birthday money. His class had a "crazy" party that day where they dressed in their silliest, wildest, craziest clothes. Daniel had worn ripped plaid polyester pants and a striped T-shirt. He had back-combed his hair and shellacked it with super-hold spray. He had looked hilarious, and he had joined the rest of us in laughing as he went out the door.

When I picked him up, I told him we were going straight to the bank; I wasn't taking him home to change clothes because I was in a hurry. He nearly went into convulsions.

I tried to point out that nobody at the bank cared how he was dressed; they just wanted his money. "Besides," I said, "a lot of kids dressed up today; nobody's going to look at you or be surprised."

No deal. He refused to get out of the car. I ended up carrying the signature card out to him for signing.

A WAY THAT WORKS

The mandatory prerequisite for building self-esteem in your kids (and yourself) is communication with the head of the human family, our Heavenly Father. Communicating with Heavenly Father means using effective prayer.

We've heard all our lives about the importance of prayer. You've probably tried to practice the principles taught from the pulpit. So have I. But I had to learn an important lesson about daily prayer before my practice became very effective.

My family starts the day with morning prayers. At the end of the day, we gather again for scripture reading and prayers (S&P). We encourage the kids to remember their personal prayers, and Gary and I pray together in the privacy of our room just before we go to sleep.

When we miss these strengthening times (and we do miss them more than I care to admit), everything falls apart. This fact was dramatically illustrated during one of our many (too many) moves.

Something's Wrong Here

I felt like I was pushing against the wind or swimming through warm fudge. No matter who I told to do what, few did anything. Those who tried to follow directions forgot their instructions or misinterpreted them.

Eric, Mike (a foster kid), Micah, and our home teachers struggled to move our travel trailer away from the carport and position a pick-up truck so it could be loaded. A tire on the trailer went flat, and the truck bogged down in a mud hole. Somebody misjudged the turning radius, crumpled the truck's rear fender, and nearly took off the side of the porch. The hitch cracked; Eric smacked his funny bone, and Mike fell down the front steps.

My sister-in-law, Sherry, and two of my nieces showed up to help me pack, and the girls started arguing with Linda and Shannon (a foster daughter). Sherry looked around and said, "Everybody's sure touchy today—it's crazy out there," referring to the chaos under the carport.

Switching On the Receiver

Suddenly, I realized that we hadn't had prayers that morning.

Gary had left an hour before everybody woke up (his job at this time required a 150-mile commute, a ten-hour day, and a six-day week). Since it was Saturday, nobody wanted to climb out of bed very early. By the time I poked, prodded, and kicked them all into standing positions, the high priests quorum and some of the Relief Society sisters had arrived.

Sherry helped me assemble everybody in the front entry, and I asked our home teacher to offer the prayer. Immediately following the "amen" tension decreased, voices changed pitch, and the rest of the day went smoothly.

By "smoothly" I mean we finished our move and nobody screamed at anybody else. Mike broke a lamp, Micah faded from usefulness in typical thirteen-year-old fashion, Eric dropped one of my file drawers, and Linda argued that she should be able to go out with her friends because she didn't feel good enough to work any more. No, we didn't experience miracles—just a basic calmness that enabled me to cope.

Let me repeat: you'll accomplish very little if you don't stay in touch with the source of all strength.

Now, let's zero in on helping your kids understand their uniqueness as sons and daughters of God in order to develop their self-esteem from an eternal perspective.

Now, What Did That Mean?

Self-esteem is developed or destroyed during the years teenagers search for identity and leave home. Contrary to the negative connotation of "selfishness" it has assumed, *self-esteem* means that a person values himself or herself. A person with high self-esteem doesn't take herself very seriously—she can be corrected without falling apart. Every kid that I've encountered who has problems has suffered from poor self-esteem.

I'm not talking about "pride" or narcissism here, either. *Self-esteem* closely parallels *self-confidence*. I liked the metaphor of a "three-legged stool" from Linda's "Teen Skills" class to help teenagers visualize the basis for self-confidence.

In the same way a stool will collapse without all three legs, self-confidence is based on three crucial principles:

1. Feeling appreciated—feeling loved, accepted, listened to, and supported by others.
2. Feeling skillful—being able to identify what you do well.
3. Taking responsibility—being *active* rather than *passive,* having a sense of control over what happens to you, not blaming others, and staying calm and avoiding negative behavior.

Let's take each leg of the stool in turn.

FEELING APPRECIATED

Everyone wants to feel special—especially teenagers. But teenagers can be hard to appreciate. Don't be overwhelmed by the negative feelings that can develop.

Like you, I get testy when I come home from work and find nothing but a gnawed turkey leg in the refrigerator, dishes piled in the sink and over the counters, the grass so tall it needs a scythe, and the telephone on the verge of melt-down. When I assemble my half-dozen or so teens to quiz them about the state of the house, they have the audacity to be surprised at my mood!

"Hey, Mom, I worked my butt off in that basement, but somebody messed it up again."

"It was clean, honest. I've washed dishes all day."

"I can't imagine why the bathroom is still dirty—I scrubbed it on my hands and knees for hours . . ."

No matter how irritated I am by my offspring's lack of accomplishments, I must remember to use "I Feel" statements rather than to yell at them for being lazy slobs.

AND (a BIG "and") I must find something to genuinely appreciate before I criticize. Sometimes I have to stretch to come up with anything!

When I try to keep the appreciation leg of the stool from collapsing, I keep two points in mind: be genuine, and be specific.

Being genuine is a must. Teens are equipped with hypocrisy detectors. If they sense you're patronizing or "buttering them up" they'll turn off and turn away.

Being specific is just as important. Saying "You're nice" is so vague that it's meaningless. But saying, "I like the way you laugh at my jokes" or "You always know when somebody needs a hug" lets your kid know what pleases you and which behavior should be repeated.

The pairs of compliments below illustrate the difference between "vague" and "specific." With practice, you should be able to devise specific statements you can use without sounding like a hypocrite.

"You look nice today."
"That shade of red lights up your eyes."

"You're a lot of fun."
"You know how to make me smile in spite of myself."

"You're so helpful."
"Wow, you loaded the dishwasher, wiped the cabinets, and swept the floor in only twenty minutes. And you did it better than most people could in an hour!"

"You're thoughtful."
"You noticed your little sister was getting frustrated, so you spent extra time showing her how to tie her shoelaces."

FEELING SKILLFUL

The second leg of the three-legged stool is to help kids feel skillful. The worst thing you can do to adolescents is call them names—label them as stupid, slow, or worthless. At the moment you may rightly think your kid is the laziest person on two legs, but you must still focus on your feelings instead of attacking him.

As you try to help your teen feel skillful, you will use techniques similar to those you used to make her feel appreciated. Your attitude should be genuine, and you should be as specific as possible.

I try to be careful not to set my kids up for failure by demanding performances beyond their capacities. Teenagers don't notice details—not like their mothers do, anyway. If I say, "Remember to do your chores today," my kid will say "Okay." But he or she will almost certainly have an entirely different perspective about chores being "finished" than I have!

See the Appendices for a discussion on how to brainstorm with your teenager and help him or her figure out "skillful" areas.

The following exercise, which was adapted from some Sunday School Course 17 materials, is a good one to use to help a teen feel "skillful."

WAYS TO INCREASE SELF-ESTEEM
1. List ten reasons why God loves you.
2. Repent of those things that are keeping you away from your Heavenly Father. Forgive yourself for those things you have confessed and forsaken.
3. Think of past successes.
4. Think of times you felt of greatest worth. Then figure out why you felt that way.
5. Live as if you already had the character traits that you desire.
6. Think of someone you know who is a lovable person. Ask yourself, "What does he/she do that makes him/her that way?" Follow the example.
7. Master a new hobby or skill.
8. Develop a positive attitude.
9. Make a list of your strengths. List ten things you can do.
10. Write and act upon your growing list of resolutions for self-improvement.
11. Realize that you have been given at least one gift and an open invitation to "seek . . . earnestly the best gifts." (D&C 46:8.)
12. Get your patriarchal blessing if you don't already have it. Study your blessing for specific personal gifts and talents.

I don't wait for family home evening to tackle an activity with my kids, because—like the average teen—they don't want to "brag" or be "snotty" (a teen word that means "to think you're better than somebody else," which is a big no-no). Instead, I take out the "Ways to Increase Self-Esteem" or I brainstorm during one-on-one times.

George Burns once said, "I would rather be a failure at something I love than a success at something I hate." Help your teenager discover just what she loves to do and encourage her to follow her dreams.

Sometimes we parents have difficulty letting children make their own way, especially if their talents and interests are much different from ours. But each of us must live our lives for ourselves; we can't live somebody else's dream.

TAKING RESPONSIBILITY

The third leg of the three-legged stool involves accepting responsibility, which means:

- Being *active* rather than *passive*; having a sense of control over what happens to you
- Not blaming others
- Staying calm and avoiding negative behavior

Be Active Rather Than Passive

I repeatedly tell my children and myself that we have no control over anybody except ourselves. When I'm so mad at a kid I could turn around and walk away forever, I remember that my anger won't change a thing. Anger will just upset my stomach.

I have a quick temper. Maintaining my balance and smiling through squabbles challenges me more than anything. When I give in to annoyances, slam around the house, or yell at my kids, I find myself in turmoil. As long as I'm calm and in control, everybody else gradually simmers down—no matter how provoked, tired, or hungry.

Sometimes I have to admit that I just can't cope at the moment—that's when I lock myself in my room to meditate and pray. And I don't come out until I've cooled off and am ready to face life again.

As old-fashioned as it may sound, I know that when I'm in control and at peace, my home is peaceful. A peaceful mother means peaceful family dynamics. And mothers aren't the only ones: Dad's attitude is just as important as Mom's.

The second step in being active rather than passive is exercising control over what happens to you. Control involves knowing where you want to go and where you want your life's journey to end.

Set Attainable Goals without Sabotaging Them

Research into adolescent physical and mental development indicates that teenagers haven't had enough experience to fully understand how their behavior sabotages their goals. It helps if you and your teenager sit together and write down what he or she wants out of life. The Young Women Personal Progress Book outlines exactly how to do it. The same technique works for boys.

The following are examples of common goals for LDS kids:

Long-Term Goals
    Serve a mission
    Marry in the temple
    Graduate from college or technical school
    Be able to support my family
Intermediate Goals
    Find an after-school job
    Pass all my classes
    Attract a girl (boy) friend
Short-Term Goals
    Be on time for school
    Understand algebra
    Go to the Homecoming dance with Mandy

Once the goals are written down, discuss with your child exactly how those goals can be achieved and how they build on each other. For example, a temple marriage follows activity in the Church and appropriate dating. Finding an after-school job means practicing punctuality and responsibility, as well as turning in applications and asking for references. Being on time for school requires getting out of bed early enough to dress, eat, and travel there.

With most of my kids, I've written their goals with them, sometimes in the form of a "letter to myself" to be opened in six years. This is a good activity to use with Early Teens.

Try Not to Blame Others

"It's not my fault!" is a common teenage lament. All of us at one time or another want to blame our problems on someone else. Kids are masters at this technique. Teaching your kids to be responsible and accountable for their moods and actions is one of the toughest jobs you'll have—but also one of the most important.

When I taught high-school English, I was amazed at the number of kids who did not take responsibility for their school work and learning. The assumption was that I should be able to teach them in spite of themselves. I pointed out that I couldn't inject them with knowledge, but that they had to reach out for it.

Too many kids ignored instructions written on the board, chose to talk to friends while concepts were explained, and "forgot" to do the reading assignments. When they failed one of my quizzes, they blamed me for being a bad teacher.

You've probably noticed your own kids acting like my students.

My kids will blame a sibling for "making me mad," "being such a jerk," and "not doing his part." Somehow, they haven't internalized the basic free-will law of the universe. They think the Golden Rule ("Do unto others as you would have them do unto you") means "Do unto others as they do unto you." In a teenager's world, "He hit me first" or "He called me a wimp" is justification for getting into a fight.

Taking responsibility is a life skill we all need, both at home and in the workplace. One of my foster kids was fired from her job, because she always took offense with customers and her fellow employees. If somebody accidentally bumped into her, she lashed out.

Stay Calm and Avoid Negative Behavior

An important part of accepting responsibility is staying calm and not taking offense—especially where none was intended.

Psychologists advocated a few years ago that when you felt angry, you should "let it all hang out" in order to avoid building up rage. During that period, I read an article about family relationships in the Church. The article, published in a national magazine, was rather critical about the way Church leaders squelched negativism. The author mentioned that the family being interviewed "didn't allow the children to express anger." Although the children seemed happy and outgoing, the author wrote that denying their feelings would "probably lead to serious emotional disturbances."

In my opinion, "saying it like it is," screaming and yelling whenever the fancy strikes us is not a positive way of dealing with life's downside. In fact, recent studies reveal that when a person reacts angrily, he or she actually reinforces and escalates the anger. I've watched this phenomenon at work in my children and myself. For example, if I'm irritated by something and I snap at the perpetrator, my tendency to snarl a few minutes later is much greater than if I'd kept my mouth closed until the irritation passed.

I've seen people who griped and moaned about their situation. The more they complained, the worse they felt—until they were eventually completely depressed (or they flipped out).

An important part of avoiding negative behavior is maintaining an atmosphere of respect. Respect in a family is crucial if love is to grow. There must be respect between parents and kids and between kids and their siblings. I usually have a copy of Mosiah 4:14-15 posted where we all can see it:

> And ye will not suffer your children that they go hungry, or naked; neither will ye suffer that they transgress the laws of God, and fight and quarrel one with another, and serve the devil, who is the master of sin, or who is the evil spirit which hath been spoken of by our fathers, he being an enemy to all righteousness.
>
> But ye will teach them to walk in the ways of truth and soberness; ye will teach them to love one another, and to serve one another.

Although kids should be able to work out their differences, you may have to interfere if you notice one person being "the goat." Quite often one child's negative feelings about self will translate into merciless tormenting of a younger brother or sister. The negative kid can't stand seeing flaws she hates in herself showing up in her brother or sister.

I've dealt with this situation several times, both with my own kids and my foster kids. In some cases I just "lay down the law" and forbid any kind of mean or belittling remark. I say, "You may not call your sister a 'witch' or a 'snotty wench,' and she can't call you a 'pompous, bloated pig.'"

I dream up suitable consequences for breaking the "No Put-Downs" law, and those consequences vary with the kids and conditions. If the offender has money, I fine him. Sometimes I make her sit at the kitchen table until she writes a letter of apology, or I stand him in a corner—whatever is most impressive and eliminates the problem.

Direct and Immediate Action

However, if the put-downs are chronic and neither kid is clearly the aggressor, I take more drastic action. I set up a family conference for everyone involved, and I insist on certain ground rules.

1. Each person will have as much time as he or she needs to state feelings without interruption.

2. No name-calling or "You-Centered" words are allowed; everything must be couched in "I Feel" terms.

I act as a moderator and summarizer. If I'm really organized, I use a tape recorder and spend time writing down each person's point of view. Then I give the squabblers a copy of the summary.

An Example of Breaking the "Fighting" Habit

For instance, a certain brother-sister combination in our family spent several years tormenting each other to varying degrees. I knew their main problems were dramatic similarities in temperament and outlook, but I couldn't convince either one to lighten up or give the other a break. Finally, I shooed the extras out of the room and sat Brother and Sister down. "You will each tell the other how you feel," I told them. "State your point of view as clearly as you can, and no interrupting."

The session involved indignant yells of "That's a lie!" "I did not" and "He (she)'s exaggerating." I grabbed each kid a couple of times to keep him/her from stomping out of the room, and a lot of tears were shed.

My summary demonstrated that both kids put the other in an awkward position with friends, made jokes at the other's expense, thought he/she was "better than anybody else," and always ignored the other, except "to be mean."

It's been a couple of years since that confrontation. While Brother and Sister still exasperate each other, I've noticed that they tend to cooperate and even enjoy one another's company occasionally.

SUMMARIZING YOUR OPTIONS

Finally, remember that you cannot do everything for your teenager. We parents must strike a balance between abdicating our responsibilities and taking away our teenager's free agency. Building your teen's self-esteem is a complicated, long-term task. Adapt any of my ideas for your circumstances. Your love and respect, coupled with a dependence on your Savior, are key ingredients to the recipe for raising teenagers who love the Lord with all their hearts and who love their neighbors as themselves—teenagers with self-esteem.

CHAPTER 6

Discipline Strategies That Really Work

Once you are able to talk to your kids and they know how much you love them, you can consider influencing their behavior—that's what discipline is. The key to successful discipline is understanding the paradox of a teenager's being part child and part adult. Unfortunately, you will seldom know which part you face at any given time.

My discipline style developed from a series of false starts and misdirected lurches. My mothering years are full of mistakes, tears, and prayers; I'm so thankful for the twin principles of repentance and forgiveness! I finally figured out how the adolescent mind works. My knowledge didn't come easily, because I had to be willing to think like an infant, a six-year-old, and a grownup—all at the same time.

Disciplining teenagers involves understanding teen logic, handling your anger appropriately, avoiding contention whenever possible, and maintaining consistency.

In addition to these key concepts, you should know how to handle the most common subjects of family fights: curfews, dress standards, and use of the phone.

Finally, you must be able to set appropriate consequences for unacceptable actions—the definition of punishment.

UNDERSTANDING TEEN LOGIC

An incident involving Gary Willis illustrates the fancy mental footwork most teenagers can execute.

One day when G.W. was about sixteen, and the proud owner of a new driver's license, he wanted to go to the Midnight Movie (something he *always* wanted to do) with Ron, his best friend in all the world. Since he'd just been out the night before and because his room hadn't been cleaned in centuries, I said, "No."

He also asked to take the car, but at our house cars are only driven by kids who do their chores, maintain a decent grade-point average in school, and attend seminary. That gave me more reasons to say no.

He tried several generic arguments:

"For Pete's sake, I never get to do anything."

"But I was too sick to go to seminary."

"I had a lot of homework."

"It [his room, the garage, the inside of the car, the filthy kitchen sink] looks fine to me."

Finally, with a parting "Nobody ever listens to me," he slammed out of the room.

An hour later he returned. While he was gone, muffled thumps, crashes, and cracklings filtered through the walls; dust billowed from his door.

"I've cleaned my room, swept the garage, washed the car, scrubbed the bathroom, and organized Dad's tapes alphabetically. Now, can I go for a little while? Just to hang out at Ron's?" G.W. panted audibly, a carefully crafted dust smudge on his forehead.

I wasn't as experienced in teen logic at the time, so I relented. "Okay, but be sure you're home by 11:00. It's Sunday tomorrow, and you were out until 12:30 last night."

He flashed me a dazzling smile. "Thanks, Mom. You're the best," he said as he hugged me. This gorgeous kid could have charmed a shark into becoming a vegetarian.

Things Are Not Quite What They Seem

I assumed he'd take his bicycle; but you notice, my instructions did not say, "Don't drive the car." Of course, he knew not to drive the car without express permission, but because he'd originally asked to take it *and* to go to Ron's, he now figured my granting of permission to go to Ron's included the car. That's just the way an adolescent mind works. He drove out of the driveway with the family van—with a set of keys he'd copied.

I may have let him get away with the car bit if he'd made more than a token effort on everything he listed AND if he'd returned home at 11:00. However, at 11:30 I called Ron's house; Ron's sister Chrissy answered. When I asked to talk to Gary Willis (thinking he'd not noticed the time), she told me they'd just left for the Midnight Movie.

Here's another example of the illogical loops and twists that teenage minds take. Gary Willis' line of reasoning was:

"I originally wanted to take the car and go with Ron to a midnight movie. I couldn't go because I hadn't done any of the stuff that gets me those kinds of privileges. Since I went ahead and *did* everything I was supposed to [here the logic gets a bit shaky—the chores indicated were supposed to take place over a week], then Mom let me go to Ron's. Ergo, I can drive the car and we can go to the movie."

The 11:00 deadline completely slipped his mind.

HELP! I'M TRAPPED INSIDE A TEENAGE BRAIN

Enter another session of convoluted reasoning:

"Mom usually goes to bed to read and eat candy bars at about 11:00. Then she falls asleep around midnight. We're supposed to go into her room and tell her when we get home. If I'm lucky, I can sneak into the house and get into bed without her knowing I didn't come in until 2:30. Then I'll just act like I suddenly remembered to check in."

G.W. ignored the fact that I *always* make sure everybody is tucked in before I go to sleep. I even set my alarm for curfew times. I'd been up that night at midnight, 1:00, 1:30, and 2:00. I was just stumbling down the hall again when I met G.W. at 2:30.

Dressed in a T-shirt and briefs, he yawned and rubbed his eyes. "Oh, hi, Mom. I'm sorry I forgot to check in. I just woke up and remembered." Then he smiled sweetly and put his arms around me.

WHEN I TELL PARENTS THEY HAVE TO LEARN TO THINK LIKE A TEENAGER, I DON'T MEAN THEY SHOULD BE TAKEN IN BY THE THINKING.

Gary Willis was a master of manipulation. He befuddled me more times than I care to admit, but I finally caught on. And I can thank him for the lessons I learned. Some of the younger kids don't thank him, however.

Take a Deep Breath and Count to Ten

How I dealt with all G.W.'s oddball thinking and blatant violations points up a most important aspect of discipline: NEVER REACT WHEN YOU'RE ANGRY. *Always think through how you will respond, and make sure your response fits the offense.*

When I realized my con artist son actually thought I'd believe his idiotic statement, I exploded, "Don't give me that sleepy-I-just-remembered crap! I checked your bed a half-hour ago at 2:00 and you weren't in it! You deserve to be grounded until you're eighty-five. Get out of my sight. I'm so mad right now I can't be responsible for what I say or do. I may beat you to death. We'll talk in the morning."

"Oh," was all he answered.

EXPRESSING ANGER APPROPRIATELY

The above confrontation illustrates three principles of handling anger around teenagers:

First, only get mad when your anger will accomplish something. G.W.'s behavior had been clearly out of bounds, so he and I both knew my anger was justified.

Second, keep the focus on this particular escapade. While I let G.W. know in no uncertain terms how I felt, I didn't call him names or refer to the dozen other times he'd pulled the same kind of stunt. I stayed focused on the present.

Third, take your time to respond, and make the Lord a partner in your response. I knew I was too upset to think or react rationally, so I decided to "sleep on it." Actually, I was going to "pray on it" because the series of rule-breaking was beginning to frazzle me.

First: Use Anger Judiciously

People who live with teenagers are usually in a state of constant turmoil. Screaming can become a habit; it's much better to try to speak in a normal tone of voice. Sometimes, your efforts to control your temper may make you sound like somebody with a computerized larynx. But if you reserve your loudest comments for the most important confrontations, you will be much more effective.

If you scream all the time, on the other hand, you will be tuned out. You'll end up using stronger and stronger methods to get your kid's attention, and you could find yourself wielding a two-by-four to convince him to pick up his socks.

Second: Focus on the Here and Now

By avoiding personal attacks and just describing how I felt, I kept Gary Willis from becoming defensive. Since he already knew he'd overstepped his limits, he accepted that some form of punishment would be forthcoming.

I've discovered that teenagers, like two-year-olds, learn best if their actions directly correlate with the consequences. Sometimes that correlation is painful, but if it's fair, the teen will tolerate it, and behavior changes.

Gary Willis earned a two-week, Class-Three grounding for his Midnight Movie escapade. In our home, a Class Three means no television, no telephone, and no going out with friends. In G.W.'s case, it also meant no driving for a month.

Third: Take Your Time to Respond

By waiting until my rage cooled on the night of G.W's movie escapade, I had a chance to tap into help from a higher plane. I was able to think everything through and devise a suitable punishment. As I said earlier, the only way to know for sure whether you're doing the right thing is to trust the promptings of the Spirit.

As the years have marched on and as various teenagers have lived in our home, I've leaned progressively more and more on prayer as a parenting tool. I don't think it's coincidence that, although the foster kids we handle are increasingly damaged and difficult, the household has never been more peaceful.

Barring bloodshed over who used the last clean towel, I lock myself in my room with the Book of Mormon for fifteen minutes every morning. This fifteen minutes takes place after morning prayers with the family and during hair spraying, teeth brushing, and shoe finding by the current crop of high-school kids who leave the house first. I emerge in time to pass out hugs, lunches, and "have a fun day" as the five dash out the door. Then I turn my attention to my grade-school kids who leave an hour later.

MAINTAINING CONSISTENCY

Once a punishment or course of action has been agreed to, sticking to a plan can be uncomfortably difficult for a parent. After going through enough similar situations with several teenagers, I finally learned to trust my instincts and the whisperings of the Spirit.

One of the hardest discipline tests we ever faced occurred during one of our sons' high-school graduation. We learned that when the Spirit whispers, we must listen without arguing.

Some of his friends had rented a fancy house for an all-night party, and our son wanted to attend *the* Grad Bash of the year. However, when Gary and I asked for names and phone numbers of parents who'd vouch that drugs and alcohol weren't part of the scene, he couldn't—or wouldn't—give them to us.

At first, he didn't believe that we would actually stop him from a once-in-a-lifetime experience. But when his explanations ("Look, there'll be security all over the place") and pleas ("Man, everybody who's anybody will be there") failed, he spent the night alone in his room.

I remember how bad I felt as I walked by his door and saw my handsome son lying on his bed, tears trickling from his closed eyes onto his pillow (we made him keep his door open, because he'd snuck out his window a few times).

I thought, "Maybe I *am* overreacting—after all, he has been pretty good lately." Then I thought, "If the party were on the level, he would be able to tell us who was chaperoning." A few weeks later he admitted that heavy drugs and drinking were a planned part of the festivities and he was glad we'd kept him away.

But Everybody Else Can!

Now that I've given you my views on the three things to keep in mind when disciplining your teenager, let's turn to typical areas of contention in the most serene homes: curfews, dress standards, and the phone.

As you might guess, curfew causes more conflict than any other single issue. For some reason, kids want to stay up all night. The surest sign of their maturity is their lack of interest in partying and their increased interest in sleeping—at appropriate times.

I've devised an effective curfew set-up, but it's by no means the only way to go. Use whatever works best for you in your situation;

some kids respond better to indirect guidance while others want and need very short reins.

Curfews (meaning the time when a person must be home) should be *specific, consistent,* and *enforced.* If any of these three requirements is missing, you might as well have no curfew at all.

Curfews

Teenagers ought to be consulted about appropriate curfew times, but they cannot have the last word (although they will try their darndest). At my house, kids in the three teen phases have three different curfews. These curfews reflect each teen's developing maturity and allow him or her to participate in kid stuff while being protected from danger.

When my children reach twelve years of age, they come under the rules designed for Early Teens. Those rules are 9:00 on school nights. Sometimes 9:30 is appropriate, but every twelve- and thirteen-year-old needs to be in bed and asleep no later than 10:00 on school nights.

On weekends or holidays the time is 11:00 if the kids have a particular activity planned. That hour gives plenty of time for going to the movies or hanging around with friends.

Middle Teens have a 10:00 p.m. deadline on school days and a midnight curfew on weekends and holidays.

Late Teens have the same school-day deadline, but they can stay out until 12:30 or 1:00 a.m. on weekends and holidays (except on Saturday nights, which would infringe on the Sabbath). Again, they must have a specific reason for staying out that late—no "just hanging around."

Curfews Must Be Consistent

Make sure that you stick with whatever curfew you establish—write it down if you need to. And don't let your teenager talk you into changing "just this once." If a special occasion warrants an additional hour, be sure that you aren't granting more than one every few weeks or month. If you are, you should come up with new curfews, because consistency is much more important than exact times.

My curfew hours come with certain other stipulations: The kids cannot go out two nights in a row, except for sanctioned school or Church activities. One of the main reasons for this stipulation is that I want our home to be more than a way station for eating and sleeping. Friends are very important to teenagers, and no parent can fight that fact, but family activities are just as important as activities with friends.

Occasionally, one of the kids objects to "being treated like a child" or "being forced to report in all the time." But I point out that I tell *them* when I leave and when I come home; people who care about each other observe such courtesies. I also apologize profusely if I forget and fail to tell anybody what I'm doing.

As I said, **exact hours and terms aren't as important as how dependable you are.**

Curfews Must Be Enforced

How do I know the hours I set are obeyed? I make sure the time limits are strictly observed. Without fail, my children are required to check in with me when they come home—night or day. They are also required to tell me when they leave.

I have to spell this rule out absolutely, and it includes when they leave to "take somebody home." And when they return. I'm a nervous sort, and can never really rest until everybody is accounted for.

I also insist that each returnee give me a hug and a kiss. This simple act of affection allows me to keep tabs on more than their bedtimes.

Various friends have different ways of tracking their kids. As you may notice, I keep the reins on my kids rather short—that's my style. I'm uncomfortable with disorder and confusion; I use schedules, charts, and lists.

Other people might find my regimentation irritating. However, I have noticed that most successful parents use some kind of schedules or records. When things are written down, there's much less room for "I didn't know," "I forgot," and "You didn't tell me."

If you have trouble remembering or being awake until your kids come home, you might consider setting a "curfew alarm" in your room (so you can sleep if you want to). Then require your teen to turn it off before it rings. If it rings, set it ten minutes earlier for the next time your teen has a night out.

For every five minutes after curfew your teen comes in, require her to come in ten minutes ahead of her normal hour next time. It won't take long before she exerts great effort to meet her deadlines.

You Will Not Leave This House in That Get-Up

Another major area of potential conflict between parents and teenagers involves dress standards, including hair and makeup. Kids try on outfits and hairstyles for the same reason they try on different personalities: to see how they fit in with the world around them. Sometimes their get-ups can be pretty bizarre.

My older girls wore rhinestones with their jeans, army suspenders and combat boots with their skirts, and their blouses inside out. Eric grew his hair to his shoulders and wore it in a ponytail. Roch dyed his hair orange and cut it into a mohawk. G.W. wore one pair of shoes, without socks, until they literally disintegrated and fell off his feet.

When my children first defied the laws of logic and good taste, I suffered profound embarrassment. I thought my motherhood certificate was at stake.

How could any competent parent allow her child to look like a yard sale reject? But I learned to relax—after all, just what was at issue here? I certainly wasn't the one who looked ridiculous—my kid did.

So, I have a simple code for dress standards: **clothing and makeup must be clean and modest, and nothing can be done that's irreversible.**

Linda tested us the hardest on the clothing standard. At fourteen she went through a weird phase where all she wanted to wear was black: black stockings, black shoes, black sweaters, black skirts, and black pants. Even her underwear was black. She dyed her beautiful blonde hair black, then smeared on very pale makeup and outlined her eyes in black. She walked out the door every morning looking like a corpse, but I bit my tongue.

Dying her hair was okay, because—as much as I hated how she looked—her hair would grow out. All the black clothes were okay because they were modest. However, when Linda wanted a black eagle tattoo, I put my foot down. And when she tried to pencil in a death head and vampire-like spider on her forehead, I stopped her. Bizarre is okay, but satanic and violent images are not.

Never Trust Anybody Over Twelve—Or Under Twenty

Enforcement might involve a doorway inspection and frisking. I found that out through experience. One of my foster daughters wanted to wear a very revealing miniskirt to school, but we refused to let her. When I found out she stashed it in her backpack to change into at school, I made her open the pack before she left the house.

"You don't trust me!" she wailed.

She was right. All teenagers lie if they think they can get away with it.

The lying isn't really pathological; it stems from the child part of their natures, which has difficulty separating reality from what they wish were true.

The third subject for contention in my house has to do with using the phone.

Reach Out and Talk Forever

Gary and I have always installed a separate line for our kids that could only access local numbers. The "kids' phone" was a wonderful convenience and it really wasn't very expensive because nobody could call long distance.

If possible, I suggest you install such a convenience—for your sake more than your teenagers' sake. If you own a computer and have Internet capability, a second line is mandatory!

Controlling the Yakkers

Whether or not you have a second line, you should try to limit the amount of time the kids use the phone—whether they receive or make calls. If you don't establish guidelines, your garrulous youth will spend every waking moment (other than those spent in front of the television set) discussing who ate lunch with whom, who's going with whom, and the general condition of adolescent society.

If you don't have a second line, you absolutely must limit the calls, or your friends and relatives will *never* be able to reach you between the hours of 3:00 p.m. and midnight.

Contrary to Ma Bell's advertisements, "call waiting" doesn't work. Oh, your chattering teen will hear the beep, but he'll ignore it. Then your friends and relatives will think you've moved, gone on an extended vacation or suffered a horrible accident, because the phone will ring and ring and ring . . .

The guidelines I try to follow are: Each teen can spend no more than twenty minutes per day on the phone. On weekdays, calls cannot be received or placed before 8:00 a.m. or after 9:00 p.m. On weekends and holidays, calls cannot be received or placed before 10:00 a.m. or after 10:30 p.m.

These guidelines are flexible, however. Genuine emergencies like calling for a ride to school or checking homework assignments can be taken or placed at other times, within reason. Those kinds of emergency calls should be limited to three minutes.

Your teenager will consider "Bob breaking up with Sue," "what to wear to the dance," and "Why won't Tanya talk to me?" to be genuine emergencies. Use your intuition here; remember how volatile and tender teenage emotions can be.

I've been known to ignore the twenty-minute deadline when my kid explains that "Sue is really depressed," "Bob's dad lost his job so he can't afford a tux, and we have to figure out where he can borrow one," and "Tanya saw David at the movies with her worst enemy." However, if the friend needs an in-depth heart-to-heart talk that will take longer than half an hour, I encourage my teen to talk to the friend face-to-face.

Setting parameters on telephone use accomplishes a lot more than freeing up access to the phone. The telephone is a convenience for the whole family, not just a couple of people, so teens learn to be considerate. And since teenagers like to use the phone, it can be a motivational tool. You can require that chores and homework be finished before your teen takes a call or initiates one.

Basic Etiquette

I want my children to answer the phone politely and to take reasonable messages. "Players' house" is an okay greeting and is certainly better than "Hullo?" However, I prefer, "Hello, this is the Players' house, Nathan speaking."

If the caller asks for somebody in the family, I expect the answerer to exert some effort to find out whether the person is home, especially if the call is for me. A few years ago, my boss called me at home when I'd left early because I was sick. One of my sons answered and told her that I'd gone Christmas shopping. My son didn't bother asking anyone else or even checking my room.

I also expect the answerer to ask, "May I ask who's calling?" and "Would you like to leave a message?" Gary and I often work at home, so business calls come in at all hours. Inept phone behavior can have economic impact!

EFFECTIVE CONSEQUENCES

Every cause has an effect, every action a reaction. Punishment can be part of how you help your children replace teen logic with adult logic.

When dress standards, curfew, telephone rules, or other family edicts are violated, punishment is in order. If kids aren't punished for doing wrong, they become confused and resentful. If they understand and accept the fact that they did something wrong, they expect a consequence.

However, punishment must be fair and fit the offense. As I emphasized earlier, it should never be meted out in anger, and the suitability of the punishment should be agreed to by both parties.

Rules should be clearly defined and developed with the teenager's input. That adult/child cross comes into play: certain things need to be handled as they would be for a two-year-old; others need the input of an adult.

Another thing I do is ponder the effects of various actions I could take. When Gary Willis tried to convince me, against the evidence, that he'd been asleep at home for three hours, I wanted to hit him. Oh, how I wanted to hit him! But physical punishment never accomplishes much and almost always makes the situation worse.

While I don't allow rude, blatantly selfish, or dangerous behavior, I try to let the consequences fit the act. "D" grades (and C- in certain cases) mean too much time has been spent on the telephone deciding whether to paint a scooter light or dark blue or in front of MTV watching rock stars dressed like turkey buzzards. I lock up the telephone and television until the errant one brings a note from his or her teacher testifying to a satisfactory grade level.

Tickets for speeding and reckless driving mean a teenage driver hasn't developed a healthy respect for a powerful machine that can kill. Because physical safety is at stake, I confiscate the car keys, ground the driver, and levy my own fine above and beyond the ticket price. The amount of the fine and the length of the confiscation depend on the circumstances behind the ticket.

Grounding: An Impressive Consequence

Grounding, which means to restrict or eliminate activities, is kind of an all-purpose punishment. Use it when nothing more creative or appropriate comes to mind. Grounding is especially effective when kids have violated curfew or skipped school. If your child cannot come home on time or goes where he's not supposed to be, logic dictates that his wings be clipped.

Sometimes the kids call grounding "house arrest" because they can do things with family members. This wrinkle in the punishment is my sneaky way of promoting family unity. The groundee often becomes so bored that movies or an ice cream cone with a little sister or brother looks pretty good.

Some of my kids' friends have been grounded for six months for breaking curfew or for talking back to parents, but I find that less is better when disciplining teenagers. A one- or two-week grounding emphasizes a point, while a long, drawn-out punishment just antagonizes the groundee.

I've developed Class One, Two, or Three groundings to give me more freedom in dishing out punishment. Class One is the least restrictive; it lasts one week or less and means the teen can't attend parties or spend the night with friends.

In addition to Class One consequences, Class Two eliminates television and video viewing and use of the telephone. Class Two groundings last one to two weeks.

Class Three pulls out all the stops. It can last four weeks or longer. Groundees must return home from school within fifteen minutes of the time class lets out. I also eliminate the use of radios, stereos, and any other favorite recreation. In extreme cases, I add a week or two to the length and restrict lunchtime activities.

In other instances, grounding includes no contact with a certain friend, detention during lunch at school (this can often be arranged in cooperation with school officials), or the requirement to write a detailed letter of repentance. Whatever grounding means, the consequences should be clear to everybody involved—ideally, before anybody has to be punished.

SOMEBODY HAS TO BE IN CHARGE—HOPEFULLY, IT'S THE PARENTS

An adolescent psychology workshop facilitator told us, "He who has, has power over he who wants." That means that if we parents want something more than our teen wants it, the balance of power shifts to the teen.

Let me illustrate with the example of a foster daughter who gave her family fits. She didn't have the excuse of a poorly parented past like most of my other foster kids. Her mother and father, as well as two grown brothers, beat themselves up trying to keep this kid on the right path. They were all active Church members whose bishop advised them to "get her away from her friends." So she came to us from another state.

At first, Kim thought a foster family who "lived in the woods" would be fun. She enjoyed the uproar she had caused at home and was very willing to come. Then she realized the Player family rules were a whole lot more restrictive than her own parents'. She wanted out. She even faked suicide attempts to force us to let her return home.

With her parents' permission, we took her to a juvenile detention center with bars on the windows and double locks on the doors, surrounded by barbed-wire fences and patrolled by guard dogs. Since she had been examined by a psychiatrist and we knew she wasn't psychotic, our ploy worked.

The admitting officer said, "Kim, this is the end of the road. This is where kids come who can't make it at home and who can't make it at a foster home."

Later, I sat and talked with her. "Your mom and dad and your brothers love you a lot, and I care about you. We're not going to let you hurt yourself [referring to the suicide 'attempt']. If that means we have to lock you up, then we'll lock you up."

Kim became a model student and daughter after that (well . . . maybe not *model* . . .). She had a few struggles after her year with us, but today she is happily married and pursuing a teaching career.

Another of my counseling patients had his father running in circles and not daring to take the car keys away from him because he "needed the car to attend early-morning youth symphony rehearsals." The father was a gifted musician who saw a similar gift in his son and was willing to "give anything" for that son to use his talent.

So you must pick your power struggles carefully! You won't get very far in raising your teenager if you want everything more than he or she does. It doesn't matter what the arena of the struggle is, either: a mission, good grades, or even eternal life!

A FINAL WORD ON DISCIPLINE

Raising kids isn't easy. They wear you to a physical frazzle when they're babies and drive you crazy when they're teenagers. These part-child, part-adult puzzles will provide you with your most humiliating and most rewarding moments.

In the end, self discipline is what it's all about. Like you, I want my children to grow up to be happy, well-adjusted people. Their adolescent years, which seem to stretch into eternity at times, are my last chance to shape them.

Discipline, founded on communication, comes at first from loving parents, but—in the end—must come from inside each person.

Developing an internal mechanism for self-control should be the aim of every grounding or other disciplinary action. Finding a flexible balance that fits a teen's changing needs can be difficult but is worth the effort.

How Can I Prepare Teenagers for Life and Teach Them to Work?

CHAPTER 7

Getting the Most Out of School

The third most common question people ask me (and I ask myself) is, "How can I prepare my teenagers for the challenges they'll face in life?" A related question is "How can I teach them to work?"

The greatest influence on your teenager outside of your home, school is primarily your child's responsibility. So, don't get caught up in your kid's school work to the point that *you* sweat over the grades and burn the midnight oil trying to finish a procrastinated report.

However, you *can* do quite a bit to encourage academic and social success.

SOME BASICS ABOUT SECONDARY SCHOOLS

Middle schools and junior-high schools are crazy places—just about as wacky as the adolescents who attend them. Things don't get any better in the upper grades, either.

Magazines and newspapers decry the mess we've made of our public school system. Not many kids graduate from high school knowing enough to support themselves; some are barely literate, and the picture grows bleaker every year. Teachers are hard-pressed to survive each day, and some schools look like battle zones. What can be done?

You could wring your hands over the state of education; maybe you could be more positive and write letters to your congressmen. You could opt to send your kids to private school, or you could teach them at home.

Better yet, you could work with the public school system to make sure *your* child gets an appropriate education. An involved parent is the single most important indicator for school success.

Why do I advocate public schools? I happen to believe that, as imperfect as American schools are, they're much better than anywhere else in the world. They strive to educate *everybody*, regardless of intelligence and ability to pay.

And that's a big plus. Enjoying the benefits of democracy means we have to make a few compromises. And until vouchers become part of the system so that parents can choose between schools (and consequently help public schools be more competitive), I'll opt for public schools.

If you send your kids to *private* schools, you'll end up paying lots of money in tuition—and you'll still be expected to volunteer and be involved. So, why not become involved in the public education you've already paid for with your taxes? Remember, however, that all your decisions should be based on prayer and personal inspiration about what is best for your own child.

Public Education's Main Problem

Every school in the country struggles with apathetic parents. Working parents think their child-care problems are solved once their kids are in school. Moms who stayed home with babies head back to career tracks once their youngest child enters first grade. Everybody expects schools to provide academic, social, and personal training—an education, plus the benefits of a stable family.

I've seen the modern education system from both sides of the fence—as a teacher and as a parent. When I would schedule parent-teacher conferences for my seventh- or tenth-grade English classes, barely fifteen percent of the parents showed up. And I taught in an upper-middle-class neighborhood! The only kids who did very well enjoyed clear parental support. Few kids achieved anything without their parents' attention.

We parents can expect classrooms to teach our kids to read, do math, and develop logical thought patterns, but we can't expect them to take our place in teaching moral and ethical values.

Nobody cares as much about your child's success and happiness as you do; there is no substitute for a caring, involved parent. Granted, being caring and involved takes a lot out of you. The more kids I have the more I feel as if I ought to give up and educate everybody at home. At least then I wouldn't have to worry about shoving them out the door every morning.

Pros and Cons of Home Schools for Teenagers

Home schools, especially for young children, have grown in popularity over the past few years. I have a great deal of admiration for parents who educate their own kids.

If you are dedicated to your children's welfare *and* are willing to spend HUGE amounts of time preparing and following through, you can run a successful home school.

Your children can gain an excellent academic education. I've observed that average home-taught kids score higher in creativity and achievement on standardized tests than average public-school kids. However, I've concluded (based again on personal observation) that social skills outweigh academics in importance by the time kids reach fourth or fifth grade. Those upper years of elementary school provide the basis for social development in middle and high school.

Because social and human relationships are the most important parts of an adolescent's education, I don't recommend home schools for kids beyond second or third grade. At least, I don't for any kid *I'd* have to teach at home!

If you are determined and consistent, you can counteract many of the negative effects of social isolation by being sure your child has opportunities to interact with peers. Community organizations like Campfire, Little/Pony League, and Boy and Girl Scouts give ample opportunities for socializing.

I know parents who combine home school and public school in equal parts to gain the best of both worlds. Their children have the advantage of one-on-one academic instruction, while they enjoy orchestra, games, camping, and sports with friends.

What I'm basically saying is what I keep repeating throughout this book: Ponder, pray about, and think through your parenting decisions. Don't worry about "expert opinion" or somebody else's ideas. Only *you* are qualified to determine what's best for your family.

If you have the time and energy to devote to a home school or you would rather send your kids to a private school (and have the money for tuition), go for it! Otherwise, seek out a partnership with your local school and do your best to make it a place of learning and success for your child.

Becoming Your Child's Public-School Liaison

Overcrowded schools and harried teachers don't need to become problems. Your presence and efforts can mitigate the worst situations. If you are in the classroom with your child several times a month, the lowest-rated school will have little negative effect.

Assess your personal strengths. What could you help with at school? Do you own a business? Are you a member of a profession or are you a skilled craftsman? Do you know how to organize and complete a task?

I've taught remedial reading and creative writing to my children and their classmates. Gary, a geologist, has taken classes on field trips and taught lessons on fossils and earthquakes. Others I know of have set up writing centers, tutored basic math, typed programs, and helped keep the lunchrooms orderly.

Another important aspect of volunteering to help your own child is that you also help his or her classmates. Your tax dollars will go further.

Now, let's turn to a discussion of actually shoving your kids out the door to whatever school they attend.

ORGANIZING AND SIMPLIFYING THE SCHOOL DAY

Every morning I hear screams of "Where's my lunch?!" "I can't find my shoes!" "All right, who spilled the corn flakes and didn't clean them up?" and "Why do I have to wear socks?"

Experience has taught me that the hours before and after school are capable of reducing me to a state just this side of idiocy. In hopes of saving you from a similar fate, here are a few tips for handling the chaos middle- and high-school kids manage to create.

Five Ways to Save Your Sanity
  1. Anticipate problems before they arise. As in everything else, being aware of what could happen enables you to be prepared. Keep Murphy's Law in mind: anything that *can* go wrong *will* go wrong.

2. Maintain a sense of humor. By the time you've read this far, you already know how valuable your ability to laugh can be.

3. Keep a notebook in your purse or pocket. The notebook enables you to jot shopping lists, keep track of kids' sizes and peculiarities, and note those bits of wisdom that flash through your mind.

4. Tape up a series of charts around the house. I've explained my chart philosophy in earlier chapters. You'll see some particular applications for charts as I go into specific times of day. Most of the detailed examples are displayed in the Appendices.

5. Hang a large calendar with plenty of writing room for each day. Post the calendar where everybody can refer to it. Each kid above the age of middle school should be responsible for charting his or her important activities.

We usually spend part of family home evening going over the week's activities. The kids must also remind their father or me in time for us to provide transportation, sign permission slips, and so on—otherwise, I can't be held accountable . . .

But I DID Tell You, Mom!

And what happens when they forget to mention a championship debate tournament in another state that they volunteered me to chaperon?

Good question. Ideally, I draw myself up and say in my most regal, motherly manner, "I'm sorry dear, but your sister already signed me up to hiss prompt lines and stumble over props in her Shakespeare competition this weekend."

Realistically, I scramble around, claiming I.O.U.s for babysitting and packing the only suitcase we own that doesn't have to be taped shut. Then I pledge a year's oven cleaning to my best friend whose daughter is in the same play if she'll take my place.

I manage to make the bus about the same time as my son, who suddenly remembers he left his file box on his bed. Eighteen other fifteen-year-olds also left their file boxes on their beds, so the bus driver sits back in his seat and hums tunelessly while the coach mutters obscenities under her breath.

We're finally loaded and en route for Castle Dale or thereabouts over a very bumpy road when I realize I forgot to go to the bathroom.

No, the bus isn't equipped—ours is a poor school district.

When I say everybody *must* remember to write things on the calendar (and I must remember to look at it), I really don't have any recourse if my kids fail to do so. Memories of their mother's near nervous breakdown on several occasions probably motivate them as much as anything.

As far as handling the everyday emergencies, the school day divides into two basic parts (at least as far as I'm concerned): *before school* and *after school.*

Taming Morning Turbulence: Before School

Outside of the Rocky Mountains, LDS teenagers' school days start at approximately 5:30 a.m. because of early-morning seminary. I've always insisted that my kids attend seminary—just like I insist that they attend school and Church. Spiritual education is equally as important (if not more so) as academic education, so LDS kids should attend seminary.

The Bishop's Handbook includes a section about seminary attendance. Saying they should go to seminary and actually getting them inside their seminary classrooms can be two different matters, however. All of my kids have been enrolled in seminary and most of them at least earned "attendance certificates."

Their attitudes toward attendance have ranged from one son who never passed a single quarter to another son who earned straight As in early-morning seminary when he could have had released time.

I tried everything I could think of to convince the sluggard to attend. To be fair, I should note that he was a "night person" and biologically incapable of functioning before noon—at least that's what he tried to tell me. He was also incredibly brilliant but never earned an A average until he was a married returned missionary.

If I could remember to enforce the rule, I was most effective with, "If you don't attend seminary, you don't go out on the weekends." But that rule meant I had to be aware of whether or not he actually went into the classroom if I succeeded in rolling him out of bed and dropping him off at the meetinghouse.

Other before-school problems involve the *Bathroom Use Schedule* and the *What Should I Wear Dilemma.*

The biggest hassles my family faces in the early-morning hours are related to the fact that nobody has a private bathroom. They all need at least an hour to shower, shampoo, and ponder the meaning of life. At one point, we coped with one bathroom for ten people.

Remember the fourth way to cultivate the gift of prophecy? Tape up charts! An essential chart is the Bathroom Use Chart. Such a chart decreases the screams of "Make her get out! I still have to brush my teeth" and "He's been in there popping pimples for an hour and won't let me have any shampoo."

The Bathroom Use Chart changes periodically as the number of users increases or decreases, but in general it breaks the morning into sections that reflect how many people must use which bathroom. Everybody gets a section based on when that person must be where.

For instance, during his senior year, Eric's time was between 6:00 and 6:30 a.m., because he had to be out the door by 6:50. Gary Willis, whose schedule didn't require much before 10:00, took his time after 8:30 a.m.

Each person had first claim on his or her time slot but could trade with someone else, as long as the trade was *mutually agreeable.*

Not only did the Bathroom Use Chart stipulate *when* somebody could use the bathroom, it outlined certain rules for that use. The chart posted beside the mirror began with "Flush!" and "Wash Your Hands," proceeded through "Wipe Out The Sink," and ended with "Pick Up Your Underwear," "Put Away Your Stuff," and "Turn Out The Lights."

Sometimes, the kids actually read the charts and (less often) followed one or two of the directions.

I Don't Have Any Decent Clothes!

The other problem area in the morning is the Great What-Shall-I-Wear Debate. The Great Debate usually degenerates into "He's wearing my sweater without my permission" and "Linda kicked me for coming in the girls' room, but she goes in the boys' room all the time!"

Therefore, another chart delineates certain ground rules about clothes. I don't usually post the chart unless we've endured a lot of fights, but the kids know the basic rule: *Nobody touches anybody else's clothes without permission.* This goes for Mom's or Dad's clothes, too—

although filching from parents never seems to be a sin of the same magnitude as "borrowing without asking" from a sibling.

I insisted on other rules that facilitated getting out the door in peace, like no TV or computer games in the morning. Plus, I asked each child to tell me when they go out the door, so I'm not running up and down three flights of stairs looking for somebody who left ten minutes earlier. Such rules reminded me as well as the kids.

At one point (when ten of us lived in a three-bedroom, one-bathroom house), I taped a "Forget Anything?" chart by the front door. It consisted of large red letters that read:

BREAKFAST?
TEETH?
BED MADE?
BOOKS AND INSTRUMENTS?
MEDICINE?
FIELD TRIP?
COAT?

I posted a similar reminder sheet whenever we had a turnover in kids, and I kept it up, depending on how responsible they seemed to be.

The Pause That Refreshes

Pausing before everybody has to leave and praying together does more to keep us on an even keel than all the rest of the activities and lists put together. It's hard to continue yelling at your sister for wearing your earrings when she's just knelt with you.

Avoiding Confusion After School

During most of the years two or more teenagers occupied the premises, the kids arrived home at three or four different times. As a result, my lists and charts tracked who should be home when. Other standards after school were:

1. *Take everything to your room—don't drop your backpack, books, or shoes in the entry.* When eight to ten kids sauntered through the front door shedding books, shoes, coats, and whatever, the entry soon resembled Mt. Everest.

2. *Check with me within fifteen minutes of when school lets out.* If somebody had to stay after school for a rehearsal or activity, I

expected a call. I dispensed groundings for lateness from school just as I did for breaking curfew.

3. *Fix a snack and eat it BEFORE 4:00 p.m.* If I hadn't put a time limit on snacks, the boys would have emptied the refrigerator and left the rest of us without any supper.

4. *Start ONE HOUR of homework immediately.* If certain kids avoided homework immediately after school ended, they never managed to get around to it at all.

WHAT HOMEWORK? I DID IT ALL AT SCHOOL

A major area of conflict that can lead to serious problems is *homework,* a word that distresses parents and nauseates kids.

As I said, I insisted that homework be started immediately after the kids came home— during snacks if necessary. Every kid had to do at least one hour of study a day. If they didn't have any homework, they were still required to sit and read an approved book (no comics or trashy novels).

I provided a quiet study place and all the materials, but I didn't do much else. I did work with a child who needed extra instruction in reading, times tables, or spelling. I just made sure the end result was the child's, not mine.

Closely akin to homework is remembering things like library books, show-and-tell exhibits, reports, and musical instruments. School is a kid's main occupation; at school your child learns accountability as well as information. Like you, I hated to see my darling penalized for forgetting his library book or clarinet, but I wasn't doing him a favor by rushing the required item to school. He just learned to rely on me instead of himself for such tasks. A few consequences helped him shift his priorities.

My kids knew better than to call their dad or me at work and ask us to run the item over "just this once." But I wasn't as heartless as I sound. Before I left my kids to their own devices, I taught them memory tricks and other ways to keep track of their belongings. I also volunteered whenever possible at their schools and visited everybody's classrooms several times a year.

A Different Aspect of the Homework Issue

What if a child is doing homework but is still failing? This tricky situation (which doesn't happen very often) has one of two answers: First, your child may be going through the motions but not bothering to follow instructions. In other words, she has the ability to succeed but is more interested in who snubbed whom at lunch, Jesse's break dancing on the teacher's desk in English, and Jesse's suspension for rowdiness.

The second possibility could be either a physical or learning problem.

Physical problems should be checked out and remedied by your family doctor; your child may need glasses, hearing aides, orthopedics, or whatever. Learning problems are a bit more difficult to diagnose.

You've probably heard terms like *hyperactive* and *dyslectic* get tossed around with abandon. The only way to determine whether or not your teenager has such difficulties is through testing and evaluation.

Certain clues can signal a trip to the psychotherapist or doctor, however:

1. Your child is continually frustrated with schoolwork. You see your child seated in her study place, but grades don't reflect the effort.

2. Your child is touchy and avoids homework altogether (this could also be laziness—it depends on the child).

3. When you help your child or ask questions about course content, his answers confuse you.

You can encourage a struggling student by not being judgmental and by speaking in a friendly tone. The last thing he or she needs is to be called lazy or oblivious. Instead, say things like, "What's the main point of the story you just read?" or "Let me go over the instructions with you."

Sometimes just giving kids a sympathetic ear and helping them understand directions can solve the problem. A lot of students get through six or seven years of school without ever being taught how to study.

Other times, you'll need professional help—tutors, education specialists, or therapists. These professionals can be expensive, but if their input is necessary for your child to receive his or her guaranteed public education, your fellow taxpayers must help you pay for them.

Most school districts have resource centers where you can find answers. If they don't, the law says they must provide help from private sources. Many struggling school systems save money by telling parents, "We don't have anyone on staff to conduct those kinds of tests."

Don't be put off if you think your child is learning disabled; be prepared to make phone calls and follow up on leads. Persist in your search. Contact your state representative if you run into too many obstacles. Because learning-disabled kids are often passive and unable to assert their rights (even when they seem aggressive or defiant), you owe your children enough time and energy to make sure they get the help they need.

I'm Not Late . . .

Middle Teens, for some reason, like to hang around school for hours with their friends. They become very adept at making up excuses that sound pretty plausible if you don't listen very closely. I used to be more naive than I am now. I believed my kids when they strolled through the door and said, "I had to stay after for a test in Mr. Beezlybob's class." However, I caught on when Mr. Beezlybob called me to ask why my foster daughter had failed to attend a makeup session for the sixth day in a row.

When kids don't come home on time and don't do their homework immediately, I lose track of who is supposed to be doing what and when. Or remember that Eric did his homework, and I transfer that memory to Micah (who finished approximately three assignments in eight years of school).

Teenagers not only grow rapidly, but their intellectual growth and their ability to exercise self-control shift into high gear. Note, that I said that their *ability* to exercise self-control shifts into high gear; I didn't say they were now totally in control and you can breathe a sigh of relief. Instead, you have to stick to the rules you've established.

DEVELOPING AND REWARDING RESPONSIBILITY

That's not always easy. I vividly remember an incident a few years ago that illustrates how kids can manipulate a mother's built-in guilt buttons.

"Mom, you're mean! I hate you! Why can't you go back for my instrument?" Micah, then ten years old, bounced angrily on the back seat.

Gary gripped the steering wheel and accelerated slightly as we made our daily twenty-mile commute from Shell Beach to San Luis Obispo, California. I sighed and repeated my answer to Micah's request that we turn around and get his clarinet, "Because we're already on the way. Daddy and I would lose an hour at work; Linda would be late, and so would you and Nathan."

I took a deep breath. "Micah, you've forgotten your instrument four times in the last month. You forgot it Tuesday! We keep going out of our way to get it for you. We just can't do it again today."

At one time, Micah's anger and tears would have made me uncomfortable enough to postpone my schedule and grant his request. I squandered hours ferrying forgotten lunches, homework, band instruments, and library books to school, baseball games, and Scouts.

Even now, like most moms, I enjoy being needed by my family. I feel self-righteous delight as I forgo my own convenience or pleasure to do things for them. But I've learned that when I continually shield a child from the consequences of his or her actions, I stifle emotional growth. In addition, I retard my children's development of personal accountability. I constantly fight the temptation to be a "good mommy" by doing for my kids what they should do for themselves.

Look, You're the One in School . . .

Once in a while I run up against a kid who defies my best efforts: planning, supervising, organizing, and even bribery fail. I often dashed to the library with one particular child and stayed up until the wee hours helping him put a forgotten report together. Finally, by the time he was in middle school, I ran out of patience. I figured he'd never change until he understood the consequences of his actions.

Warned at the beginning of the semester about a project, I helped him plan the writing of ten book reports. Then I asked about his progress every few days, but didn't nag. He always assured me he was right on schedule as he ran out to play. But two days before the due date, he confessed that he still hadn't started.

The old me would have scurried around and gathered most of the needed information. But the new me clucked sympathetically and returned to my own work.

The C-minus he managed to squeak out embarrassed us both, but mostly him. I reminded him and myself that the more I had covered for him, the more he had let me.

I had taught him the skills he needed to succeed in school, but I couldn't take over his responsibilities. By the time he finished the year, he had brought his grades back to where he wanted them.

SPECIAL PROGRAMS AND EXTRACURRICULAR ACTIVITIES

Motivated kids can wring tremendous rewards from their high school years. The key word here is *motivated*. Methods of motivation are as numerous as the number of times a day an adolescent goes through a mood swing.

Remember that your teenager is a curious combination of adult and infant. Addressing the adult part of his or her personality is usually most effective. Adults like to save time and money—such an appeal to the wallet may help when you talk to your child about using high school to prepare for self-sufficiency. Ideally, when kids graduate, they should be able to land a job that pays better than McDonald's or Burger King. If they want to enter professional training, they can save themselves months, and sometimes years, of effort.

Many high schools have advanced placement programs that a lot of eligible kids don't fully use. Eric earned twenty-two credits during his senior year and entered college as almost a sophomore. Such an early jump on his education saved him a lot of time after he returned from his mission.

Conversely, Gary Willis didn't bother with advanced placement classes; he was too busy collecting love notes and sleeping through history. But his mission in Brazil not only changed his character and enhanced his spirituality, it made him fluent in Portuguese. Brigham Young University, like most colleges, offers credit for students who have learned another language (specifically as missionaries). Language skills can come from living in a foreign country, taking courses, or individual effort.

Most colleges allow students to challenge language classes by taking tests for credit. Sometimes taking the tests requires fees, but those fees are significantly less expensive than tuition.

Benefits Beyond Academics

Your child's high-school education shouldn't consist solely of academic work. Extracurricular activities like chorus, band, and athletics provide a basis for scholarships and work/study programs, as well as give teens an outlet for volcanic energy levels.

None of my kids has been a world-class athlete, but most have developed their muscles and team spirit by participating in track and field, water polo, and swimming. High-school coaches worth their salaries will give the stars exposure without neglecting the ordinary kids.

Eric's swimming coach in San Luis Obispo, California, deserves a spot in my book (and a star in his heavenly crown) for his dedication to young people. Handicapped by a stroke when he was two, Eric suffered constant pain and weakness. Most coaches wouldn't have wanted a partially paralyzed kid who limped badly, but this coach encouraged Eric to join the team. His criteria was how hard a kid practiced—not the kid's innate ability.

Eric never missed a practice and never missed a meet. His best place in any competition was last, but he practiced so hard he often came home bruised and bloody.

Eric's left side was so much stronger than his right that he'd end up in the wrong lane and collide with other swimmers. Or he'd build up such momentum that he crashed into the sides of the pool. His exertion paid off. He managed to halve his personal time, and his teammates voted him "Most Improved Player."

Every Kid Can Find Something

Extracurricular activities other than sports teach personal development, cooperation, and motivational skills. My kids have traveled with the debate squad, marched with the band, and painted scenery for the school play. Some have been stars and others have not, but they've all enhanced their self-esteem and enjoyed themselves.

If your kids aren't interested in theater, music, or drama, they can still find a niche. Various clubs let teens explore career interests: consider Future Business Leaders of America, Junior Achievement, Candy Stripers, and others. Participating as officers or committee members also teaches cooperation, organization, and group dynamics.

Running for a studentbody office and working in student government teaches the political process. Kids learn early to be responsible citizens and internalize the importance of voting in a democratic society. Such state and national programs as Boys and Girls State and Presidential Classroom give kids an education in civics unmatched by any textbook. Students who participate in these programs gain a sense of control. They learn that grassroots involvement can influence laws and the direction of society.

So the next time you get ready to shove a kid out the door to school, think about all the great things that could be waiting for her when she gets there. And remember: using the tactics in this chapter can help your teen's school years be simpler and much more fun . . . or at least tolerable!

CHAPTER 8

Raising Responsible Drivers

A main source of conflict and poverty in most families is a sixteen-year-old with a driver's license. I was unprepared for the economic and emotional realities when my oldest daughter arrived at the magic age of sixteen.

Because the steering wheel of my van felt like a piece of clothing I could never take off, all I could think of was finally having another body to help out with carpooling.

Now that my nine have all passed the age of sixteen, I'd rather they rode bicycles or let me do all the driving. One child plowed twin furrows in the newly seeded lawn; another thought "don't hit your brakes on the ice" meant "grab the emergency brake, instead." As soon as I think I've seen everything, another kid comes up with a new aspect of the same old nonsense.

Insurance companies agree with me—they would rather nobody younger than twenty-five drove at all. They claim ninety-five percent of all accidents are caused by people that age, although they'll often insure girls at lower rates. Insurance company actuaries have proof that boys are not only involved in more accidents than girls, but boys' accidents are more deadly and cause more property damage.

The first time you try to put a teenage son on your policy, you're in for one of the most frightening experiences of your financial life. Much of the expense depends on where you live—and how many boys between the ages of sixteen and twenty-five hold a driver's license and live under your roof.

At one point, with three such drivers in our house in California, our premiums ran nearly $2,000 every six months. That figure dropped sixty percent when we moved to Utah. It dropped again when Eric left on his mission.

You and I need practical, clear advice on how to keep our kids alive and ourselves out of bankruptcy. Although my way to enlightenment about teen drivers is littered with blown engines, speeding tickets, mangled fenders, and gnawed fingernails, I've learned some things that may help—and that I wish I'd known fifteen years ago. The same discipline system that shapes successful students and brings family harmony can produce young drivers who contradict insurance statistics.

Keep three points in mind when your kid starts begging for a learner's permit:

1. *Driving is a privilege, not a right.* You are not required to provide a car, gas, oil, and insurance for your children—although they'll try very hard to convince you otherwise.

2. *Kids will do anything to drive.* The car keys are my most effective disciplinary tool.

3. *Kids who drive have limitations.* Teenagers who can drive can relieve their driving-weary parents, but you should recognize that the combination of lack of experience and "teen logic" can bring serious, even tragic, consequences.

DRIVING IS A PRIVILEGE, NOT A RIGHT

This fact supersedes all others, but because driving has become so important in our society, your children will expect a driver's license when they turn sixteen in the same way they expect their home to be equipped with a television set and a stereo.

Don't be deceived; as a parent, you are legally and ethically obligated to provide food, shelter, and clothing for your minor children. You are also required to teach them correct principles and send them to school. Nowhere is it written that you must allow them to operate a motorized vehicle!

I'm continually surprised by the number of parents who impoverish themselves to give cars to their kids on a sixteenth or eighteenth birthday. I'm even more surprised by the number of parents who wring their hands and worry about a teenage driver out with the family car, but who never take control of the situation.

Most of us let our kids get driver's licenses, paid their premiums, and bought their gas because they freed us from chauffeuring duties. I was lulled into this thinking because my oldest two were relatively responsible girls.

Girls are not as expensive to insure as boys, because they are not as likely to use a car as an extension of their egos/machismo. Boys sense the power that ton of metal and rubber can give them. There's something pretty heady about having control of such a machine.

Evidence of this attitude is obvious in my family. My oldest son wrecked our new car when it was less than a month old, then went on to blow out an engine in the not-so-new-but-still-expensive second car a year later. His brothers have racked up similar, albeit less costly, figures (wrinkled fenders, gouged paint, and broken axles). Then it suddenly dawned on me: I didn't have to put up with this non-stop demolition derby! Driving wasn't as necessary for my sons as breathing or eating (although each tried to convince me it was). They *could* survive without driving to school each day. They could (shudder . . .) walk or (convulsion . . .) ride the bus.

Paying for the Privilege

If kids want to drive that much, they can get jobs and pay for their own insurance and gas. If they balk at funding their driving, they should relinquish their driver's licenses; a law in many states requires insurance to be paid on everyone in a household who has a driver's license.

Let me pause here and assure those of you with girls that your daughters can be just as costly in terms of damaging your car. My daughters have side-swiped a Mercedes, mangled a fence, and cracked an engine block. However, the first two casualties happened when they were on family errands. The cracked engine was a result of ignorance, not rampant testosterone.

Taking my own advice is hard, however. Because I gained my knowledge slowly, the non-drivers screamed like wounded ducks whenever I mentioned they would be held to a more stringent standard than their older siblings. So I tried not to scream back; I answered that I'm a reasonably intelligent person who learns from her mistakes. And did I ever make some mistakes! Through grim experience, I've learned that power without responsibility is the main problem with driving (and cars) for teenagers.

Power vs. Responsibility

One of my counseling patients buffaloed her parents into letting her drive the family jeep wherever and whenever she wanted. Yet she refused to wash dishes, make her bed, do laundry, tell her folks where she was going or abide by any kind of curfew.

When I asked a friend I'll call Barbara why she didn't just confiscate the keys from her oldest daughter, she said, "Oh, but she'd get so mad!"

Why are so many of us afraid of our children getting mad at us? What will the child do? Scream? Slam doors?

I told Barbara that she should tie driving privileges to taking responsibility around the house. Barbara, a mother of five who worked full time, struggled to motivate her daughter and came to me in desperation.

"But what if she takes the jeep, anyway?" asked Barbara.

"Call the police," I answered.

Barbara was horrified. "How could I do that? I don't want her to go to jail!"

Therein lies the problem—Barbara was so worried about what might happen if she crossed her daughter, she was unable to take control and maintain family power where it belonged.

Authoritative moms and dads know that, whether their kids like it or not, parents must have the final say in how a home is managed— if they don't, the logical order of the universe is violated and chaos reigns. When our kids know we will do everything possible to be sure they're safe from the consequences of their choices, they blithely let us continue shielding them.

The following are the three worst mistakes I made when I bought into the idea that everyone sixteen and older has an inalienable right to a driver's license and access to a car:

MISTAKE #1: PAYING FOR EVERYTHING

I do mean everything. I've actually handed out the $15 application fee and sent for the birth certificate! My kids all know how to write their names, and they mail letters to dozens of friends and missionaries around the globe—you'd think they'd be capable of such correspondence for themselves. They are, but since I went ahead and took care of the written work, they happily let me.

Gas, maintenance, and insurance are major expenses. I was always hearing, "I need a few bucks for gas." And I always coughed up the cash or forked over a credit card. No more!

MISTAKE #2: BELIEVING MY KIDS ABOUT CAR MATTERS

I didn't remember that all teenagers lie—if they can get away with it. The "Can I take the car to run over to Angie's for a minute?" is a ploy I've fallen for an embarrassing number of times.

My question, "How long will you be gone?" is usually answered with, "Five or ten minutes—max." That's when the "10 factor" of teen logic comes into play: teenagers invariably stick on or subtract an extra zero whenever they deal with money, time, and distance—depending on whether adding or subtracting will be most in their favor.

Today, I write the time down when a kid leaves and when she returns. I always do this, even when I must do it in lipstick on the back of a torn envelope. The act of writing the time, mileage, amount, and other items eliminates most "10 factor" excesses—most, but not all. Remember that teens are biologically programmed to see things from their own perspective, even when that perspective defies logic.

MISTAKE #3: NOT SEPARATING "CHORE" AND "FUN" DRIVING

As I said earlier, any kid who wants to drive at my house will fund his or her own activity. "But," you may ask, "How can I expect my child to run errands unless I pay for gas?"

This is a good question and a thorny problem that I've wrestled with for a dozen years. I've finally separated the "chore" driving from the "fun" driving and proceeded accordingly. You can do the same.

Sit down with your youth and develop a definition of each. The following are my definitions; yours will depend on how many kids you have, your family's economic situation, and where you live:

Chore driving consists of: (1) *shuttling siblings* to and from lessons, practices, and such; (2) *picking up stuff,* like the dry cleaning, a jug of milk, and trash compactor bags; and (3) *taking a turn during long trips* to relieve a weary parent.

You might limit the number of miles that can be earned in any one day, however, or the family vacation could eliminate your main motivational tool.

Note: I'll talk about giving rewards for "chore driving" in a minute. For now, realize that shuttling can be highly entertaining for the youthful driver and needs no further reward. For instance, G.W. volunteered to drive Linda to dance club and cheerleader tryouts and practices. He usually hung around to watch, because he "didn't want to make an extra trip . . ."

Fun driving encompasses all driving initiated by your teenager.

This definition is by far the simplest because it avoids all kinds of communication problems. If my teen wants the car for a date, to visit friends, to attend a movie, or to "take a drive," his or her time behind the wheel is definitely fun.

You may notice that G.W's volunteering to chauffeur his sister and her friends could be classified as "fun driving" because he took the initiative and enjoyed it so much. This situation demonstrates how smart parents stay one step ahead of their kids.

Gary Willis actually received some extra "fun" miles while I gratefully accepted his gift of time and paid for the gas. So he was a willing helper. I didn't bother pointing out that those miles were as much for his benefit as mine (and his sister's—a handsome, available brother gave her considerable status).

KIDS WILL DO ANYTHING TO DRIVE

Now, for the rewards you can offer for "chore driving," and the price your kids need to pay for "fun driving." Once you have established which kinds of driving you will pay for and which your child must pay for, you need to devise a tracking method. I've used various methods; some work for a while and then become ineffective. Others sound good to me, but I have neither the patience nor the persistence to put them into effect. You might try one or more (or a combination) of the following:

• *Keep a driver's log* in the car, and record mileage. All chore driving miles should be recorded, and an equal number of fun miles allotted to the teen driver who logged them *without complaint.* Griping and growling negate the whole thing.

Caution: This suggestion takes the same careful supervision in the beginning as does the Point System. You can never really relax your vigilance—you must "spot check" frequently. A couple of my little darlings padded their miles before they realized I kept my own private log. You may find running out in the snow or 115-degree heat to check the speedometer a bit uncomfortable, but don't stint on such supervision.

Also, be careful if your child is a mechanical whiz. It's not unheard of for a kid under this 1:1 rule to disconnect the speedometer cable during his or her personal sojourns.

• *Charge $.30 a mile for fun miles.* This is a simple and effective tool to avoid arguments over whether your teen can take the car. Your kid is more likely to act responsibly if he's spending his own money. Of course, this hint means you've established a log, are checking it, and that your teen has a paying job.

Cover yourself if your teen is like mine—never having the money "right now" to pay for gas, oil, and insurance. My teen is always going to give it to me *later.* Later never comes . . .

If they can't get away with "later," they're very adept at saying they paid when they didn't. A clever teen can stretch a $20 bill to Mom into $200 worth of driving.

• *Tie using the car to the Point System.* I've discussed the Point System in other chapters. Just being able to drive will motivate your kids to earn the requisite number of points; you have a tremendous incentive at your disposal.

Use your imagination. Figure out what you want and how your teenager's driving will help you get it.

Setting Parental Priorities

A friend of mine devised a stress-free method to make sure her boys "walked the Eagle trail." In her family, earning an Eagle is the prerequisite for a driver's license before age eighteen. I think it's a great idea and announced the plan to my youngest boys—both of whom yelled a lot at my announcement.

I'm not sure what I can do at this late date, because my youngest kids will probably manage to hoodwink either their father or me into waiving the requirement. They use the standard arguments of "You didn't make Gary Willis or Roch!" and I don't think as fast as I used to.

I do know from personal observation, however, that parents who stand united on this subject have the joy of beaming through the Eagle Court of Honor. Their sons may goof off for a couple of years, but by the age of fourteen or fifteen, all of them are hard at work on Eagle projects.

I watch wistfully as my friends' sons accept First Class rank before they're even out of Primary. I've threatened, cajoled, and bribed, but none of my sluggards have risen above Second Class rank. So, take my advice: deliver the Eagle Ultimatum before ANY of your boys are out of diapers.

Although I never had a chance to make being an Eagle a requirement, driving privileges were the only way I forced one of my boys to exert any effort at all in school. Grounding, lecturing, and crying were equally ineffective. Gary and I finally laid down the law that a B average in school was a prerequisite for getting a driver's license. If my son couldn't show enough responsibility to attend class and perform above-average work, he couldn't have adult privileges.

Don't think it was easy to take this stand! My son brought home his report card and had the audacity to point with pride to a D-plus. Gary looked at the sorry figures and said, "I told you last quarter that if you didn't pull your grades out of the toilet, you wouldn't get your license. Time has almost run out. A D-plus doesn't cut it."

My son hit the roof (literally—he was tall enough to whack it with his fist) and yelled, "What? Everybody gets a driver's license—no questions asked. But not my parents. They think I'm the wicked monster kid."

Notice how my son skillfully shifted focus from his GPA to accusing his parents of hating him. His next tactic was even more slick. "Everybody in the world thinks I'm wonderful and have such a great testimony, but in my own house, I'm the devil."

Teenagers like that know that a good offense is the best defense. If you are blessed (or cursed) with such a teen, don't let him shove you off-balance.

In this particular confrontation, I was proud of Gary. He didn't rise to the bait; he said, "Driving is an adult privilege. Adults take responsibility and follow through on their commitments. Until your grades demonstrate adult actions, you won't be driving."

This section is probably as good a place as any to give you a related piece of advice: If you can, **buy a special car for your teenagers to drive**. An armored car or tank would be my vehicle of choice, but not many are available. Just be sure the car has a lousy paint job, multiple dents, a reliable engine, and great tires.

Our "teenagers' cars" are always at least fifteen years old, because we assume (correctly) that fences will be knocked down, light poles backed into, and driveways missed during the first few years each kid develops his or her driving skills.

Should High-School Kids Own Cars?

Buying a car for the kids in your family to drive is *not* the same as buying a kid his or her *own* car, however. I'm not sure why, but teen ownership of a vehicle always causes problems. I guess the difficulty may be that ownership is too much responsibility too soon.

My high-school English classes provided me with evidence against letting teenagers own cars long before any of my children arrived on the scene. Without exception, every student who bought or was given a car dropped at least one grade point. One of my super "A" kids slid into the "C" category after taking possession of his sixteenth birthday present. Why? He worked extra hours to fund insurance and gas money and had less time for studies.

Another student defied his parents' authority and drove his car at will. His reasoning? "It belongs to me—you can't tell me what to do."

If your teenager is out of high school and you think he or she needs to own "wheels," don't get stuck with payments. Buying a car on time can be a learning experience for kids older than eighteen. Otherwise, it's an exercise in frustration.

I know too many parents who have cosigned for their kids and ended up making the payments on wrecked or stolen cars or on cars that weren't worth what was still owed on them. So don't cosign unless you want the car your kid wants. Better yet, don't let him or her buy a car, unless your darling is independently wealthy. Again, remember: YOU DON'T HAVE TO BUY YOUR KID A CAR! Nor do you have to let that kid drive if she doesn't have enough personal money or isn't willing to work for the privilege.

KIDS WHO CAN DRIVE HAVE LIMITATIONS

Once you've laid the ground rules and established the criteria for gaining the driving privilege, you will be blessed by that extra pair of hands for the steering wheel and feet for the accelerator and brake pedals. Certain cautions are in order, however.

Recognize that lack of experience and "teen logic" can combine to produce tragic consequences. One of the main reasons why is a mental quirk psychologist have named the "personal fable."

All adolescents function under the grand illusion that "it can't happen to me." That's why driver's education scare videos rarely work. Kids are grossed out by the films, but they never apply what they see to themselves.

Don't expect your teenager to know how to drive right away—driving takes skill and coordination, as well as close attention to details. A January 1993 *Reader's Digest* article titled "No Survivors" illustrates the dangers of teenage driving. According to the article, inexperience is the number-one killer/crippler of drivers younger than twenty-one. These kids have no idea of exactly what a car or truck can do to them or to others:

> Every week, auto accidents wipe out the equivalent of an entire senior class at a typical American high school. More than 6,000 people between ages 15 and 20 are killed on roadways each year.
>
> Alcohol is often assumed to be behind the shocking statistics. But in two-thirds of the cases—including the ones in this article—drinking plays no role. Instead, the culprit is an equally deadly concoction of carelessness, over-confidence and inexperience. Each day many good, decent young people simply make lethal mistakes. (Per Ola and Emily D'Aulaire, "No Survivors," *Reader's Digest*, January 1993, p. 39.)

Most states now mandate driver's education for drivers younger than eighteen, and I highly recommend enrolling your kid in private lessons if your school doesn't offer driver's education. You should also provide as much behind-the-wheel practice for your child as your fingernails and heart will allow.

Gary spends countless hours with our kids, giving them the practice they need. I usually refuse to ride with any of them until a year into their licenses, because my nervous system can't take the strain. By refusing to ride with anyone, I avoid hurt feelings and "you don't trust me" accusations. I'm grateful for Gary's greater courage, because our kids need that practice time.

Neutralize Deadly Errors

Don't fall into the trap of thinking your teenager is more skilled than she really is. Even when your teenager has taken the relevant class, he needs practice to develop an appropriate level of skill.

Dolly mangled the front end of the "teenagers' car" (a 1974 Buick Skyhawk) when she drove her elementary-school brothers and sister one icy morning in Oklahoma. Born in Anchorage, Alaska, she'd been around a lot of winter driving, so I assumed she could handle the conditions. I handed her the car keys without a second thought, because she'd had her license more than a year.

As she drove, she remembered being told not to hit the brakes if she started to slide. So when she hit a slick spot, she yanked on the parking brake. She spun out of control and slammed into the curb. Luckily, nobody was hurt, and the extra dents didn't really stand out on that already-battered automobile.

Dolly needed to be shown how to slow down in such a situation, and she needed experience under winter driving conditions. But Dolly was my oldest, and I was so desperate for her help behind the wheel that I let her do far more than I should have.

Now, Player family drivers must have licenses for six months before they can drive another person. I also won't let my kids ride with anybody who hasn't had a license for at least six months (I prefer a year). This particular rule irritates my offspring. They have a tendency to think they know everything and to snap "I know" in response to every suggestion. They don't want to be told *anything* by their fuddy-duddy mother, whose vehicle operation skills pre-date the Stone Age.

Seatbelts Save Lives, So Make Your Kid Wear Them

Most teenagers fuss about wearing seatbelts. Their reluctance is part of their personal fable—"bad things only happen to other people." They also hate the sensation of being tied down or restricted. But none of these reasons minimize the importance of using seatbelts.

Gary and I are very strict on the Seatbelt Rule. Our cars have always had enough seatbelts for every child, and we don't move until everyone is "buckled up." We also try to insist that our kids use seatbelts when riding with anyone else.

Of course, we have no way of knowing whether or not they do, just as we have no way of knowing exactly how they behave when they're out of our sight. But they have little doubt about our reactions if we find out they've violated the Seatbelt Rule.

Being cited for not wearing a seatbelt would be grounds for serious punishment and would involve a lengthy period of giving up their car keys. Since laws concerning seatbelts are being enforced, we parents have more support in this area.

Now that I've covered three facts on maintaining a leadership position in your family and winning the Right vs. Privilege Battle, I'd like to touch on a parent's worst nightmare: what to do when your teenager makes serious mistakes involving the family car and the law.

"We Have Your Son/Daughter at the Police Station"

Drinking or taking drugs while driving is a grave offense. Obviously, the dilemma is complex and involves moral as well as legal issues.

I don't have all the answers, and I tend to overreact sometimes. But my deepest feelings tell me that if a teenager *ever* drinks and drives, he or she should have his license yanked for at least two years, whether or not a ticket was issued. My earlier admonition against long, drawn-out punishments doesn't apply here. In situations where lives are at stake, I don't think there's a margin for error.

What to do when your teen uses any kind of recreational drug is a complex and soul-searing decision. I mention it here, because being able to drive is a powerful behavior modification tool.

Where drinking and driving are concerned you have the law on your side, and you have many options. Work with the authorities to be sure your teenager experiences enough consequences to be discouraged from further such actions. Spending the night in jail or a couple of weeks in a group home may be sufficient to change disintegrating behavior.

A counseling patient of mine was caught with beer in her car. Although she wasn't legally drunk, being underage and having possession of alcohol were grounds for the courts to enter the picture.

She was put on house arrest and ordered into family counseling. Her mother had been trying to take her daughter to counseling for three years, and she had refused to go. But when the judge ordered, the girl obeyed. I had to write a weekly report to him about whether or not she cooperated.

If she hadn't cooperated, she would have gone to jail. So, she participated in her therapy and made progress. She was released from custody without having to be put on probation. Because of her age, her demonstration of sincere repentance, and the fact that she had never been in trouble before, all references to the situation were deleted and her record was cleared.

I worry, though, about the tendency of some judicial systems (especially in large cities) to dilute or even eliminate punishment for criminal behavior on the part of adolescents. A trip to the police station can become a badge of honor among street-wise kids. A few days in "juvey" is often better than life at home for the desperately poor. But we're not talking about abused and disadvantaged children in this book.

I make it clear to local authorities that I will back up their actions when my kids are involved in unacceptable behavior. I try not to be guilty of the "not my kid" attitude, which makes police nervous about being sued if they try to stop reckless driving, vandalism, and other initial offenses against society.

I prefer that my young offenders endure consequences, however unpleasant for my self-image as a parent, than that they think "nothing will happen" or that their deeds are above the law.

I'm Smarter/More Skilled Than Anybody Else

Other more common problems with kids running afoul of the law involve reckless driving and driving without a license. Both of these difficulties can be handled much better if you decide on your reaction ahead of time.

Reckless driving stems from lack of experience and/or lack of respect for a powerful machine that can kill. You want to provide the experience and instill the respect without endangering your child, property, or anyone else.

Driving Without a License is Hard to Avoid

When kids turn fourteen or fifteen (about the time they qualify for a learner's permit), the temptation to actually drive becomes overwhelming. Little children delight in pretend driving, but pretending no longer satisfies a fourteen-year-old. The process starts with, "Can I start the car?" and progresses with dizzying speed to, "Can I drive home from church?"

My Early Teens will happily freeze to death for the privilege of warming up the car in below zero weather. I've even witnessed cases of bribery where a twelve-year-old gave his entire allowance to an older sibling for the honor.

But Middle Teens are no longer thrilled by the act of turning a key and pressing the accelerator. They'll still go out to "warm up the car," but after about two minutes, they grow bold enough to slip the engine into gear and actually move a few feet.

We parents would have an easier time denying the "drive home from Church" request if all of us stuck to the letter as well as the spirit of the law. Technically, no one should sit behind the wheel of a moving vehicle without a valid learner's permit.

Take your son or daughter to the Motor Vehicle Department and get a permit before you teach driving skills. Otherwise, stay on private property and never let your kid drive publicly unless she has a permit in hand.

The difference between driving without a license while a parent is in the car and driving without a license whenever they want to becomes insignificant for some teens. My kids whine, "See, Stan's mom let him drive home from Church! I'm older than he is."

I know of fourteen- and fifteen-year-olds who sneaked out with the car keys and "went for a spin." Some convinced little sisters or brothers to fetch the keys (nobody would suspect a six-year-old of wanting to drive). Others enlisted buddies to help push the car out of the driveway and down the road far enough so they wouldn't wake Mom when the engine started.

I just wish everybody would answer, "No, you can't drive until you have a permit, and then only with another licensed driver older than eighteen in the front seat with you." It would help those of us who really hate being wicked witches by continually denying their offspring the euphoria of doing what "everybody else can."

The main thing to remember is that driving is a privilege, not a right. If you demand responsible behavior and stick to your guns, your teenager's driving will be part of his or her growing-up process. You'll endure fewer headaches and emotional wear and tear, you'll avoid late-night floor-pacing, and you will save yourself a lot of money.

CHAPTER 9

War or Peace: Convincing Kids to Help Out

"Is your room clean?" is the question every parent asks every kid. "Almost," is the typical answer. The question and the answer underscore the difference between adult logic and teen logic.

You probably want to know that the bed is made, clean clothes are tucked in appropriate drawers, dirty clothes reside in the laundry, and all books, baseball mitts, swim goggles, and teddy bears are either arranged on shelves or hung from handy hooks.

Your teens, on the other hand, define a clean room as a smudged sheet lumped along one edge of an equally smudged mattress, clean folded clothes stuffed under the bed, dirty clothes crammed in the closet or under the bed with the clean stuff, and "all my stuff" arranged in mysterious heaps and mounds.

Knowing how to work is the life skill everybody needs, and a work ethic is developed first at home and then out in the world. I'd like to give you some handy hints designed to convince your capable, but lazy, offspring to do more than indent his pillow or arrange her eye makeup according to color.

Effective parents teach their kids how to work, a skill that seems to be rapidly going out of style. As a business owner who hires people, as well as a parent who wants to see her children become happy productive people, I'm very interested in seeing that the next generation develops a solid work ethic.

Closely related to whether or not kids work around the house is whether or not they hold a part-time job. Therefore, this chapter also contains a short section that covers the issue of when and where kids should work.

Teaching teens how to work involves defining and clarifying what needs to be done, motivating kids to actually DO something, and praising or rewarding the kid (once he manages to accomplish anything).

DEFINING AND CLARIFYING: WHY ARE THEY SUCH SLOBS?

One of my pet peeves has always been how teenagers can blithely saunter through a house, dropping crumbs and dirty socks for somebody else to pick up. I've yelled, threatened, and cried—with no effect.

When more than one teenager lived at my house, I entered the living room to find an algebra book, college brochures, *Silly Cow Jokes,* one filthy sweatsock, six broken crayons, and a ripped backpack scattered over the couch and floor.

The kitchen was worse: a jelly jar spilled down the front of the dishwasher, a gallon of milk warmed beside the sink, several empty cereal bowls graced the top of the garbage can, and a bread sack lay in the middle of the floor on top of the area rug.

But as the older kids passed out of their teens, left for college, returned from missions, married, and began raising their own families, their attitudes changed. I like to think some of my hounding and training techniques actually influenced their behavior.

Changing Sloppy Habits—Patterning

You can teach your kids to clean up, after themselves, but it's exhausting and involves a lot more than nagging. The teen who drops her shoes in the family room, her books in the kitchen, and her coat in the hall will put those things away if she's yelled at. But she'll drop them in the same places tomorrow. Yelling, scolding, or threatening won't change her behavior, but reprogramming her brain will lead to change. The best reprogramming device is "patterning."

Patterning works if I have the patience to follow through. When my child saunters through the front door, slips out of his shoes (where his little brother will trip over them in twenty minutes), plops his books on the stairs, and throws his grungy coat on one of the recently recovered chairs, I (as politely as possible) ask him to back-track—to leave the house and try again.

Grudgingly, he puts on his coat and shoes, picks up his books, and stomps back out the door. Then I open the door, say, "Hi! Glad to see you," and watch him put the coat, shoes, and books in their proper places. If I'm not too weary, I repeat the process until he gets the point.

Patterning can be used with any habit you want your kid to develop or break. Intervene when you see your teen pour a glass of juice, chug it down, and leave the carton on the cabinet. Witticisms like, "Is that thing going to grow legs and walk back to the refrigerator?" might earn you a smirk from your teen, but it's better than, "You're such a slob! Why don't you ever put anything away?!"

As I continually emphasize, maintain your sense of humor and stay calm. Insist the juice drinker put the juice pitcher either in the dishwasher (if it's empty) or back in the refrigerator. You may have to stand at his side during the procedure, but if you persist with a light touch, you'll make progress. He'll put the pitcher in the right place whenever you're in the room. Sometime after his twenty-first birthday, he may put it back all the time.

Is Your Room Clean?

Many teenagers "clean" their rooms only in their daydreams, because they've never been taught what a "clean room" means. Define your minimum standards: "Clean" can mean anything from "basically picked up" all the way to "corners vacuumed, windows and mirrors washed, and carpets shampooed."

If your son or daughter is a slob and has no desire to change, don't despair. The Point System comes in handy here, too. A clean room is part of the "Picking Up After Yourself" category on my charts. Samples of my charts and lists are contained in the Appendices.

A Summary of the Point System

The three categories of the Point System are: first, *attitude*; second, *chore(s)*; and third, *picking up*. I rank all three (attitude, the quality of chores finished, and picking up after yourself) on a scale from 4 to 10. Ranking avoids all kinds of arguments. The kids know that:

10 =	Couldn't Be Better
9 =	Outstanding
8 =	Satisfactory
7 =	Average (okay, but nothing to brag about)
6 =	You ought to try a little harder
5 =	You are not contributing to the family's well-being; you lose privileges

4 or less = House arrest and/or confinement to room

When somebody wants to go out two nights in a row on the weekend, sleep over with a friend, watch a particular television program on a school night, or add an hour to curfew, I ask them to average their points and find their answer on the chart.

Two Examples of How the System Works

My Late Teen daughter wanted to watch videos with a few friends. She had gone to a dance the night before, but wheedled, "You said I could earn both weekend nights, and I've done great! I got lots of nines."

Now, this discussion might have turned into a typical argument about my always saying no, but all I had to do was take her into the kitchen and point to the sixes and sevens that crowded the chart at the beginning of the week. Her average was eight—okay for ordinary activities, but not good enough for special privileges. The "lots of nines" she bragged about were two that had occurred the day before.

Muttering a few things under her breath, Late Teen huffed into her room and slammed the door. My Middle Teen son, on the other hand, wasn't as easy to convince.

Middle Teen bustled around, picking up the newspaper and straightening the vacuum cleaner hose. "As soon as I finish this, I'm leaving," he said.

I looked up from the letter I was writing and asked, "You're what? It's a school night."

"Ooops, excuse me. Let me say that differently," grinned this good-looking charmer. "Can I go to the Moytahwa Review [the high school dance and drill team]?"

"I repeat—it's a school night. And your chore points hover in the 5 and 6 range; you know what that means," I said.

As he stood in front of me arguing, "This is a school function,"

"Mary is on her way to pick me up," and, "Everybody's expecting me to be there," I could see the pile of folded clothes he was supposed to put away two days earlier still on the back of the couch. I also could see two pairs of his shoes beside the television set and the remains of his after-dinner snack dribbling down the front of the stove. His "picking up" points for the day would be at their usual 4 level.

"No way," I said.

He yelled, "I hate this stupid point system! Why does everything around here have to be so regimented?"

When I merely sat quietly, he tried another tactic. "Come on, Mom. I did my chores today and you said you'd think about it when I asked to go last week."

"No," I said, "the numbers don't lie. You haven't even qualified to go out this weekend—much less in the middle of the week. Get in gear and try a bit harder so you can go to Steve's party on Saturday."

"You mean I can't go tonight? What am I going to tell Mary? She'll be here any minute."

"I'm sorry. Tell her your mom won't let you go."

"But she's driving all the way up here."

At that point the doorbell rang, and my son said, "See? She's here . . . Please? Please?"

I won't bore you with the rest of the details, but the story ended with Mary driving away without my fuming son, who stood on the front porch pounding his fist against the railing. After a few minutes, Middle Teen stalked into the house, glared at me, and stomped down to his bedroom.

Because I'm usually such a wimp during confrontations, I was very glad to have the information about my kids' past week's achievements written down. My point chart helped me to not take personally either kids' sulking and animosity, so I could better deal with the absurdity of it all.

Expectations and Reality

If my teens held down a part-time job as well as attended school all day, I didn't expect much in the way of chores during the week. They were supposed to keep their beds made and dirty clothes picked up, however. Those who didn't have part-time jobs or heavy extracurricular activities should have completed at least one significant chore a day, such as cooking dinner, doing dishes, or mopping a floor.

In addition, each kid was assigned as a "supervisor," which meant he or she made sure that one area of the house was clean while others were actually assigned to do the heavy cleaning. The job wasn't counted as done unless it looked good throughout and at the end of the day.

The above two paragraphs describe what the kids were supposed to do, but as in the Video Party and the Moytahwa Review incidents, their performance wasn't always what I wanted it to be. A friend of mine came up with a modification of my Point System that she swears works for her. Although I haven't tried it, it sounds pretty good.

When she grew weary of reminding her three boys (ages thirteen, fourteen, and seventeen) about keeping their rooms clean, she taped ten quarters on sturdy cards and hung one in each boy's room. She posted another card which spelled out the rules:

• Bed made
• Nothing on the floor except furniture
• Closet floor clear, except for shoes
• Drawers and closet door closed

Anybody who found his brother's room in violation of the rules could remove one quarter and put it on his own card. The offender had to be notified of the loss and had thirty minutes to rectify it before losing another quarter.

At the end of the week each boy got the quarters still taped to his card. My friend swears this method worked. She says nobody came to blows, and all three kids developed the habit of keeping their rooms clean.

Like the "get your Eagle" requirement for a driver's license, I can see how careful set-up and supervision of "quarter cards" could succeed. And I wish I'd known about it earlier.

Everyone Lives Here—Everyone Works Here

Thirty-something years of tussling with my desire for order and my kids' desire for relaxation have taught me how to reduce the general workload. I now operate under three maxims:

1. Take off your shoes. This idea grew from necessity. My house in Alaska was surrounded by woods and mud. Lots of that mud came inside on people's feet, so I posted a sign on the front door, "Please Remove Your Shoes." I've continued the shoes-off request over the years because it eliminates a lot of vacuuming, sweeping, and mopping.

2. Pick up your own messes. Somehow, I have to convince my kids that when they peel a banana, they shouldn't drop the skin for somebody else to throw away. As I said earlier, patterning helps sharpen their awareness, but I haven't found anything that works all the time.

3. Do more than your share. While mothers already do more than their share, kids live by the motto "That's not my mess." My Point System allows me to reward kids who do something without being asked or reminded (a big factor in the "attitude" category).

I divide household tasks into major categories, with categories assigned to individual members. If we have four categories and eight kids at home, two kids cover each category. I don't give myself or Gary a category, because we're the eternal substitutes—we do the chore if nobody else will.

What About the Dog?

I added another category when Rajah (a half-coyote pup) and Lucky (a border collie/St. Bernard cross) joined the household. We'd had several dogs, a few cats, hamsters, rabbits, white mice, and goldfish over the years.

Pets can be wonderful for the whole family, but I don't think anybody should have them if the parents are the only ones who do the work. What I think doesn't count for much, though—we always have some kind of pet. And Gary or I always end up taking care of it.

If you are stuck with the care of a cat, dog, or goldfish (the poor thing would die otherwise), I suggest you hold a special family home evening about pet care.

When it's handled properly, a pet can benefit your teen in many ways. It teaches him empathy and accountability. It gives him practice in service and the rewards of love from a devoted, living being.

Sharing with and Caring for Animals

Discuss God's purpose in creating animals. Tell your kids that animals have souls, and that they can think and feel. Find out as much as you can about your particular pet(s) and educate your family. If your teenager is agitating for a critter companion, try to obligate her to do the research *before* she brings the animal home, or you might experience what I did shortly after Linda graduated from high school.

Linda insisted that she wanted a dog to accompany her when she went jogging in the early morning. Our previous dog had died the year before, so the rest of us were amenable. Gary and I laid down the rules:

The dog must be an adult.

The dog must be housebroken.

Linda must take complete financial and physical care of it.

The dog must be large and healthy enough to live outside.

Linda argued with us on the last point. "Why have a dog if it has to be outside all the time?" she asked. She wanted the dog to sleep on the rug beside her bed.

Nathan, Brian, and Micah were excited and volunteered to "help" her build a dog run and "clean up poops." I tried to caution Linda not to latch onto the first dog she came across. She assured me that she'd be the epitome of sensibility.

Two days after she received permission, Linda brought Rajah home. Rajah was big, but that was the only way he resembled the dog she'd been told to get.

Rajah's teeth indicated he'd barely been weaned. He definitely was *not* housebroken. While Linda paid the shelter fees and bought Rajah a food dish, collar, and leash, she changed her mind about wanting a sleeping companion.

Rajah spent his first and last night in the house the day he arrived. I'd told the kids, "You want a dog; you clean up after him." When I went to the kitchen for my early breakfast, I found evidence of Rajah's busy night. The table had been dragged nearly to the carpet (Linda had tied Rajah to one of its legs).

The sugar canister lay shattered in a sticky slurry beside the back door, and the newspaper we'd put down to begin "paper training" was shredded from one end of the kitchen to the other. The house reeked, and I wasn't going to do anything to change its odor.

Linda decided she wanted to "be independent" and moved out a week later. She didn't take the dog with her . . .

Discuss why your family wants this particular pet, then have your kids decide whether they want the pet enough to put up with the messes and the hassles. If everybody agrees on the need for the pet and on the responsibility to share in its care, make a chart that reflects what needs to be done and that tracks who should do it.

Finally, post the chart and remind your teens if you have to. Reminding is the hardest part for me. I can define tasks and draw up charts, but once I tape them up, nobody looks at what I've written. And I'm easily distracted, so I don't follow up enough.

Individual Accountability

I contend that *not being home for your chore is no excuse—get your own substitute.* But I hate disorder, so I probably handle more of the household chores than I should have to, because I can't stand seeing a mess pile up. If I were more tolerant, I know I could save myself a lot of aggravation. Use whatever parts of my advice suit you, and discard the rest.

The most recent Player work divisions were:
- Cooking (including shopping for the food and washing the pans)
- Dishes/kitchen
- Dusting and vacuuming (cleaning the living room and family room)
- Bathrooms
- Taking care of the dog
- Entry and outside (including hauling the garbage, picking up trash, and sweeping the walks and porches)

Washers and Dryers—Blessing or Curse?

You'll notice that the chore divisions did not indicate anybody in charge of laundry. Everybody did his or her own laundry at my house—at least they were supposed to. Laundry skills were necessary for my mental well-being and for my kids' survival as adults.

"Do your own laundry" meant no tossing dirty clothes in front of the washing machine. Dirty clothes stayed in baskets in each person's room until that person was ready to wash, dry, fold, *and* put away. I also tried to keep baskets in each bathroom for soiled linens and towels. But those baskets were always carried off by someone. I occasionally thought about nailing them to the floor.

Anyway, when somebody did a load of laundry, he or she was supposed to add to the load from one of the bathroom baskets. Since the majority of my children were known to run a full wash for one particular pair of pants, I was sometimes forced to get nasty on this point.

I didn't assume the kids knew how to wash clothes just because they'd reached the age of twelve, either. One of my daughters showed me a pile of rumpled, dingy clothes and said our washing machine was broken. When I watched her cram the entire contents of her laundry hamper in at once ("to save time"), I figured out the problem.

Sometimes I taped a laundry tips chart (see example in the *Chore Charts and Lists* Section of the Appendices) above the machine—especially when we had new foster kids or one of my own turned "laundry age." Part of the challenge, as usual, was making sure my kid *read* the chart once it was posted.

You can probably come up with more creative motivations, but I asked my teens to put their initials and the date next to each step. This requirement messed up the chart and necessitated replacing it frequently; a sheet of notebook paper taped next to the chart would work almost as well.

As I've indicated in other parts of this book, lists and charts eliminated guesswork and statements that began with, "But I thought you said . . ." When I wrote things down, I was much better off.

Motivating Teens to Do Something

Now that I've given you a general description of KP around my place, let's turn to four of the basic categories: *cooking, dish-doing, vacuuming,* and *bathrooms.* These four will give you an idea of how I've tried to simplify household tasks and motivate my lazy offspring.

Eat, Drink, and Be Merry

Cooking (including shopping and washing the pans) headed my list. We all have to eat, so cooking was one of those skills I figured that anybody who wanted to eat should learn. The best place to learn is at home, because the inevitable mistakes won't cause too much bother.

I've endured watery soup, cold scrambled eggs, burned toast, and all the other results of inept cooking by Early Teens. By the time the kids were Late Teens, they could usually put a balanced meal on the table without too many disasters.

The chart and checklist detailed in the Appendices hung in our kitchen and, as with the laundry chart, I did my darndest to make sure the kids looked at it. Their chore points depended on whether they completed all the steps, although some of them could have cared less. When I was alert and diligent, I had fewer confrontations and the household functioned fairly well.

Temptations for Young Cooks

Watch for certain pitfalls as you encourage your teen's cooking skills. Most of my kids created huge messes that they ignored because it was someone else's job to do the dishes. Knowing how to consolidate steps so that fewer pans are used doesn't come naturally. Neither does wiping up spills as they occur—both reasons why #10 on the Cook Chart requires the person who messed up the pans to scour them.

Work along with your teenager—it's a great opportunity for friendly chats while you give tips and demonstrate efficiency. But don't do all the work while she lounges against the cabinets to watch. And don't be too picky about results. Teenagers like to eat, and they know what tastes good. If they burn the vegetables or cremate the chicken, they'll remember next time not to set the burner on High just before they leave the room.

Otherwise, let your teenager figure out a procedure that suits her. Nothing irritates a teen more (well, not much anyway) than being told to do something a certain way—especially when they condescended to actually start a job. So, as long as the job was done, I didn't demand any particular technique.

Cooking can be very rewarding; creative kids usually enjoy it once they get started. Monitor your hungry sons to be sure they don't eat everything before the rest of the family can partake, though.

Dish-Doing Duties Simplified

My kids hated to do the *dishes*. Our biggest chore wars, accompanied by episodes of my blowing my stack, clustered around who was supposed to do the dishes.

When I was a kid, I lived on a homestead without sewers, running

water, or electricity. I washed dishes in an enamel pan with water heated on the cook stove. Of course, I drove my mother just as crazy as my
kids drove me by waiting for the water to heat, waiting for the water
to cool down, and other such stalling tactics.

My kids didn't have the handy excuses I did; water temperatures
were adjusted by a twist of a faucet handle. They had a dishwasher (at
one time we had two) that dramatically simplified the job, but they
still stalled, whined, and wandered off. As bad as they still are, they
were much worse before I put together my "Dish-Doer Chart."

Temptations for Young Dish-Washers

I've discovered that teen dish-doers try to get away with certain
shortcuts. The "there's-still-something-in-the-serving-dish" ploy was a
favorite. I continually opened the refrigerator door to find the shelves
stuffed with tenderly covered bowls and plates that contained one tea-
spoon of juice and one peach pit, a smear of tuna fish, three green
beans and a soggy potato chip, and a single piece of petrified cheese.

Not only did they "put away" nonexistent or inedible food in
order to avoid washing the dish, but they left in the serving spoon
and/or fork. Winding three yards of vinyl or tin foil around those
utensils took a lot more time than washing would have, so I failed to
understand what was gained by the strategy.

Another interesting tactic was the "put-back-the-putrid-peas-Mom-
just-took-out" maneuver. Circumventing this maneuver took talent. I
learned to pull off the covering and either scrape the peas into the dog's
dish or dump them into the garbage disposal. Nobody has yet retrieved
things from those two places, but I wouldn't put it past them . . .

A third subterfuge called "the pans-are-soaking" was difficult to
contradict. Your best bet is to keep pot scrubbers handy and to inspect
the dish-doer's work, or you'll run up against a variation on the theme
called "it-looks-clean-to-me." I guess some of my teens really did have
such poor eyesight that they couldn't tell the kettle had held chicken
broth not long ago . . .

Teenagers think that if they do a lousy job on the dishes, bathrooms, or whatever enough times, you'll decide the hassle isn't worth
the results. This thinking illustrates why you must persevere in the
face of overwhelming odds.

Your daughter, who never understood that big pans go *under* smaller pans or comprehended that greasy drips down the front of the cabinet do not magically evaporate, will one day alphabetize her spices and color-code her dish towels.

Your son, who always managed to arrange a water polo practice or marathon research paper whenever his dish night came around, will stun you by single-handedly clearing away Thanksgiving dinner *without* being asked.

But Somebody Messed It Up Again

Dusting and vacuuming were relatively simple jobs. When I told my kids to "do the vacuuming," I meant that everything that was carpeted should be vacuumed, and all the furniture that stood on the carpet should be dusted. That definition took into consideration that crumpled candy wrappers, pieces of the newspaper, and dirty socks would automatically be picked up and disposed of properly.

When (or if) my kids responded to my request, they thought they'd finished if they'd managed to haul the vacuum cleaner into the middle of a room, turned it on, pushed it around for thirty seconds or so, and switched it off to become a piece of playground equipment for one of the grandkids. Since your teenager probably acts the same way, use the checklist in the Appendices to lessen those blank looks and grieved, "Well it looks fine to me."

Just as they try all sorts of ways to avoid doing dishes, kids expend tremendous energy avoiding or postponing vacuuming and dusting chores. I've found dirty underwear stuffed under the couch cushions, crumpled paper behind the bookcase, and pizza-stained napkins in my top desk drawer. Since errors and omissions in the living room were less obvious (and less hazardous to health) than the cooking and dish-doing chores, I tended to let my kids get away with more in this area. I shouldn't have, but I did. Cleaning and polishing the living room has always been a sort of therapy for me. I enjoyed making everything look nice, so I never said much.

And that was probably my main problem. My kids were smart—they knew just how far to push me before I turned into a mom version of a marine sergeant.

Don't Forget to Lift the Seat

Although a cluttered living room or family room didn't bother me (much), I couldn't stand dirty bathrooms. My kids thought I was a fanatic, but I wanted every surface in every bathroom cleaned every day. That's what I wanted; what I got was the privilege of doing that scrubbing and disinfecting myself. Then my kids used my bathroom, because theirs was dirty. I couldn't win.

But I tried. I posted my "Clean Up the Bathroom" chart in each bathroom (see Appendices); I placed another chart above the toilet in the kids' bathroom that read, "FLUSH! WIPE OFF THE SEAT! WASH YOUR HANDS! PICK UP YOUR UNDERWEAR!"

Then, when my energy level permitted, I used patterning. I didn't think I'd been very successful until a few days ago. One of my grown sons remarked that he'd taken a can of cleanser with him to work and cleaned the men's bathroom, because it was "so gross." Hang in there; someday you, too, will overcome.

Besides cooking, dishes/kitchen, vacuuming and dusting, and bathrooms, other categories of chores I used were outside (including hauling garbage, picking up trash, and sweeping the walks and porches), taking care of pets, entry and closets, and garage.

Exactly what these divisions of work included depended on the number of able bodies littering up the premises at any given time. Whether either Gary or I worked at home was also a factor, because these methods took close supervision and effort in the beginning, with random checks thereafter.

PRAISE AND REWARD A TEENAGER'S EFFORTS

One of the reasons kids fight so hard about doing chores is they're afraid the list will go on and on. Avoid penalizing a good worker.

I'm usually so grateful (and amazed) when one of my kids actually plunges in and finishes something that I ask that willing laborer to do something else. Therefore, my teenagers think, "If I do my job right away, I'll just get given more to do. I might as well goof off and avoid the extra load."

Also, we parents have trouble motivating our kids because we forget to praise. Once Eric, Linda, and Micah showed they could do something halfway right (like making a bed without giving it a stirred

look), I tended to count on Eric, Linda, and Micah plugging helpful-
ly along in that chore without any more hassles.

Convincing any kid to do anything really hinges on praise. No matter how thick you lay it on, your teen will accept your words as truth.

You can praise in diverse ways. The Point System is one means,
but you have to be sure your kid sees the points as soon as you record
them—otherwise, she will argue about them days and weeks later
when she wants something.

Your kid may blush and say, "Aw, Mom!" when you tell a neighbor about the great job he did trimming the hedge or raking the yard,
but he loves to hear you talk about his good points. In fact, praising
your teen to a third party is one of the most effective methods you can
use, as long as you are sincere and don't dwell on the subject too long.

Keep one last caution in mind: No matter how provoked, **don't yell**.

Dr. William Chambers, a child psychiatrist at Columbia
Presbyterian Hospital in New York, said in the early eighties, "Once you
start yelling, kids know you're feeling powerless. Powerful people speak
quietly. . . . Simple conditioning is a lot more effective than yelling."

I have a hard time keeping this caveat in mind, and I do yell once
in a while. Actually, I cry and yell at the same time. But I try not to
do it very often.

A sporadic outburst reminded my teens that I was a human being,
not just a mom whose sole function was their convenience and comfort. They scurried around for a few minutes and occasionally accomplished quite a bit before they lapsed back into their slovenly ways.

TO TAKE A JOB OR NOT TO TAKE A JOB

Now that we've talked about specific household tasks, let's consider whether your teenager should hold an after-school or weekend job.
You might think this is a moot question, because teenagers are very
expensive members of the family. But sociologists and psychologists,
who have studied the subject of teen workers, have recently come up
with some interesting conclusions.

Most experts now believe that unless real economic hardship
exists, kids younger than eighteen should work only one hour a day
during the school year. Jobs in family businesses have not been studied, and the conclusions don't hold for summer times or vacations.

Psychologists reason that personality development and education take priority over earning money. Kids who work more than five or six hours a week have lower grades, drop out more readily, and participate in fewer extracurricular activities. That's not all: they have less time for family activities, and if they work on Sundays, their spiritual welfare suffers.

Who Benefits?

I've grappled with the "to work or not to work" dilemma since Dolly and Sherri had jobs in a day-care center run by the Church of God in Tulsa. Their working six or seven hours a week gave them money for clothes, lunches, and track meets—especially when we struggled to make ends meet.

Dolly's experience added to her education for her career choice in early childhood development. Sherri's working in a nursery gave her compatible experience for her home health nursing career.

However, others of my kids have been on payrolls at a fast-food restaurant, a local theater, a clothing store, and a supermarket. When they worked more than one hour on school days, their grades, their behavior, and our family peace suffered.

Rarely did the extra money translate into anything positive, because they spent it all on themselves or their friends. Whenever I asked for assistance with the phone bill, utilities, or gas, I was answered, "I don't have any cash." On the other hand, if I offered the opinion that a dance, a concert, or some other activity/purchase was a money-waster (from my point of view), my kid said, "It's my own money."

However, your teenager might be an exception like Eric was. He earned twenty-two college credits during his last two years of high school while maintaining a 3.6 GPA, traveled with the debate squad, played trombone in the marching band, sang with a competitive choir, and averaged thirty hours a week mucking out Albertson's bakery. Believe it or not, Gary and I had to pay him to quit. We were concerned he'd collapse under the strain.

Taking a Stand on Teen Labor

I've severely limited the number of hours my kids could work during high school, especially if we had enough family income to provide allowances or a job in the family business. I tried to tie the money they wanted to work that needed to be done around the house—per the Point System. If they didn't want to do their chores and they had jobs or allowances, they were fined. The money went into a central kitty for the family or savings accounts, whichever was most appropriate.

Each kid started the week with $15 or $20, or whatever I could afford. Then I added or subtracted from that amount according to the following scale:

10 Points	=	+$2
9 Points	=	+$1
8 Points	=	OK
7 Points	=	-$1
6 Points	=	-$2
5 Points	=	-$3
4 Points	=	-$4

Money rewards attached to earning points helped me educate my kids that money symbolizes action; good intentions don't produce money.

The Root of All Evil

Money and the earning of it can reflect positive or negative values. I wanted my teenagers to understand their needs and not to assume they would be happier if they had more money. So I didn't want earning their allowance or holding a job during their school years to take on undue significance, nor did I want to confiscate all of their hard-earned cash from outside jobs. You, too, ought to reflect on just what you are teaching your kids when you interact with them on the subject of money.

Perpetually granting cravings for name-brand clothing, stereos, boom boxes, and money-munching activities feeds a teen's innate materialism. Allowing them to spend everything they make from a job is just as bad as buying for them. On the other hand, continually denying their wants and keeping them deprived won't teach them generosity or love of work.

I generally insisted that the kids put half of what they earned into a savings accounts, after paying their tithing. They could use the remainder as *discretionary income.*

Holding a job, working around the house, taking responsibility, and following through with their commitments are all life skills that will serve your teenagers well.

How Can I Stop the Fighting?

CHAPTER 10

Diffusing Sibling Rivalry

Another common question I'm asked is, "Why do my teens always fight, and how can I stop it?" When most of us decided to be parents, we visualized happy days with smiling tots.

Unfortunately, most kids not-so-secretly yearn to be only children.

The competition for lap space and the car keys makes me want to turn in my resignation about twenty times a day. Little kids fuss and fume at each other, but big kids can get downright nasty.

Teaching kids to "love one another" takes more commitment and energy than any other parenting task. I've seen parents really blow it by trying to treat everybody the same—ultimately impossible. Also, without meaning to, we parents tend to reward obnoxious behavior because we just want "A LITTLE PEACE! DO YOU HEAR ME? PEACE!" Rather than focus on the situation and teach kids to deal with their emotions, we ignore whatever we can. The noisiest kid is noticed, while the quiet ones (translated: those who don't bother us) are ignored.

Have you ever been guilty of the following statements?

"Shame on you! You're the oldest—you should know better."

"I don't care who started it, both of you shut up!"

"Don't be so stubborn; she didn't hurt your sweater, did she?"

"Why don't you ever finish a job like your brother?"

So how *can* you stop the fighting? I haven't completely stopped it among my kids, but I have reduced the frequency and duration of family battles. Correcting common mistakes we parents make involves these considerations:

- The fairness issue—Mortal life requires us to live under a paradox.
- Charity—Our kids must learn to sacrifice for one another. They must understand that emotions can be changed, and they must practice communicating their emotions in a positive way.
- Special reasons for fighting—similarly aged siblings, toddler and teen siblings, and adults as siblings.

THE FAIRNESS ISSUE

"It's not fair!"

"How come she got more points than me?"

"It's not fair!"

"Why can't I stay up, too?"

Kids are obsessed with "fairness." By the time they become adults, however, they figure out that life isn't fair, and all their complaining won't make it so. But what's a parent to do in the meantime? How can you and I explain this complicated paradox? And if we can't explain it, how do we survive the assault on our logic and sensibilities?

"It's not fair" usually echoes through the house at specific times. Some of those times are downright silly. Others stretch even an adult's understanding and coping powers, such as when loved ones disappear through divorce or death, illness strikes, or jobs and livelihood disintegrate.

First, we have to recognize and accept that although natural and social law govern the universe, life isn't fair. Bad things happen to good people; innocents suffer.

But Why Can't I . . . ?

Although life doesn't seem fair at times, we all need to see the universe as orderly, where consequences follow actions. That's the paradox. And because natural order coupled with an absence of fairness is difficult to understand, "It's not fair!" can become an excuse for laziness and apathy. "Why try? Nothing ever turns out the way I want it to, anyway . . ."

Developing a Sense of Control

In order to learn to take control of their lives, adolescents must practice making decisions and experiencing consequences. The results of their actions gives kids practice in coming to terms with the paradox of free agency and accountability.

A situation where one child must be treated differently in a family can be a learning experience for all involved. If you have a handicapped or seriously ill child, your family has been blessed. All of your children will learn empathy and selflessness, but not very easily . . .

Eric, who had a stroke when he was two, suffered a series of mysterious seizures when he was eleven. His illness meant he often came home from school during the day or didn't leave the house until lunchtime.

When any of the other kids "didn't feel well," they griped about my pushing them out the door anyway. "How come Eric can stay home when he wants to and I can't?" was a frequent complaint.

However, such grumbling didn't really bother me, because Eric's cheerful struggle with his handicaps usually disarmed the murmurers. Even though he missed a lot of school and had the perfect excuse for not working, he never fell behind in his studies and he maintained honor roll grades.

Cause and Effect

Learning that actions have consequences can be painful for the child and hard for the parent. I've left some kids behind when an unexpected trip materialized and the rest of us went to the beach for a couple of days. Those left behind wept and wailed and cried "No fair!" but they'd cut classes and ignored homework so many times they couldn't miss any more school. The kids who went were current in their studies and attendance. Missing such outings has been the most powerful tool I have to teach responsibility. Seldom has a child missed more than one "special day." But how should you handle an unpleasant consequence for accepting responsibility? The paradox comes into play when a child does his or her best, but something bad happens.

I Did Everything Right . . .

"Mom, why did Breathless have to die? It's not fair!" My fourteen-year-old foster daughter, Anna, wrapped her arms around herself and rocked back and forth.

I remembered her devotion to the newborn lamb. She patiently fed it every two to three hours, climbing out of a warm bed to fix bottles of smelly formula and standing in the cold while Breathless fed. She surprised me with consistency and devotion that lasted for weeks.

Breathless followed Anna like a puppy and climbed into her lap when she sat on the front steps. Anna spent hours romping with the little animal or holding her in her arms like a baby, while Breathless nibbled and kissed her mistress's chin.

Then Breathless developed an infection in her tail. When the infection began, the vet told us to give the lamb antibiotics. Unfortunately, the kids didn't realize such medicine must continue until all the pills were gone, and I forgot to remind them. Now, Breathless was dead.

It didn't seem fair at all. Anna had tried as hard as she could. If anyone was to blame, it was me, because I didn't explain the medicine's purpose or how to use it properly. But placing blame wouldn't comfort Anna or help her grow from a sad experience.

Instead, I tried to focus Anna on the positive parts of her time with Breathless. We took Breathless' body into the desert to become part of nature's cycle. Then we held an informal memorial service. I encouraged Anna to remember all the things she loved about her pet.

The other kids gathered around her, expressing their sympathy and reminiscing. "Remember the time Anna put a diaper on Breathless and slept with her?" said big brother Danny. They laughed and cried together for the rest of the day.

The Prodigal Son—The Ultimate Paradox

When he first encountered the parable of the prodigal son as we watched the video produced by the Church, one of my sons became very upset—just like the son who stayed home and served the father. "It seems to me that the bad kid got the best deal. His dad didn't yell at him; he hugged him and threw him a big party."

My son's reaction was pretty typical for an adolescent, because teens tend to live in the moment. I pointed out that being welcomed back with open arms couldn't erase the years of misery the prodigal had suffered.

My son and I talked about that suffering. The prodigal son didn't need to be yelled at—Heavenly Father doesn't yell at us or make us suffer more. The natural consequences of our sins are sufficient punishment.

The prodigal son lost many years to his unrighteous actions, but his father's love never failed him. Contrary to his own opinion, the righteous son wasn't completely righteous, either. He was jealous and angry when he should have rejoiced in his brother's repentance.

We all must recognize our own failings; we have enough to handle without worrying about whether others have been "punished enough." The prodigal son was given a cloak and a piece of jewelry, and a fatted calf was killed for a great feast. But everything else belonged to the righteous brother who had served faithfully. He hadn't squandered his birthright. He'd developed and nourished it, so he was much richer.

After this explanation, my son felt better; I think he understood what I was trying to teach him about family dynamics and bearing each other's burdens. And it was clearer to me, too. Once kids at least accept that their lives will never be "fair," they're ready to learn about charity.

CHARITY: THE FOUNDATION OF A SUCCESSFUL LIFE

Moroni 7:47 reads, "But charity is the pure love of Christ, and it endureth forever. . . ."

When your thirteen- and fifteen-year-olds are screeching at each other about who used the last drop of shampoo or your sixteen- and seventeen-year-olds are on the verge of fisticuffs over who gets the teenagers' car this weekend, you may think there's no hope.

Let me reassure you that you really can stop, or at least reduce, the fighting. Plus, if you believe the Book of Mormon, you know that you are commanded, in no uncertain terms, to not allow the fighting: ". . . neither will ye suffer that they transgress the laws of God, and fight and quarrel one with another, and serve the devil. . . ." (Mosiah 4:14.)

The Differences Between Emotion and Reaction

Kids must become aware of how they respond—what kinds of emotions they have and how they typically deal with those emotions. Then they can gain control over and channel their negative emotions into constructive areas.

Sometimes a kid's negative feelings about himself translates into teasing and tormenting a little brother or sister. The older kid can't stand seeing things he hates about himself showing up in his sibling. This situation is very common, but that doesn't mean it should be ignored. Sometimes, I simply forbid nasty remarks, period. But I also do role playing and help the kids learn to identify their emotions more clearly.

Know What's Happening

Identification is the first step to control. You can't have power over that which you don't know. So, teach your kids about their feelings. Emotions are neither bad nor good in themselves; they just are.

Kids, especially Early Teens, should understand that they're not at the mercy of their emotions—they can control how they react. In order to do so, they must separate feelings from reactions. Anger needn't lead to punching or kicking or name-calling.

First, identify what a feeling is. A *feeling* or an *emotion* is a reaction experienced inside a person as he or she responds to external stimuli. Most kids use only the four categories of happy, sad, scared, and angry. They are unaware of the vast spectrum of feelings they're capable of experiencing. We parents must teach them to discriminate and to be able to describe their feelings accurately.

Quest International utilizes an analogy called "The Rainbow of Feelings." The colors of red, orange, yellow, green, blue, and purple define various types of emotions. Activities in the student workbook illustrate that emotions can shift and change from one color to another. These activities can be appropriate visual aids to help your teen understand his or her feelings.

After your child grasps just what his or her feelings are, explore the differences between feelings and reactions. Some *feelings* include being excited, jealous, mad, or disappointed. *Reactions*, which involve actions, might include screaming, crying, hitting, laughing, or sleeping.

The distinction between the two concepts is vital—teenagers tend to mix them together. Then they rationalize inappropriate reactions with "I was mad," "She hurt my feelings," and "I couldn't help it."

Emotions Can Be Changed

Self-control comes after definition and understanding. When we understand and communicate emotions, we govern them rather than being governed by them.

Although emotions are neither bad nor good, they have positive or negative effects. Research shows that people who are quick to anger suffer heart attacks at least twice as often as people who don't react with anger. The same research indicates that colds and indigestion follow stress. A study of the correlation between our immune systems and our emotions has revealed some tantalizing information. People do die from broken hearts!

The field of mind-body medicine has gained tremendous prominence in the last fifteen years. Such diverse scholars and thinkers as Bill Moyers (producer, writer, and publisher), Bernie Siegal (cancer surgeon), and Norman Cousins (sociologist) have explored the influence of emotions on physical well-being. Modern science is only now beginning to prove what the gospel has taught since Adam.

Gaining a testimony, an emotional occurrence, has a profound physical impact. Glorified, immortal bodies and those bodies that are completely under the control of God have the power to run the universe. I'm intrigued by the very real light that shines from the faces of those who live as they should.

The act of laughing or thinking positive thoughts brings about a chemical change in a person's brain. The following exercise teaches kids about controlling the way they react to their emotions.

Exercise
Sit or lie down in a comfortable place and close your eyes.

Think about something very pleasant. Recreate the scene and the emotions you felt: seeing Forest Gump *with Todd, holding Nicholas in Church after his blessing, listening to G.W.'s homecoming talk, and so on.*

Relax and experience those neat feelings; remember how good you felt.

Now, switch to an unpleasant scene. Recreate it in the same way you did the pleasant scene: flunking algebra and being told you're ineligible for the state debate trip, listening to Amy tell you she thinks you're an idiot, watching your best friend dance with the guy you like, and so on.

As soon as you have entered the scene completely and feel awful, switch back to the pleasant scene.

Notice how the negative emotions disappear as you focus on your positive experience.

This exercise demonstrates how people choose their reactions. Whatever we tell ourselves becomes reality. Your teenager can learn that she will leave behind sadness, anger, despair, self-pity, and jealousy by substituting joy, delight, amusement, sincerity, and trust. Those feelings will come when she reads the scriptures, ponders Christ's love, and prays.

Express Emotions Positively

Encourage kids to control their impulses and to consider the effects of their behavior. I bought all my teenagers sterling silver CTR rings when they turned twelve and told them to look at their ring before they responded to something one of their brothers or sisters said.

Another tactic is to say something positive. At my house we talk about giving each other "warm fuzzies" or "strokes." I also use another gimmick borrowed from *Skills for Adolescents*:

> All of us carries a positive and negative bucket with us all the time. Each time we hear something positive about ourselves, a drop is added to our positive bucket. Each time we face rejection or ridicule, a drop is added to our negative bucket.
>
> We tend to "lean" toward negative or positive feelings, depending on which "bucket" is fuller at any given time. Our feelings about ourselves are directly related to what we "carry" in our buckets." (Unit Three, Session Five of *Skills for Adolescence*, published by the Lions Clubs International and Quest International.)

In addition, kids shouldn't hurt other people under the guise of "expressing how I feel." Instead, encourage your teen to discuss emotional situations and their range of possible responses.

Conscious Change

Besides thinking positively and avoiding grim or depressing situations, emotions can be changed through service to others. The quickest lift comes from doing a kind deed.

As I strive to show my kids how to serve one another, I've developed stratagems that work most of the time. I encourage my teens to give each other notes, to be "secret angels," and to make small gifts.

Our family home evenings built around "What I like about—" are simple and effective. We pick one family member to be honored and focus all the neat things we can think of on that person. We also spontaneously go around the room, saying one or two positive things about each person present.

I remember one incident at our house where I used positive reinforcement and physical contact to help an Early Teen son change his feelings. Thumps, scuffles, and thuds reverberated through the ceiling, followed by an indignant squawk from Early Teen.

"Mooommm! Middle Teen sister hit me and sat on me just because I wanted to go to the bathroom!"

"Shut up you little toad—I just tried to get you to calm down."

"Calm down?! You sat on me and hit me and threw me across the room . . ."

"This is my bathroom. You use your own; I don't want you peeing all over the seat."

The screams and bellows of rage from upstairs increased in intensity and decibel until Gary stormed out of the kitchen and took the stairs two at a time. He reappeared, gripping Early Teen's elbow.

Full of twelve-year-old fury, Early Teen struggled to free himself. "Why don't you grab her? She's the one who started it! You never say anything to her. It's always me. She's Miss Perfect and you never believe me."

"Sit down and don't move until I tell you to," said Gary, shoving his son into an armchair.

Early Teen curled into a ball, hugging his knees and pressing his face against the back of the chair. "Go away! Leave me alone! Just get out of here."

I sighed. Here we go again—another sibling war in progress. I went upstairs to talk to my daughter.

She looked at me with wide-eyed innocence. "I don't know what got into him, Mom," she shook her head. "He just freaked out. He nearly broke the door down."

We stood on the landing. I looked down at Early Teen, who glared up at us with angry tears dripping from his chin.

"You have got to stop antagonizing him," I told her. "You know just which buttons to push and set him off like a skyrocket."

"Oh, he's just being dramatic. He'll get over it." My daughter's self-righteous tone elicited an "Oh yeah?" and a disgusted noise from her brother.

I rolled my eyes and went back downstairs. I leaned over him and kissed his hair. He twisted away from me, "Go away."

"Honey, I'm sorry you feel so bad," I said. "Come here and let me hug you."

"No, go away. You never believe me—just Miss Perfect!" Tears flowed again. "I hate her; I wish I had a baseball bat. I'd bash her so hard! I wish she'd go away and never come back."

"Do you really want to hurt your sister?" I said. "Think of how bad you'd feel if you actually lost control and did something to injure her."

I stroked his hair and tugged gently on his arm. "Come on, sweetie. Let Mommy give you snuggies." (The silly language seems to work with my kids, but you have to use whatever tactics suit you.)

"Ugh," he said, but he didn't pull away. I tugged again, and he followed me to the couch, where I put my arms around him and continued telling him how much I loved him and how sorry I felt about his misery. Gradually, his tense body relaxed and his tears dried up.

Every time he said, "She's a jerk, and it's her fault I'm so mad," I countered with, "You are choosing to be mad at your sister. She was dead wrong to push you around and yell at you, but you chose to react."

When he tried to change the subject and argued, "Why don't you punish her?" I answered, "I'll deal with that girl later. Right now, I want to show you how you can make yourself feel better."

The whole situation, from first scream to last "Thanks, Mom; I'm okay now" took about an hour. My son's attitude for several days continued to be sunny and sweet; he did lapse once in a while, but the skirmishes were brief.

REASONS FOR THE FIGHTING

As mentioned earlier, King Benjamin's words in Moroni 4:14 tell us in no uncertain terms that we cannot allow our kids to squabble.

Their fights have different reasons; understanding the reasons helps me figure out solutions. Sometimes the fights break out because everybody is close in age. Some problems develop because the discrepancy in ages is too great. Still other problems result from some of the siblings reaching adulthood.

Same—or Nearly Same-Age Siblings

Most kids yearn to be only children, to have their parents' undivided attention. Because more than half of my children were very close in age, this "occupying the same age bracket" accounted for the majority of eruptions around our house.

My main objective for this group was to acknowledge each kid's innate territoriality while building his or her ability to share. In order to do that, I had to remember and instill two adages.

1. A person's own space is inviolate. Territoriality is an inborn human instinct. Some privacy is necessary. Every kid must have an "own" place—even if that place is no more than a bed, a single drawer, and a section in a too-small closet. Nobody can snoop in drawers, closets or other private places. And everyone has the right to define which places are private and off-limits.

2. The kids must not be selfish, however. Certain things are common property, such as the house, clothing, and food. Trying to make common property private or private property common provoked many sibling wars. Most of my kids' avenues of contention involved either clothes or food.

Territorial Clashes over Clothes

"Mooommmmm!!! Micah (Eric, Roch, Whoever) is wearing my pants again!"

"I don't have any clean pants!"

"Well, what am I supposed to wear, then?"

Things really got out of hand when I had five teenage boys who all wore approximately the same size. The Wardrobe Wars reached record heights the week before Eric left for his mission in Minnesota. Perhaps Eric's attitude stemmed from the fear of not having enough clothing; maybe he figured he would freeze to death up there. Whatever motivated his actions, I verged on locking him in his closet until the day he entered the MTC.

I found myself screaming, "Shut your mouths immediately! One more word and you both will comprehend a whole new dimension of bodily pain!"

Of course, they continued the bickering and arguing and, of course, I didn't really beat them to death. I stood the two combatants in separate corners.

Then I said, "Most of the clothing on your back, Eric, was bought by either Dad or me, or you bought the clothes with money you didn't have to spend on food and a roof over your head. Therefore, you will remain imprisoned in that corner until you decide it's okay for Micah to wear anything you don't take to Minnesota."

I turned to Micah and said, "You will refrain from raiding Eric's drawers or closet without his permission. But you can pick up anything off the floor that you'd like to wear. You, too, will keep your nose to the wall until you're both civil to each other."

I left the room. Seconds ticked by—about thirty of them—accompanied by "See? It's all your fault!" "No, it's not—you're the dummy who had to holler," "Phooey, it's your fault I'm going to be late," and "If you don't shut up, we'll never get out of here."

Finally, I heard, "It's okay, Mom, we made up. Now, can we get out of the corner?"

That episode illustrates how I kept the peace—pertaining to this particular subject, anyway. **First**, I reminded the fighters that they'd be naked if it weren't for their parents—so, technically, they had no grounds for argument.

Second, I punished them appropriately. Standing a fourteen- and a nineteen-year-old in the corner is a fitting consequence for behaving like a two-year-old.

And, **third**, I left the burden of solving their squabble on them. I gave them a neutral setting where they had to figure out a solution. I didn't act as a judge, jury, or prosecutor; if they continued acting like two-year-olds, they'd continue reaping the consequences.

And there was another benefit: my giving permission to Micah to wear anything laying around on the floor was a blatant attempt to get

Eric to pick up his clothes.

Territorial Clashes over Food

Besides their wardrobes, I hate it when my kids fight over food. They remind me of hyenas crouched over a dead zebra, each trying to grab the tastiest morsel. I'm still struggling with this aspect of family dynamics, but a few tactics help:

First, divide the amount of food available into the same number of units as you have children. I've even been reduced to writing people's names on the sticks of caramel apples, the labels of yogurt cartons, and bread wrappers.

Second, if you don't have equal portions (for example, you have a cake instead of individual cupcakes), assign one kid to do the dividing and another to choose first.

Third, a friend of mine who was very wealthy bought a refrigerator with individual, key-locked compartments. When she brought groceries home, she put them away either in the family compartment (to which she had the only key) or specific kid's compartments (to which each kid had a key, as did she). A less expensive alternative could be to section off places in the refrigerator and label them with freezer tape and a grease pen.

Finally, rotate cooking and shopping chores weekly. Whoever is in charge must stay within the budget and develop acceptable meals and snacks for everybody. This activity helps kids understand what goes into their food supply.

Other Types of Conflicts

Besides clothing and food, kids fight over other kinds of things. For some reason, they go out of their way to annoy each other.

Some of my kids are so touchy they bellow if a sibling breathes too loudly. Others, I'll admit, have quirks of the "fingernails grating on blackboard" variety.

It requires the wisdom of Solomon to deal with, "Ugh, Micah's slurping his nose again," "Make Linda stop clicking her tongue at me," and "Nathan's rapping is giving me a headache." I generally use role playing, communication enhancements, and listening skills.

In stubborn cases, I separate the combatants—as in Eric and

Micah's confrontation over pants. A time out often lets the moods settle and the differences dissipate. When I see that truly negative feelings are developing, I pray for guidance to know how to deal with the
situation. Then I approach each combatant separately and in private.

I start the discussion with a reference to Moroni 4:14 and emphasize that current actions have allowed Satan to invade our home. I listen to what each has to say, but I don't take sides. Most of the time a
prayer together resolves the issue. Other times, one particular child
needs to ponder alone a little longer.

Toddler and Teen Siblings

Most teenagers love and dote on the babies in their families, but
balancing a toddler's need to explore with his big sister's need for privacy always required fancy diplomacy on my part. I attempted to
explain that two-year-old Nathan was fascinated by Dolly's tape player. He didn't stuff the cat food in the cassette slot or pry off the knobs
to be destructive. He just liked the cat food's consistency and the neat
scratches he could make with a screwdriver.

However, along with my explanation, I gave Dolly a simple lock
that kept her brother out of her room. While I sympathized, I giggled
with her about the time *she* painted the dog blue, put raisins in her
ears, and papier-mached my car.

Dolly learned compromising skills and how to deal with a pesky
two-year-old—valuable lessons she's used in the last few years with her
own babies and toddlers.

To Babysit or Not to Babysit

Another aspect of having babies and teens in the same family is the
babysitting dilemma. Obviously, you should be able to expect some
babysitting as part of your teenager's family responsibilities.

Big kids must look out for little kids, because such interaction
gives them practice in parenting and sensitizes them. It's also good for
the baby to learn to love and trust people beyond his or her parents.

But the baby shouldn't be the teenager's complete responsibility—
the baby's main custody belongs with parents. Ensure that adult obli-
gations aren't foisted off on teenagers who are, by definition, imma-
ture and unready to be parents.

In order not to expect too much too often, my general rule has been to assign babysitting when I do something for the family—like grocery shopping, work, Church meetings, and so on. But when I go out for pleasure (such as for parties, movies, or window shopping), I pay my teenager for his or her time. If I couldn't afford the going rate, I negotiated. "Would you watch the baby tonight for five dollars (or use of the car, or whatever)?" I always secured the teen's cooperation before I left. I've seen too many cases of big brother or sister resenting the younger because of forced and too-frequent babysitting.

I also avoided trouble by enforcing my "no hitting" rules. None of my kids have ever had spanking privileges. However, I know from a painful older sister experience (mine) that younger kids will harass their sibling sitters unmercifully and push the limits. So I told everybody that *I* would punish any offenders when I returned.

There were never any arguments, either. If the one in charge said he was defied or disobeyed, I put the offender in the corner, made him sit on the time-out chair, or administered a spanking if I thought it was appropriate. Backing up the sitter is crucial.

I didn't leave the sittee at the mercy of big sister or brother, either. Everyone knew where the responsibility and accountability were placed. Where much was given, much was expected.

Adults as Siblings

Your grown children, especially if they live nearby, can cause unique family problems—and provide unique blessings. I have grandchildren who are close in age to my youngest kids. Nathan's nephews and nieces take the place of little brothers and sisters he'll never have (except for the foster kids we'll continue to take until he's grown). He has the benefit of babies to teach him about fatherhood, and I don't have to go through any more pregnancies!

The same concerns can surface here, though, as with kids who are distant in age. Nathan and the other kids should be expected to take care of nephews and nieces whenever their services are needed. And they should do a reasonable amount for free (although I encourage the young parents to reward them with thanks and some tidbit or two). But if they're sitting so Dolly and Roland or Gary and Norine can go out on the town, then they should be paid whatever their siblings can afford or negotiate.

Boy, Can Things Get Complicated

An experience during a spring break dramatically shows just how screwy family communications can get. Dolly and Roland had brought two-year-old Nicholas and four-year-old Cameron over for the day. The house hummed with activity on all three levels. I was chatting with my mother on the phone when Dolly stormed into the room, followed by Sherri.

"Mother! You've got to talk to Micah. He just hit Sherri and laughed about it," said Dolly.

"Yes," chimed in Sherri, "I don't know why, and it hurt. And he wouldn't apologize."

Dolly lowered her voice and said, "Mom, he's liable to become a wife abuser."

After talking to both girls for a few minutes, then talking to Micah by himself, and finally bringing everybody together, I was able to piece together what had happened.

The story illustrates the pitfalls and bridges that exist in our family dynamics.

Fifteen-year-old Micah and twelve-year-old Nathan built a space station for Cam and Nicky in our unfinished basement playroom. Linda, Dolly, and Sherri played UNO with twenty-one-year-old Roch and Roland in Micah's room nearby. After a while, Micah (bored with entertaining his nephews and little brother) tried to join the game.

In typical fifteen-year-old male fashion, he made several dumb comments that failed to get a reaction from his siblings, who were obviously enjoying playing cards without his company. Then he flopped down on the waterbed and said, "Let me have some cards, guys, okay?"

"We're in the middle," "Just wait a minute," "What are the boys doing?" and "Stop sloshing the bed" answered his question. Micah reached over to Sherri, who was closest to him, and flicked her on the head with his knuckle. Nobody, not even Micah, could remember what he said as he did so, but Sherri yelled, "Ow! Micah, that hurt. Get away."

At this point, eyewitness accounts become a bit sketchy and conflicting. Nathan, Nicholas, and Cameron had followed Micah into the room, so it was pretty crowded. Dolly, in typical eldest sister fashion, said, "Micah, stop acting like a jerk and apologize."

"That didn't hurt," said Micah.

"Then why is Sherri crying?"

"I didn't do anything—I was just kidding around," said Micah.

"You always hurt people," interjected Linda.

"You need to watch yourself," said Roland.

"Yeah, Bro, chill out," said Roch.

The argument heated up, with Dolly becoming angrier and Micah more defensive. Sherri cried, and Linda, Roch, and Roland contributed to the general squabble.

Finally, Dolly said, "I don't think you're sorry at all, and I don't want you acting like that around my boys—you're not a good example."

Then she herded Cameron and Nicholas out of the room. And Micah yelled at everybody else to get out.

When I came down to find out what had happened, Micah, with tears running down his cheeks, said, "I didn't mean to hurt Sherri, Mom." Micah went on to tell me how upset he was by Dolly's reaction. "I take care of Cam and Nicky all the time for free, and she doesn't even care."

I managed to bring everybody together in the family room, where I acted as an interpreter.

"We have a classic case of miscommunication and overreaction here. On one hand, the grown-up kids were yukking it up and having a great time playing cards together. On the other hand, the youngest kids—Nathan, Cameron, and Nicholas—were having fun, too, in their make-believe space station. Micah enjoyed setting up the game for them, but he wanted to be part of the adult group—not one of the little kids.

"Micah asked to be let into the game, but the big kids didn't realize what he wanted and ignored him. Micah's attempts to join the adults were misguided and unclear. But you misinterpreted him, so everybody contributed to the quarrel."

Listen to Each Other

My explanation enabled me to help my family continue honing their communication skills. As in your family, our dynamics change over time. Kids grow up and leave home, but they continue to play the roles they've always played.

These roles can be positive or negative, and, although they can be modified (usually, with tremendous effort), they will always exist. Dolly will always be our "Big Sister," Nathan will always be "The Baby." Linda will always be "The Littlest Girl." Everyone has a role. Whether or not these roles are played out in a righteous, nurturing way depends on individual choice and accountability.

For example, Dolly must recognize the influence her actions continue to have on her siblings, and she needs to understand how she can help or hurt them. Everyone will always have a tendency to baby Nathan, but he still must be held accountable for conducting himself maturely and making wise decisions.

Reducing the number of fights in your household requires you to expend more energy than a marathon dancer, more tact than a Middle East negotiator, and more patience than Job. But you can succeed if you keep in mind that life is a paradox, kids can be taught to control their emotions and serve one another, and that different age groups mean different challenges.

CHAPTER 11

Encouraging Suitable Friendships

"Please let me be pretty and popular" wafts heavenward from the bedsides of ninety-nine percent of all teenage girls. Boys whisper, "Please let me be good-looking and popular," with "Make me a jock" tacked on at the end.

Teenagers don't pray for wisdom, patience, or eternal life. They can't see beyond right now. They want to be valued for who they are, not what they might become.

Crucial to their emerging sense of self, their ability to make and keep friends determines the kind of lives they will lead. You may wonder whether anybody, let alone a parent, can influence a teenager's choice of friends, but your ideas and desires have a more profound effect than you might think. You can do a lot to ensure constructive friendships.

The Right Kinds of Friends

Friends can make a parent's job easier or more difficult. Most of my sons served honorable missions because of encouragement from their friends. All three daughters insisted on temple weddings because they wanted to follow the examples of their friends.

Conversely, some friendships can devastate a kid's life. One of my counseling patients fell in with the "wrong crowd" at school. As a freshman, she was flattered by the attention of older, more experienced kids—especially a certain senior boy. Within four months, she was pregnant and in trouble with the law.

Another teen found himself on house arrest for truancy because of a friend. The friend continually manufactured ways to "get out of class" or "do some serious partying." Instead of resisting and doing what he knew was right, the teen went along with all the suggestions.

When Janet, a foster child, was placed in our home, her first words were, "I like to be with my friends." That meant she left for school an hour early and came back one to two hours late every afternoon. Her "friends" not only encouraged her tardiness, they gave her cigarettes, helped her cut classes, and accompanied her on shoplifting sprees.

All of these examples show how friends can shape your kid's life. Dealing with the negative and reinforcing the positive require great effort on your part. Certain observations may make the effort easier.

Be alert to times when your child will be more likely to attract the wrong kinds of friends. **The most critical times involve moves and life events.** Major life events can be as simple as attending a new school or graduating from one level to another. Or they can involve either or both parents losing jobs, divorce, or the death of a close relative. Major life events also include positive things. They can be as anticipated and celebrated as a mission call for an older sibling, the marriage of a sibling, or a family member leaving for college.

SIGNIFICANT LIFE EVENTS

Kids are vulnerable when they leave familiar territory behind and must adjust to a different climate, geography, and/or customs.

But, I Don't Want to Go!

I list *moves* as number-one for potential friend problems because the undisciplined, "bad" crowd greets and accepts newcomers much more readily than any other. As a high-school teacher, I've watched the process repeatedly.

The kids who are busy with studies and extracurricular activities rarely pay attention to new people. Girls clump together with their best friends, laughing and swishing their hair, trading blush and eye shadow, and giggling about who might ask them to the dance. Boys hang out with their buddies, punch each other in the arm, burp and scratch, and make bets on Monday Night Football.

I think the innate insecurity of both boys and girls makes them reluctant to reach out to a new person. "What if the new person turns out to be a 'loser'?" they think. "Then I would be a loser by association!"

Kids who have nothing better to do are more likely to say "Hi" and invite a newcomer to tag along. They also have a greater need for blanket acceptance and are more willing to take a chance on an unknown entity. That's not all: their activities are validated by how many others they can convince to do the same thing—a main reason for gangs. It's also a well-known fact that kids with low self-esteem have a need to control others—hence, their efforts to recruit friends.

If you don't want your teenager falling in with this kind of group, take steps to help him or her adjust to a move.

Gary and I have moved our gang twenty-three times since Dolly and Sherri arrived on the scene (we adopted them in 1967). Eight of those moves were of the gut-wrenching, life-changing variety. We've moved kids of every age from infancy through seniors in high school. We've moved them from Anchorage, Alaska, to Martinez, California; to Bakersfield, California, back to Anchorage; to Tulsa, Oklahoma; to Houston, Texas; back to Tulsa; to San Luis Obispo, California; and—finally—to Cedar City, Utah, which I hope is the last move.

As if eight cross-country moves weren't enough, we've also made fourteen moves within one town or another, thirteen of which put us into different wards. We've endured tremendous guilt as our kids wept and wailed and gnashed their teeth. They've accused us of destroying their lives, and—at times—we've agreed with them.

But in retrospect, I can see that each move produced important, positive influences on us individually and as a family. We were successful, because each move was always preceded by family fasts, family councils, and prayer. Then we took steps to ensure that our family "transplanted" successfully.

Successful Kid Transplants

The gardener/plant analogy holds in many parent/child relationships, but it's especially appropriate for families on the move. In conjunction with calling on spiritual resources, I approached moving kids in the same way a gardener moves seedlings: preparing the plant, encouraging it to root, and nurturing it in the new location.

Exactly how you prepare your kid varies with her age and personality and your family's circumstances. The same "hardening off" a tomato plant gets will deflect problems before they start. Encouraging rooting often gets ignored in the bustle of moving, and nurturing can be overlooked as the whole family adjusts.

Some of our moves were more difficult than others, and I wish we'd done certain things differently. Our last move was probably the hardest, but it was the most successful because we leaned on the Lord and our new ward family even more than during other moves.

Preparing, encouraging, and nurturing transplants means helping everybody in the family feel a sense of control over what is happening. Some things will have to change, but some can remain the same. I've discovered that certain aspects of moving are consistent, no matter what aged kid I'm shuffling around, while other aspects of moving are more age-related.

Preparing the Plant

Being members of the Church has become our most important coping device. The gospel is the same whether you live in South Carolina, Sacramento, or Singapore.

The sense that we are all sons and daughters of God, part of the human family, has sustained us when nothing else could. Instant friends greeted us in each new location, ready to offer support and encouragement.

Where appropriate, my "transplanting" suggestions correlate with the Three Phases of Teen.

Early Teens—A Touchy Group

Although kids of all ages become clingy and more dependent after a move, twelve- and thirteen-year-olds seem to have the most difficult time. Humor is probably your best coping tool, both for you and for your kid.

Roch, in the fifth grade at the time, reacted the most negatively to our move from Alaska to Tulsa. He hated fitting into a new school, so he decided to stay home. When "I don't feel good" or "I feel awful" stopped working, he hid his shoes.

Everybody else walked to school, but Roch slumped down in the driveway and refused to budge. He lay there as his brothers and sisters and the rest of the kids in the neighborhood trooped by. Since most of them ignored him, he yelled, "I'll stay here until I die!"

Fifteen minutes of driveway theatrics finally forced me to drag him to the van, shove him in, and drive him to school. At the front gate, I opened the doors and shoved him out. These maneuvers continued day after day. Roch's problem was solved after Gary finally witnessed the struggle.

After finding Roch's shoes in the dryer, wrestling them onto his feet, walking Roch's limp body to the end of the driveway, then draping Roch over his shoulder and carrying him to school, Gary asked, "Does he do this *every* day?"

When I nodded, Gary sat down at the typewriter and composed a letter from the "Oklahoma Theater of the Absurd." The letter congratulated Roch on winning First Place in Family Drama for "capturing the essence of a fall day in Tulsa." Gary folded and sealed the letter and delivered it to the school.

Roch rushed home that afternoon, waving the letter and exclaiming, "Look what I got!"

We all had a good laugh, and Roch stopped hiding his shoes. He still continued to sleep in his closet, though, sometimes evading my eagle eye for several hours.

Finding a Common Ground

Roch taught me that young adolescents (like all of us) need some control over what happens to them. Feelings of helplessness lead to resistance, quarreling, and disobedience of varying degrees. The more helpless Roch felt, the naughtier and more destructive his behavior became.

In order to gain a sense of control, teens ought to be involved in a pre-move or house-hunting trip. After our not-so-fun Tulsa move, when we knew we had to relocate again, we began holding family councils to discuss our options.

Each kid voiced (sometimes noisily) his or her preferences. "My own room," "big enough trees for a hammock swing in the backyard," and "garage workroom" were written into a notebook for whatever realtor we hooked up with.

We also discussed our economic limits. We had lost all of our equity in our Tulsa home; Oklahoma's housing market had collapsed, and we had been victimized by a shady contractor. We had nothing to transfer to another house. In addition, Gary had been laid off; our income had plummeted from six figures to about minus $15,000.

Family councils, as well as a great deal of soul-searching and reading in the Book of Mormon about what happened to the Nephites when they prospered and forgot the Lord's commandments, helped the kids scale down their expectations. For lots of reasons, they learned to be poor.

Moving from a 6,500-square-foot mansion where they enjoyed their own rooms and a swimming pool to a three-bedroom, two-bath apartment took place with minimum tears and tantrums. The five boys shared a bedroom with wall-to-wall beds, while the three girls shared a room approximately the same size as Dolly's walk-in closet in the Tulsa house. They were happy to have their own beds.

The whole family knew we had to leave Tulsa, and we desperately needed guidance about where to go. Since we couldn't afford to take everybody to look for our new location, Roch and G.W. were selected to represent the kids' point of view. Our trip over spring break 1987 involved looking at several different locations between Tulsa and the West Coast. It took two weeks and covered more than 3,000 miles.

Encouraging the Plant to Root

After a move is made and the first confusion of settling in is over, many people—including teens—suffer mild to severe depression. The best way to fight it is to reach out to your new community.

You might join a newcomers club or organize one. I found large, active groups in Tulsa and Houston—a product of the mobile petroleum industry. But almost any community will have resources for telling new people about their town. The local chamber of commerce is a good place to start, as is your new bishop and Relief Society president.

If you move with a large company, ask the personnel office about available services. Many medical insurance policies cover counseling that can keep depression from escalating. LDS Social Services and talks with the bishop of your new ward are sources of help that are even more readily available.

Consider joining community groups that can involve your kids, such as the PTA, band mothers, baseball parents, or other support groups available through the schools. None of these activities cost more than a few dollars and a little time.

I've baked cookies or brought other treats for my kids to share with their new classmates (after checking with the teacher). Most of my kids have brought slides and mementos of their Alaska birthplace, which gave them something to talk about with interested classmates. You should figure out what makes your teen unique and figure out a way to share.

Nurturing the Transplant

As soon after a move as we could, Gary and I made it a point to volunteer our professional services and our bodies in various ways at our kids' schools. I've put together a creative writing unit that has endeared me to a dozen junior-high English teachers across the country. Gary gives a basic geology lesson, complete with slides. And we've both accompanied busloads of kids and teachers on field trips.

You might consider throwing a couple of parties for local kids within a few weeks of your move. A house full of giggling, running young adolescents is a sure recipe for a headache, but the headache is worth it if your teenager makes new friends.

While helping your kid reach out and find new friends, try to expedite his or her connections with old friends. Usually the letters and phone calls taper off in a few weeks or months, but just being able to reconnect with familiar roots builds confidence around new people.

Middle Teens—Unique Challenges

Most of my suggestions for transplanting Early Teens are valid for this group, too. But because of their level of maturity, kids fourteen and older can be both harder and easier to move than younger teens. Although they're older and should know better, these kids have more destructive methods of reacting than younger teens.

Vandalism, drug problems, and other self-destructive behaviors are apt to develop because these kids feel so out of control and isolated from their old friends. Now is not the time to try new discipline methods, but you can't forgo your usual standards, either.

Also, don't make the mistake of "going easy" by ignoring defiant behavior because "the poor kid is having a hard time." Inconsistencies will only confuse the situation and make your teenager more apprehensive and upset. Soothe your child while coaxing out the adult parts of his or her personality.

The child part wants you involved and becomes anxious, but it doesn't want you to be obvious. As Eric said at one point, "I wish you were invisible, Mom, so you could see my classes and teachers." The kids withered with embarrassment if I showed up in the school's cafeteria, but they smiled with pride when I made a surprise appointment for a fast-food lunch.

Special treats like a candy bar with a note tucked into a folder or backpack let your child know you share the worry and the love. Lots of hugs and "I love you" are important for all ages.

Take Concerns Seriously

Kids need to worry aloud about hard classes, no friends, and pimples. If you figuratively pat your kid on the head and say, "Everything will be perfectly okay," you're not going to make many points. "I understand. Let's think of ways we can make things easier" is a much more helpful statement.

Worry about schoolwork can be mitigated by setting up study schedules and planning approaches to the school day. When your kid flunks a test or brings home a D, review his past accomplishments.

Letting him know that you're going to do your best to ease this transition boosts a teen's confidence. "A" papers pulled from scrapbooks or remembered together will reassure kids who start to doubt their abilities.

Some teens who had difficulty in the past with schoolwork might find they perform better in a new environment. They aren't hampered by old mistakes or bad habits. However, some gifted students who were used to top grades could flounder when transferred. I recommend easing into honors classes. More demanding study can come when the stress of being new is over.

Late Teens—But It's My Senior Year!

Moving kids during the last half of their high-school years can be devastating to the whole family—especially when the move takes place during or shortly before the senior year. This last year is often a culmination of many years of effort and friendships. The senior prom, the homecoming game, and other "last" events mean a lot to kids.

But no matter what extracurricular activities or special classes are planned, in my opinion, nothing can take the place of family involvement for this crucial age. Circumstances have forced us to move four of our kids during their junior or senior years. I never considered leaving them behind with friends. I did consider leaving one with family—but not for very long. Gary and I tried hard not to move during this critical time, but we've never had any other choice. We either moved or took out bankruptcy.

I know I'm in the minority on this subject, because most of my friends and relatives in the same situation chose to let their senior stay in the old school to graduate with his or her class.

Here's how we tried to make the tearing away less wrenching:

1. We acknowledged the sadness and dedicated a fast Sunday for the particular child to gain inspiration about easing that pain. Gary also offered a father's blessing, which was usually accepted.

2. We made the senior's concern top priority for any decisions and actions we took, such as when G.W. and Roch accompanied us to search for a place to live after our Tulsa adventure. Gary and I narrowed the choices and then let them pick from among the acceptable options.

3. In the new location, we continued to make the senior's wishes top priority whenever possible. Here, again, being members of the Church made things easier. We found dates for the Junior Prom, Senior Ball, and Homecoming dance among our ward family. Kids who would have missed those opportunities were able to go. If necessary, we footed the bill for the event, too.

How the Wards Helped

Priesthood and Young Women's groups always gave our kids wonderful support. Classes and quorums held birthday parties, welcome parties, and other ice-breaking activities directly for our kids. In three different areas, our girls were "kidnapped" for a surprise breakfast, the boys were serenaded, and welcome notes were pasted to our cars in the Church parking lots.

Although every ward we found was great, I'd like to honor two wards that were absolutely magnificent in welcoming and nurturing our stressed, sad adolescents: the San Luis Obispo (California) 1st Ward and the Cedar City (Utah)17th Ward. In both moves, we could have lost, emotionally and/or spiritually, at least one of our children, but the ward members' "beyond the call of duty" approach saved us.

San Luis Obispo First Ward

The SLO 1st Ward's youth and young adults literally enfolded the kids into their midst. For the first time, our children tasted what living among other active LDS kids could be like. Our move from Tulsa to San Luis Obispo took G.W. away from friends who used drugs and was directly responsible for his decision to go on a mission two years later. Roch's political ambitions were realized in a way he might not have experienced in Tulsa: he was elected SLO High School's student-body president six months after we moved there.

Not only did seven people bring food over the day we moved in, we were invited to dinner as a family (no small feat) several times during our first weeks in town. People continued to bring dinner and treats by at random intervals for months. Dozens of priesthood and Relief Society members showed up for three days in a row to help us unload the moving van and unpack. Most of the costs for G.W. and Sherri Lynne's missions in Curitiba, Brazil, and Spokane, Washington, were met by anonymous members (with full cooperation of the SLO 2nd Ward). Their support continued even after we'd moved to Cedar City.

Cedar City 17th Ward

Gary moved three months before Linda and I joined him and the boys; I had to finish up a teaching contract at Cal Poly, Sherri was on her mission, and Dolly was married. Angie Day, whose family lived across the street from our first house in Cedar City, began writing Linda before we moved there. She became one of Linda's best friends, and remains so to this day.

Three young women made Linda their secret sister—one of them for an entire year! I never found out who left the California Snowman, flower arrangements, cards, cakes, cookies, and other treats, but those sweet girls surely earned a star in heaven. Their gifts usually came when Linda was most miserable. And everyone in the family enjoyed the spirit the gifts brought.

Linda wasn't the only one who had a secret sister, either. I found several beautiful things on my doorstep, too, including a handmade "mop" doll. As in San Luis Obispo, bread, casseroles, brownies, and cookies arrived in a steady stream. We received more Christmas goodies for our first Christmas than I'd made in any of the three previous years.

Although G.W. and Sherri hadn't left on their missions from the 17th Ward and the San Luis Obispo wards were still supporting them, the Cedar City 17th Ward accepted them as their own. The ward gave them plaques to hang in the foyer and threw them great homecomings.

Cedar City 17th Ward members helped lift the financial burden of Roch's and Eric's missions to Tulsa, Oklahoma, and Minneapolis, Minnesota. The cards and letters they sent to our missionaries were as important as the money.

Summary of Successful Moving Techniques

Official studies rank moving only slightly below a death or divorce as a stress-producing event. Whether you transplant Early, Middle, or Late Teens (or all three), keep in mind the analogy between tender plants and growing kids. Preparation means involvement of everybody before the moving van loads; then you must carefully nurture your transplants in their new location.

LOOK OUT! CHANGES AHEAD

Besides moving, your family can endure other changes that impact how your teenager makes and keeps friends. Like all children, adolescents have a hard time with change. They tend to regress a bit and to take fewer chances. Graduation from elementary school into junior high (or middle school) and from junior high into high school can cause major problems.

Family upsets are even more disorienting than graduation milestones. When I look back on my children's most difficult periods, I find they coincide with disasters. Gary Willis' most serious problems occurred after Gary was laid off from his six-figure-income job. As a buffer for all our economic problems, our high-school boys began hanging out with the elite crowd, who just happened to be the kids with too much money and too much time. And none of them were members of the Church. Several of those kids ended up suspended, in jail, or dead.

We tried a lot of things to counteract the undesirable influences; some of them worked. But, frankly, our most effective strategy was leaving the problems behind in Oklahoma (although undesirable friends *was not* the main reason we left). If your child's friends cause similar problems, moving might be your best way out, too.

Less Dramatic Changes Can Cause Problems, Too

Change doesn't have to be as dramatic as divorce, unemployment, or death. Sometimes a teenager feels so disoriented and unhappy about a sister's marriage or a brother's leaving for two years that he or she seeks affirmation by throwing in with the lowest element around.

So what's a parent to do? Excavate a dungeon under the house? Implant a beeper? Insist that every buddy your son brings home supplies three references?

I've seen parents cope with "friend" problems by choosing their children's friends. Choosing your kids' friends rarely works. Teenagers are struggling with their own identity and trying to break away from their parents to establish themselves as independent people. If you like somebody a lot, your kid is apt to reject that person on general principles.

You can't choose friends for your child, but you can encourage friendships (if you're cagey). However, don't let on that you are doing anything in particular.

TECHNIQUES FOR ENCOURAGING FRIENDSHIPS

I believe in the "wait and see" philosophy of child rearing: I watch for a while before I make any judgments or pronouncements. Whenever a new kid comes into our home, I give them the benefit of the doubt, but I keep the reins short. Relaxing of rules for my kids comes after they've demonstrated responsibility in chores and schoolwork. As unobtrusively as possible, I also watch the interactions between my child and the new friend.

Don't be afraid of eliminating a friendship that proves to be destructive. If a friend convinces or persuades your child to violate the family standards, then that friend should not be welcome in your house, and your child should not be allowed to associate with that friend.

I know the preceding paragraph might horrify people who think my advice is "too controlling," and I don't claim to know everything. But I have yet to see any long-term damage result from barring an undesirable friend. And I've seen a whole lot of damage result from not restricting the influence of a "bad" friend.

Your teenager should realize that a true friend wants the best for him. Real friends will encourage him to do what he ought to—not just what he wants to do at the moment.

Guess Who's Coming to Dinner?

Your major quandary will probably be defining exactly what a "bad" friend is. Bad friends do not necessarily dress like charter members of the Hell's Angels. Nor are they always the young men with shoulder-length locks and earrings in their nostrils or the girls in tight pants with purple hair.

Many of my kids' worst friends have worn ivy-league clothes and have driven fancy sports cars. They looked like models for Eagle Scout advertisements; some of them *were* Eagle Scouts. But their minds were stuck on pornography and drugs, and they wanted company while they broke as many moral laws as possible.

Although these youthful hypocrites looked pretty good, their filthy attitudes and ideas become obvious fairly quickly. After they'd been in the house a short time, I figured them out through some judicious eavesdropping and casual observations.

Why Wouldn't I Like Him?

One of my sons answered my "Why don't you have a party here?" with, "My friends wouldn't like it here." Then he admitted the reason they wouldn't like it was because we didn't allow smoking or drinking.

If for some reason my kids don't want me to know their friends, then I smell a skunk! Most kids know their parents are observant; a clear indication that a friend is undesirable is a child's keeping certain friends away from home.

My sons with the smoking/drinking pals inspired my "Rule of Friends." Simply stated, the rule says, "For every visit to a friend's house or haunt, you must bring that friend to our house for a visit."

You can expand or change the rule for your particular circumstances. You might insist that you meet any friend who will associate with your kid beyond the confines of your home. A study date, a walk, or a rehearsal are all examples of associations that seem innocuous but could lead to trouble.

I know it sounds Victorian, but Gary and I insisted on meeting the parents of any boys who dated our high-school daughters. My brother was even more old-fashioned—he not only met the parents, he interviewed every would-be date for his seven daughters. The girls knew that if they wanted to go get ice cream with John or Bill or Tad, John or Bill or Tad would have to spend a half-hour being grilled by their father.

A couple of the girls wailed that a certain boy would dump them rather than endure the fatherly interview. Paxton answered such concerns with, "Fine! He's not the kind of guy I want you to date."

My kids were not allowed to spend the night with anyone whose parent(s) we hadn't met. Sometimes you can fudge a little on that one and let a teenager go to a slumber party given by someone in the group if one of your friends knows the parents. As in every aspect of parenting teenagers, rely on the Spirit and be flexible.

An LDS Parent's Most Powerful Aid

The only times I've failed in my quest to keep my children safe from bad influences are when I've ignored spiritual promptings. For example, although I was uncomfortable giving permission, I allowed Daughter X to stay behind when the rest of us took a family trip. Daughter X, then sixteen, argued that she had to work and wanted to "hang out by myself for a little peace and quiet."

She had been sick the weekend before and still owed money on a loan she had taken out for a school trip. We were also living in a *one*-bathroom, three-bedroom house while we built a new home. We were all a bit nutty from our confinement (one of the reasons we took the family trip), so I reluctantly agreed that she could stay if her married sister checked up on her and if she had an approved friend spend the night.

When we returned home two days later, Daughter X blurted out that the neighbor had called at 4:00 in the morning to chew her out for the dog's barking. She was full of righteous indignation about how she "didn't know we were supposed to keep Spock inside at night" and how "Laurie could have solved the problem by bringing Spock in—she didn't have to wake me, but the neighbor was being unreasonable and a snot and insisted on yelling at 'the person who lived in the house.'"

If you're experienced with teenagers, you will have spotted certain clues in the preceding rush of words that alerted you to trouble as they did me.

First, the long, involved story is a clue that something is being covered up. Second, the complaint about the neighbor was supposed to divert me from the real problem. Righteous indignation is almost always a cover-up.

On Your Toes, With Your Ears Open

Getting to the real story can be tricky—especially if your teenager is prone to lying (and, as you know, most of them are). I try to listen without interrupting, occasionally asking questions designed to draw out more information.

In this instance, I asked her why the dog was outside. She said, "Because he was going nuts inside and wouldn't shut up, and he was tearing the house up."

Eric (Spock's caretaker) chimed in with, "Did you walk him and feed him that day? Did he have water?"

Daughter X answered that she had indeed walked, fed, and watered Spock, and she couldn't understand why he was so "hyper." Then she added, "Tab and I went to bed, and Spock wouldn't let us sleep."

The name "Tab" prompted my question, "Wasn't Laurie the one who was spending the night?"

Daughter X said, "Yes, but Tab and Kara spent the night, too; only Kara and Laurie wanted to talk to the boys."

The word "boys" raised another red flag, and I said, "Boys? What boys?"

At this point, Laurie, who had just changed her clothes, left very quickly. (Laurie and Daughter X had just driven up when we returned; they'd been at a friend's farewell—another reason Daughter X hadn't wanted to leave town.)

The story finally came out that a couple of boys had come over both nights we were gone and "wouldn't leave when I told them to." The boys, friends of Kara and Laurie, hung around until "after curfew when I made them go outside. Laurie and Kara went outside to talk and Tab and I went to bed." Apparently, Spock had been distressed about the strange kids hanging around the house in the wee hours of the morning—as well he might!

Gary made Daughter X give him the boys' names and phone numbers so he could call their parents. We had a weepy, remorseful evening, and she endured a two-week grounding, as well as the assurance that she wouldn't remain behind again until she was a little old lady with great-grandchildren.

The Acid Test of Friendship

With all my hints about detecting difficulties with friends and avoiding confrontations that could lead to problems, one gospel concept is more crucial than any other. Understanding that *everybody is responsible for his or her own actions* is the key to maturity. Unfortunately, teenagers rarely comprehend that responsibility. Not many adults comprehend it, for that matter.

Yet, accepting responsibility for actions makes the difference between successful, uplifting friendships and destructive friendships. Kids who have bad friends who lead them astray have foisted the responsibility for their actions onto someone else. It's kind of like the old cliche, "The Devil made me do it." In other words, "I was helpless against the influence."

Choice and Accountability

Don't allow your child to get away with such reasoning. Unless he was kidnapped at gunpoint, he had a choice in whether he went along or bowed out and came home.

While sitting in the principal's office, one of my foster kids said, "It was David's fault. He told me we should go downtown. Then he thought it would be funny to soap people's windows, only we couldn't find any soap, so we used paint."

Not once did that particular kid say, "I tried to leave and he wouldn't let me," or "I didn't think messing the windows was funny, so I made him do it without me."

Time and again, especially with my foster kids and counseling patients, I stress that people always have choices. They might not want to make the choice and they might not like the consequences of the choice, but they always have choices.

The Appendices contains an exercise with some situations and possible choices and consequences that you might find interesting to discuss with your teen. It also provides a range of responses that can help your child deal with friends who exert pressure to join questionable activities. Practicing such responses ahead of time gives your teen the means and will to resist.

If you find yourself with a balky teenager who is always testing your rules, have a personal interview and discuss reasons for the rules. Also, consider specific consequences for breaking the rules. And practice various ways to *avoid* breaking the rules. Role playing allows your teen to test and demonstrate adult behavior in a safe way. If you've already figured out together how he will handle certain circumstances, you can be more sure of his behavior when he faces a dilemma.

Setting up a few situations, choices, consequences, and responses as described in the exercise will help you and your teenager understand what you are trying to accomplish. By involving your teenager, you are sharing power with her and allowing her to help set the standards. Such sharing is vital as she grows from limited social ability to full-fledged adulthood.

HELPING LONELY, SOCIALLY AWKWARD TEENAGERS

If your family has always actively participated in the Church and you hold regular scripture study, family home evenings, and family prayer, your child will probably choose appropriate friends (although the best kids still do dumb things on occasion). But sometimes, no matter how hard she tries, your child may be lonely and feel left out at school and Church.

Nothing hurts more than to see the person you love in pain—the kind of pain that devastates tender spirits. Let's face it: some kids are cruel. The more certain kids need affection and friends and the harder they try to be accepted, the more other kids put them down and squash their feelings.

Being a member of the Church doesn't guarantee a kid will be thoughtful, considerate, and empathetic, either. As parents in the Church, we should be as aware of the actions of our own children as we are of how they are influenced by others. Adolescents are inherently selfish, and they must be taught empathy and service.

Sometimes you might need to take direct action and "interfere." At other times, all you may need to do is help your child communicate more effectively.

Soothing Real or Imagined Injuries

Dolly suffered some pretty intense hazing from other kids at Church and seminary. Most of the hazing was innocuous, but she took it personally. They called her "Mrs. Kimball" (referring, of course, to President Spencer W. Kimball) and "Molly Mormon," and they teased her when she balked at going along with some of their antics.

Dolly suffered neglect and abuse before we adopted her at the age of three. The birth child of an Eskimo woman and a half-Creek Indian, half-Irish man, she took a long time coming to terms with her heritage. Dolly's self-esteem was too low for her to tolerate even the gentlest teasing.

I spent hours hugging her while she sobbed about nobody asking her to dance and everybody "ignoring" her or giving her "nasty looks."

Holding Up a Mirror

Then I gave her some clear advice about how her attitude and feelings influenced the way others treated her. After telling her to think about how mad and sad she was, I took her picture with an instant camera.

As the picture came into focus, I asked her to look at her own face as if she were somebody else. "If you were a normal, insecure fifteen-year-old boy, would you approach this girl? (Pause.) Of course, you wouldn't; you'd be terrified she'd strike you dead!"

I used the picture example only once, but Dolly never forgot the lesson. Her black eyes could either shoot thunderbolts, or they could sparkle with wit and sunlight. She finally figured out how to change her feelings and, thereby, change the way she appeared to other people.

Not only did I work with Dolly to help her understand how to act, but I occasionally went to the source of a problem. One of the boys in her group who teased her unmercifully was the son of a friend of mine. I talked to Diane about Steve's comments and Dolly's reaction to them. Diane was surprised, because Steve had confided to his mom that he had a crush on Dolly. When I told Dolly, she was able to handle Steve's teasing much more happily. And Steve received a few lessons in proper admiration techniques from his parents.

Helps for Shy Kids

The same qualities that smooth relationships between siblings work in developing relationships between friends. Friendships thrive on concrete manifestations of feelings. Notes and homemade gifts, given for no particular reason, are friendship cementers. Everyone likes to be remembered. Brainstorm for ways to change things and foster friendships. After a brainstorming session, you might write the ideas down.

I've given the following "List of Secrets to Happiness and Making Friends" to several of my kids. It's a handy reminder of the things that make friendships work.

- Stop blaming other people.
- Admit it when you make a mistake.
- Do something nice every day, and try not to get caught doing it.
- Be on time.
- Don't make excuses or argue.
- Get organized.
- Be kind to everybody—whether they deserve it or not.
- Let someone cut ahead of you in line.
- Take time to be alone and reread a favorite book.
- Cultivate good manners and be humble.
- Understand and accept that life isn't always fair.
- Know when to say something and when to keep your mouth shut.
- Don't criticize anyone for twenty-four hours.
- Learn from the past, plan for the future, and live in the present.
- Don't sweat the small stuff.

(Adapted from a handout given by Diane Holmes of Cedar City 17th Ward in her Relief Society lesson.)

SUMMARY AND CONCLUSIONS ABOUT TEEN FRIENDSHIPS

Certain times, like during major moves or family changes, can negatively influence the kinds of friends teenagers make. Wise parents will pay attention during these times and take positive steps to counteract the situations. Just remember: teenagers must be *guided*, not pushed, coerced, or shamed.

When a teenager feels some kind of control, she is more likely to cooperate. She won't gravitate to destructive friendships for control over her life, and she won't become involved with undesirable behaviors.

Families who have regular prayer and scripture study together have shared values. Teenagers who feel like their opinions count will make reasonable choices, and they'll know that you are on their side. Parents who rely on the Lord and spend a lot of time on their knees will know when their children's friends are inappropriate, and they'll know how to encourage appropriate friendships.

How Can I Teach Eternal Values?

CHAPTER 12

Talking Straight About Morality

Teaching LDS kids moral values means teaching them to make choices consistent with gospel principles. That's not as easy as it sounds: teenagers mix up their eternal choices with what they want here and now. Take a look at what teen logic can come up with:

"I can sleep with my girlfriend now, but I'll repent just before my mission."

"I can have a beer or two as long as I say I'm sorry to the Lord just before I bless the sacrament."

"If it feels so good, it must be okay."

Adults instinctively understand the flaws in such reasoning, even if they can't quite articulate what those flaws are. But adolescent minds haven't developed as far. They have tremendous abilities to compartmentalize and rationalize.

To some teenagers, Christ's gift of repentance is a handy eraser that allows them to do anything they feel like doing. They think they can sin now and repent later. Other teens break the Word of Wisdom and chastity laws without realizing that what they're doing is wrong; we parents must teach them differently.

During these crucial years, teenagers need *more* parental involvement, not less. Some of my friends mistakenly think their kids are all grown up as soon as those kids can dress and feed themselves. This thinking seems particularly true in big families with lots of babies that are born close together.

Once your son or daughter is capable of helping out with changing diapers and mopping up messes, you may be tempted to think your job of intense parenting is over. It has just begun! Now begins the hardest time of all, when your emotions and spiritual strength will be tested again and again.

You should understand, too, that certain subjects are open to negotiation and others are not. Teenagers must feel that they have influence over what happens to them, that choices have consequences. They must know that their choices are within their control. Because they want control, they often insist on having everything their own way. And they make stupid mistakes—mistakes that defy logic.

If your ultimate parenting goal is to produce a full-fledged adult who doesn't need supervision, pick your fights carefully. Some things are worth arguing about and some are not. Gary likes to tell a joke that illustrates the kind of goofy fights and mixed-up thinking that parents and teens can fall into where moral conduct is concerned:

> *Debbie, a cute and popular girl who earned her Young Women medallion, kissed her parents goodbye and went off to BYU. She came home pregnant, had the baby, left it with her parents, and went back the next year.*
>
> *She came home pregnant again, had the baby, left it with her parents and returned to BYU. When she came home pregnant yet again, her long-suffering father finally exploded, "My darling daughter, where have I failed?! Why are you so promiscuous?"*
>
> *Debbie replied, "I'm not promiscuous, Daddy. They all have the same father."*
>
> *"Then why don't you marry the guy?!"*
>
> *"I can't, Daddy. He smokes . . ."*

Silly example, huh? But it's no joke when our children scramble gospel values and their actions in this way. Kids should understand which choices impact their eternal salvation and which choices can be left to personal preferences. You'll struggle to guide that understanding.

Spiked purple hair, ripped jeans, and vegetable-dye tattoos may make you cringe, but they are temporary and really don't matter. On the other hand, going steady and becoming physically intimate can bring devastating consequences.

PARENTS IN PARTNERSHIP WITH CHRIST

Because we're the parents, Gary and I set the standards for our children. But we're careful that those standards are consistent and relatively simple. The most nonproductive way of relating to teenagers is either extreme in parenting: permissive or autocratic. Remember, permissive parents run child-centered homes where kids do pretty much what they please. Autocratic parents are just the opposite—they think demanding, yelling, and punishing will bring compliance.

Luckily, the Lord has given us a better way—His example tells us to guide with love and long-suffering, but to set clear standards and stay in touch. Within that framework of standards, particular rules are established that preserve the peace or contribute to a child's eventual independence.

I feel sorry for parents who hold such notions as "I'll let my kids decide (whatever) when they grow up and can make their own choices." You'd be surprised how many educated LDS parents espouse similar opinions. They reason that they're being "enlightened" or "allowing freedom of expression," or some such absurdity.

Such thinking is ridiculous. No sane parent would say, "I'll wait until my kid grows up and can make choices before I teach her to read." As I discussed in the chapters on discipline and family communication, it's okay to set behavior standards. And it's imperative that once those standards are set, they are enforced consistently.

When a new foster kid comes into the house or somebody starts junior high, I set him or her down and explain Player's Basic Rules. There are two: "Modest, thoughtful behavior," and "Parents must know where everybody is." I base my elaboration and definition of these concepts on each child's level of understanding.

Then I explain that I assume they will follow the spirit behind these rules. As long as they do, they will enjoy as much freedom as possible. However, once they lose my or their dad's confidence, they'll face a struggle to regain it.

Sometimes, no matter how you try, you can't change another person. Free will means the right to choose. Keep in mind that *you* also have free agency, and your rights are equal to your child's rights. While you may not be able to force your teenager to be good, you can insist on minimum standards that must be followed if that teenager wants to be fed and clothed by you.

BACK TO BASICS

Moral choices for teenagers generally fall into two categories: the Word of Wisdom, and chastity/virtue. These categories cover qualities that are prerequisites to maturity and independence.

The Word of Wisdom

I'm starting with the Word of Wisdom, because of its symbolic significance and the fact that the "weakest" among us can follow it. Obeying this law involves both "do" and "don't." The don'ts are straightforward: refrain from alcohol, tobacco, recreational drugs, and hot drinks, specifically coffee and tea.

The do's are specific and have far-reaching ramifications:
• Get enough sleep, but no more than "is needful."
• Eat fruits and vegetables in their season.
• Partake of all grains, especially wheat.
• Save meat for "times of famine or cold."

There's little room for argument about what the Lord meant when he said to leave drugs, alcohol, and tobacco alone. But we can get side-tracked into arguments about the definition of "hot drinks." Did the Lord mean just coffee and tea? What about hot chocolate? And scalding soup? Our youth are quick to point out the hypocrisy in Dad's frowning at drinking a cup of coffee while he has a Coke or Pepsi every afternoon.

The Lord gave us the Word of Wisdom for two reasons: As a health law and as a token of our covenants to follow His teachings. Keep those reasons in mind when your teenager wants to argue about why "a bit of wine with dinner isn't so bad" or "one beer isn't going to hurt me." Also, consider what signals you send when you indulge in a caffeine-laced soft drink.

A few years ago, Coke introduced Jolt Cola, and my oldest boys thought it was wonderful ("Hey, Mom, Coke and Pepsi aren't against the Word of Wisdom"). I wouldn't buy the drink for them, so they bought it for themselves.

Finally, Gary and I called a family council and he announced, "We have a new order of things around here. I'm uncomfortable with the attitude toward colas you guys are developing, so I'm not going to drink Dr. Pepper [his very favorite soft drink] any more. We're not going to buy anything with caffeine in it other than chocolate. And we're going to keep the chocolate intake at a reasonable level."

When the boys started to debate, Gary cut them off with, "You are big enough to make some decisions on your own. I can't follow you around to be sure you obey this rule, so you're on your honor. Just keep in mind that these drinks will not be served in the Player house—we're talking spirit of the law here. Remember, you're a sloth-ful servant if you must be commanded in all things." That particular family council was very helpful to us in getting our point across about making choices consistent with the gospel.

Kids may argue and resist, but setting up slogans and standards will give you support where you need it the most. There's also nothing wrong with condensing family rules into short maxims—and posting them around the house.

Not in My Family

Caffeinated soft drinks may not seem that serious when compared to some other things. Many LDS parents struggle with kids who have succumbed to today's drug culture. None of us can afford to say, "It can't happen to me." It can, and it probably will in some form or another.

These beautiful, powerful spirits in our homes are God's elect, his "Saturday's Warriors." Forces beyond our comprehension seek to tear them away from the Iron Rod. I believe our best defense is a good offense—meaning that you and I must be aware, every minute, of what is going on with our children. Adolescents who get away with minor instances of smoking and sipping beer are more inclined to keep experimenting until they find themselves enmeshed in addictive behavior that needs serious intervention. Lines of communication must be open and maintained.

And don't be fooled. If you live in tune with the Spirit, you will be prompted to take action early and quickly. You can't afford to "hope everything will be okay."

My friends and relatives who have endured critical moral problems with their kids usually didn't suspect anything until their worlds came crashing down. Or if they were a bit uneasy, they dismissed their concerns with "Not my kid! I've sent her to Primary and Young Women; we all attend Church together . . ."

Remember, nobody is immune to temptation—even General Authorities have wayward kids. In my experiences with my nine and numerous foster kids over the years, I've developed a "sixth sense" about when a teen is heading for trouble. I watch for certain danger signals:

1. **Radical changes** in routine or behavior. An active, social kid becomes withdrawn and pensive—or a quiet, bookish kid gets jazzed and hyper.

2. **Mood swings** disrupt the family more than usual and cause consistent tension and stress between family members.

3. **Grades take a plunge**; a good student brings home Cs and Ds. A mediocre student fails.

4. **Basic hygiene gets sloppy**; your son or daughter loses/gains weight (inappropriately) and/or keeps odd hours.

5. **Physical evidence of "huffing"** (inhaling solvents, aerosol deodorants, marking pen, typewriter correction fluids, or furniture polish fumes) appears in the garbage or garage. Solvent-soaked rags or paper bags, empty butane lighters, and empty aerosol cans are some of the evidence. Huffing is a growing problem because kids don't think sniffing legal substances is wrong.

With the exception of the evidence of huffing, any of these signals can be consistent with the changes that come with adolescence. But when the signals persist, there is usually trouble. When you see these signs, confront your child and express your concerns. Sometimes the thought that you're attentive is enough to stop the downward slide.

Most of all, never think you're immune because you try to do everything right and your family is active in the Church. The prophets have promised none of us would lose our children if we held regular family home evenings, but he didn't promise that the process would be simple or easy. Besides, the promise means that we won't lose our children in the long run; it doesn't mean that they won't make serious mistakes in the meantime.

Affection Has Many Uses

One of the ways I keep tabs on my kids and ensure that I'll find out when they experiment with tobacco and alcohol is our nightly smooch. I insist on a kiss and hug when they check in with me. I knew one of my kids had a problem with the Word of Wisdom when he started blowing me a kiss from across the room.

As one son put it, "Mom has the nose of a bloodhound—she can smell one puff on a cigarette taken three hours earlier." My kids know that "I wasn't smoking, my friend was" is no excuse or explanation, either. If I smell tobacco or alcohol in their clothes, they're in trouble, period. Smoking friends quickly learn that my kids are grounded if they pick up the smell, so real friends refrain from lighting up in their presence.

It's easier to keep all but the most rebellious kids from smoking these days, because society and science back us up. Smart people don't smoke.

Alcohol and drugs are more difficult to detect, but they still leave some physical traces. Your parental instincts, combined with vigilance to odd odors, will alert you to take action.

Frequently, kids who are drifting into dangerous pursuits leave hints around—they want to be caught. This often-unconscious need is another reason not to ignore your suspicions.

One of my children reacted indignantly when his dad and I suggested that his clothes contained tell-tale odors. "Don't be stupid!" he yelled, "I know better than that. You're insulting me."

This kid was a champion debater and dramatist, so we believed him. "I guess we're overreacting," I said to Gary during one of our frequent conferences about our wayward son.

Because he'd managed to convince us otherwise, this same son lit up a cigarette in front of his older sister a week later. He tried, feebly, to persuade her "not to tell." Of course, she told immediately, and he was visibly relieved.

Let the Lord Help Lift Your Load

So, what do you do when your nose or instincts tell you your child has broken the Word of Wisdom? Maybe you won't have evidence as concrete as Gary and I did, but you should act quickly.

Let me caution you, however. **Everything you do and say must be done lovingly and without anger.** Being loving and calm when your child has violated gospel standards is difficult, to say the least. Pray and fast *before* you confront your son or daughter; lean on the Lord's strength to get you through this time. Contention and hostility will accomplish nothing; in fact, they will only make matters much worse.

One of the first things Gary and I do during a confrontation with one of our kids is to offer a father's blessing—an offer that is usually accepted. By eliminating our anger as much as possible, we allow a righteous spirit to operate.

Helping kids who are addicted or who have emotional problems takes a lot more than a few prayers and discussions, though. Professional medical and psychological assistance is necessary.

If you have such a situation in your home, don't delay getting in touch with your bishop for guidance—your difficulties are way beyond the scope of this book.

Considering Natural Consequences

Assuming your intervention is early enough, your next step should be to decide *with your teenager* exactly what to do. One of the reasons kids experiment with nicotine and alcohol is a desire to feel in control. Giving them some say in handling the consequences of their actions helps alleviate reasons for the misbehavior in the first place.

Reviewing the steps of repentance becomes most useful in helping teens back onto the straight and narrow. *The Miracle of Forgiveness* by President Spencer W. Kimball should be required reading for these kids, because it outlines in no uncertain terms what is necessary and it clarifies that being sorry is only a small part of repentance.

The four steps of repentance are recognition, remorse, restitution, and resolve. The first two steps, recognition and remorse, involve helping your teenager understand the seriousness of any sin and the necessity for repentance. Repentance is a continual process for all of us.

Restitution and Resolve

Consequences can vary, but should take into account the symbolic and health law functions of the Word of Wisdom. Make clear that drinking alcohol and/or smoking indicate disrespect for their Savior as well as their bodies.

A beer-drinking son was embarrassed and chagrined when I told him people said he must be one of those "liberal" Mormons. We lived in an area of the country that had few members of the Church—our actions were often the only way others knew what the Church of Jesus Christ of Latter-day Saints stood for. Like it or not, teenagers (and the rest of us) either "build up the Kingdom" or tear it down every hour of every day of our lives.

If associating with certain friends led to the undesirable actions, then those friends should be forbidden, either for a specific time period or permanently. Again, you must be guided by inspiration.

One repentant young person I know decided with her parents that she would fast twice a month for the next two months as penance for participating in a drinking party. She also voluntarily eliminated candy and ice cream from her diet for those two months.

She recognized that breaking the Word of Wisdom resulted from giving in to physical temptation, so she wanted to demonstrate that she had control over her own appetites.

Other effective consequences I've used or know about are:

- Short research projects into the physical effects of nicotine, alcohol, or the problem substance
- Spending service hours with "crack" babies or children suffering from the effects of Fetal Alcohol Syndrome
- Talking to recovering alcoholics or drug addicts
- Donating allowance or part-time job income to a local abused children's shelter or homeless facility
- Isolation and time to ponder and pray
- Reading and marking scriptures that discuss self-control and the body as a temple

The preceding list isn't exhaustive—your family's circumstances and your child's personality will impact whatever consequences are necessary.

During April 1993 general conference, Elder Richard G. Scott said, "The secret to solve problems in your life will be found in understanding and using the beneficial interactions of your agency and His truth."

Elder Scott related that a rope swing in a tall tree in his Uncle Zene's yard provided exhilarating experiences for him and his brother. One day Elder Scott's brother gave him "even more excitement." The brother twisted the rope and sent him into "a spin of ever-increasing velocity."

At first Elder Scott thrilled to the new sensation, but the spinning soon brought on nausea and fear.

Elder Scott likened his experience to those who pursue excitement and pleasure beyond normal bounds. As Elder Scott's story describes, therein lies the enigma you and I must solve in teaching our teenagers about moral agency. Many feelings are new to teens, including attraction to the opposite sex and other pleasurable sensations. Without careful monitoring, a young person's trying out new things disintegrates into activities he is not ready for or activities that belong within certain bounds.

Living close to the edge becomes addictive, and tragedy results. This idea brings us to the next area of concern for keeping our youth morally straight.

Chastity/Virtue

The gospel teaches that sexual sin is second only to murder, while the world classifies sex as just one more healthy appetite to be satisfied. Satan's most powerful tool, the elevation of lust, grips our society in a way calculated to bring down mankind.

With that kind of coercion arrayed against us, is it any wonder we parents sometimes despair? When discouragement threatens, remember that Christ's glance can destroy Satan's vast armies in seconds. Also, remember that He's with us as long as we do our best.

Avoiding the Problem

Life would be much easier if the mass media didn't constantly pound us with prurient material. The pounding has gone on so long that most of us have become calloused to it. Movies and videos that would have been rated R not long ago are now PG-13 (a cop-out rating in my opinion) or even PG. A few years ago, R-rated movies that win Academy Awards today would have been shown only in seedy, slum theaters.

All that is necessary for our destruction is for good people to do nothing. You may not participate in raunchy movies, videos, and magazines, but if you tolerate them in your neighborhood store, you're responsible.

You can't run out and picket or buy up the offending materials and burn them in the middle of the street, but you can let your children know exactly how you feel and that you won't tolerate such filth in your home. Then be sure that you don't inadvertently violate your own standards.

I bought a book by a writer friend of mine that was part of a major publisher's "Candle Light Romance" series. We writers support each other, and I was delighted to see her new release. But my delight turned to dismay when I started reading the book and realized it was pornographic.

When I had brought the book home, I had showed it to my children. Once I realized the book was pornographic, I gathered them around again, told them what I'd discovered, and let them watch me throw it away. Dozens of mainstream novels in the bookstores are as offensive as the one I trashed. Smut sells, and will continue to sell as long as people buy it.

As R-rated videos have become more and more commonplace, I've had a more difficult time keeping them out of the house. My kids who are older than eighteen and their friends have occasionally rented offensive videos and tried to show them in our downstairs playroom. However, they've learned, to their sorrow, that I mean what I say.

One of my sons who had been home from his mission only two months rented an R-rated movie with some friends. They rationalized that it had just violence, no sex. I walked downstairs just in time to catch sight of a horrifying murder. I flipped on the lights and ejected the tape.

When Kid X said, "Hey, lighten up, Mom! We're older than twenty-one here."

"Then watch this trash in your own apartment—not my house," I said. "If it's still sitting here in the morning, I'll burn it."

As I stormed from the room, Kid X said, "She means it, guys." The next time I went downstairs, they were playing a board game, "Axis and Allies."

There will always be purchasers for titillating videos and reading materials, but good people—especially LDS parents—cannot allow offensive materials to become acceptable. As a writer and journalist, I know the dangers of censorship, but we must exercise community control over what's available to our children.

But We're in Love

Besides monitoring entertainment, you must teach about honorable relationships between the sexes. Sex education is a buzzword these days, and almost every junior high and high school has some form of it. I don't think it's practical to eliminate sex education from the schools—you can expend a lot of energy and end up without accomplishing much. I know. I've gone as far as running for the school board and serving on health curriculum committees in my communities.

However, I think you can have a big impact on what is taught by keeping your eyes and ears open and participating actively.

A few years ago, school districts tried to include teaching about human reproduction in biology courses, but saner minds prevailed. Today, most educators recognize that the subject is fraught with moral and ethical issues that must be addressed.

When your school calls a meeting about materials that will be covered in sex education, be sure to go. If you miss the meeting, make a special trip to review or check out the information. I also suggest that you attend the class (with your child's permission). If your teenager is appalled at the idea, settle for discussing the day's lesson each evening.

Dolly didn't mind my going to her sex education class when she was fourteen (probably because I was on the health curriculum committee, so she could explain it to her buddies). I sat through a session about venereal disease taught by a male public health nurse.

Dolly and her friends had told me how everybody thought the guy was great, so I wanted to see for myself. He was an excellent speaker—in fact, the lesson was highly entertaining, but I thought it far more appropriate for a college classroom than a group of high-school freshmen.

He made such comments as, "turn on the dome light in the car or carry a flashlight to check out your partner before you have sex." He also told the kids to go to the clinic every time they had sex or once a week, whichever was less frequent.

When the bell rang, I walked out with Dolly and two friends. I said, "That guy didn't tell you the one absolutely infallible way to protect yourself from venereal disease."

They looked confused, so I said, "Have any of you had sex?"

They shook their heads and giggled.

"If you wait until you're married and your husband is a virgin, too, will you be exposed to VD?" I said.

More giggles and head shakes.

"Then if you both stay faithful to each other, you'll never have to worry," I concluded.

Dolly's friends (who weren't members of the Church) looked astonished. They had never heard such talk before!

What You Can Do Right Now

A happy marriage is your best teaching tool in this area. How you and your spouse relate to each other influences your kids far more than what they read in a textbook or learn in a class. If your relationship needs help, get it! Let your children see that marriage is worth investing time and effort.

If you are single, your dating behavior will send strong signals. In addition, seek out friends with good marriages to help you demonstrate the way things should be. Home teachers and ward leaders can be a single parent's best resource in this crucial area of modeling appropriate behavior between the sexes.

Also, be available to talk. Let your kids know that no question is dumb, and that you will answer truthfully or find the answer. I set aside specific times to speak frankly with my daughters, and Gary does the same with our sons. We also give our boys and girls the benefit of the opposite sex's point of view. We've found that our shy kids won't actually ask much, but they're receptive and eager when we make the opportunity.

One talk isn't enough, either. Teaching moments are all around us, especially with what's on television these days. Comment on what you see and hear; the evening news can create great dialogue. Discuss the sanctity of life and demonstrate awe for God's creative power. Reiterate that tampering with the fountain of life is degrading and wrong, but that power used within marriage is beautiful.

A chart about the differences between lust and love is included in the Appendices; it's adapted from a Sunday School manual.

Rules to Date By

Church leaders have given us direction in teaching our youth proper dating and boy/girl interactions. Your bishop has access to the booklet *For the Strength of Youth*; every teenager should have a copy of it.

As directed, attendance at dances shouldn't start until age fourteen and dating should only be in groups until age sixteen—and preferably age eighteen.

Too many times I've seen friends and relatives be talked into letting their kids date a year or two early, because their teen argues, "I'm more mature . . ." When dating is postponed until sixteen or eighteen, marriage occurs at eighteen, nineteen, or twenty—the ages most of us are comfortable about letting our kids go.

But when your thirteen- or fourteen-year-old convinces you to let him or her run with an older crowd, you can bet you'll be weeping through a repentance session with that same child at age fifteen or sixteen. I know several girls from active LDS families who were married at fifteen, and even more who had babies before graduating from high school. Many of the fathers were just as young.

Chastity Begins Early

By the time your child begins to show interest in the opposite sex, I hope you've already laid a foundation for considerate relationships. Modesty in dress, language, and actions should be encouraged from toddlerhood—not because bodies are shameful, but because they are temples for the spirit and are very beautiful.

We have a family motto that so far has kept everyone chaste and worthy of temple marriages. That motto is, "The more you love someone, the less time you spend alone together." The wording is deceptively simple.

We recognize the need courting couples have for learning about each other and developing a bond. We also recognize that everything they need to know before marriage can be done in full view of somebody else. Kisses and hugs are perfectly acceptable, and private conversations don't have to be overheard.

Our older kids found this maxim easy to follow, because they could haul along a younger sibling who happily played video games or read comic books. Now that only a few are left at home, our dating kids have to use more imagination to keep the family rule.

Our returned missionary daughter fell in love with a young man who wasn't a member of the Church. In the beginning, she told him she wasn't interested in dating anyone who wasn't potential husband material, so he decided to listen to the missionaries. He joined the Church, and they coped with a long-distance relationship.

He kept trying to convince her that she should move to Los Angeles so they could continue dating, but she refused because she knew she loved him too much to be around him unless they were married. She also knew that being a returned missionary, having strong values, and intending to be married only in the temple were no guarantees.

Love Makes the World Go 'Round

You and I must somehow teach our children to respect the power of sexual attraction. When that attraction is combined with love between two healthy young people, it becomes an overriding passion.

I've never seen anyone who could ignore that power. Another familiar story illustrates the chances we shouldn't take:

> Wells Fargo wanted to hire a stagecoach driver for a route that covered steep and treacherous territory. They condensed their list to three drivers, each of whom were asked one question, "How close can you drive to the edge of the cliff without endangering your passengers?"
>
> The first driver answered, "I can come within three inches of the edge and still keep control." The second driver answered, "I can let one wheel hang over and still stay on track." The third driver answered, "I stay as far away from the edge as possible."
>
> The third driver got the job.

Like the third driver, our youth must know to stay as far away from the edge as possible to avoid putting themselves in a situation where they might fall.

Gary and I set aside an hour every Sunday evening for "reports" from the kids about what they learned in Church that day, including sacrament meeting. We ask them to summarize the lesson and to give reasons why they think the lesson applies to them. In this way, we can apply the principles from their classes to decisions and problems they face every day. Keeping our teenagers morally clean is a daunting assignment, because all we can do is teach and set an example.

CHAPTER 13

Strengthening Testimonies

On April 23, 1992, I sat in the Gold Sealing Room of the St. George Temple. The mirrors and crystal chandelier reflected shafts of light onto the white-dressed assembly. A feeling of incredible peace swept over me as I experienced one of those profound moments that make all the stress and mess of parenthood fade away.

I sat between my returned missionary son, Gary Willis, and my soon-to-be daughter-in-law, Norine, who was also a returned missionary. Gary stood with Norine's father as one of the witnesses.

Our two adult daughters were with us, too. Sherri, who recently returned from the Spokane Washington Mission, held her sister Dolly's hand. Dolly sat beside Roland, her own eternal companion. Eric and Roch couldn't be with us, because they were both still in the mission field.

G.W.'s wedding that day marked a significant milestone for our family: Gary and I had been successful (by our definition) with more than half of our kids. On that date, all of our grown children held current temple recommends, and four of the five had served full-time missions.

The next four years brought Eric's and Roch's honorable returns from their missions and selections of their eternal companions. Eric was married in the Los Angeles Temple in 1996 and Roch in the Salt Lake Temple in 1994. Micah was called to the Charlotte North Carolina Mission, Linda married her returned missionary in the St.

George Temple in 1996, and we adopted fifteen-year-old Brian, who was sealed to us the same day Linda was married.

Gary and I knelt across the altar from each other, with Brian's hands over ours, while all eight children watched. Even fourteen-year-old Nathan was able to be there, dressed in white and holding his own recommend "to witness the sealing of a sibling."

I know how lucky we are; statistics indicate that active, worthy parents have no guarantees their children will always remain close to the Church. Most of my friends and relatives have endured the heart-break of at least one wayward son or daughter.

Gary and I are no exceptions. We've struggled with rebellion, defiance, and self-destructive behavior in our own children, as well as with numerous foster children—I've told about some of that struggle in the pages of this book.

My purpose in this chapter is to pass along some hints that, so far, have enabled Gary and me to help our kids develop strong personal testimonies. Growing up, breaking away, and all the tie-cutting that teenagers must go through—doesn't need to mean they break away from the gospel.

Most of my ideas are not unique; you've probably heard many of them in Relief Society and priesthood lessons at the same time we did. I've just adapted them to my style of parenting. And, as I've stressed throughout this book, nobody can tell you exactly how to handle your own family. Nobody but Heavenly Father, that is.

If my suggestions seem logical, go ahead and use them, but always seek confirmation from the Lord. His promptings and affirmation will ensure you're doing the right thing.

Another way to be sure you are acting appropriately, which is directly related to heeding promptings of the Spirit, is to examine the way you feel. If you are angry and tempted to explode all the time, you are probably not reacting correctly. You may feel sorrow and sadness as you struggle with your youth, but you won't blow your top.

Strengthening your kids' testimonies hinges on their developing positive attitudes and, therefore, individual spirituality. As you've probably guessed, if you've lived with a teenager for more than thirty seconds, "attitude" is crucial for learning to take place.

A kid with a crummy attitude is virtually impossible to reach—let alone moderate or influence his or her behavior. Luckily, bad attitudes can be transformed through a combination of sensitivity, persistence, and humor on your part.

Three methods can bring about positive attitudes:
1. Keeping kids in the right places
2. Teaching them about reverence
3. Observing the Sabbath day

KEEPING KIDS IN THE RIGHT PLACES

Attitudes won't change until kids absorb essentials of the gospel. And they can't pick up much in the way of spirituality if they aren't where the Spirit operates. They need to be in Church, where the Spirit is the strongest, and they need to stay away from unwholesome environments, where the Spirit refuses to go. Being in the right place at the right time means youth attend all their meetings, including sacrament meeting, Sunday School, and youth activities. Sounds simple, doesn't it?

Okay, you know it isn't simple, because your kids have left sacrament meeting to "go to the bathroom" and never returned. Or they've hugged you on their way to Sunday School classes, but failed to arrive at their destinations. Or you've dropped them off at a youth activity only to find them at the local convenience store fifteen minutes later.

Since we agree that they can't learn anything if they aren't on site where the knowledge is given out, exactly *how* can you avoid the scenarios just described?

To Force or Not to Force . . .

First, you must insist that your kids go to church. Period. This is the most significant area where my position differs from my friends and relatives. **I firmly believe that kids don't have a choice about going to school and they don't have a choice about going to church.**

I think a spiritual education is even more important than an intellectual education. But my teenagers still have their free agency. Just as I cannot creep into their minds and force them to learn algebra, I cannot force them to meditate and pray.

They must sit with us in sacrament meeting, attend their classes, and be in the room for quorum or Young Women activities. And they must not disrupt the proceedings or be rude. They can sit in a stupor, day-dream, or look out the window, as long as they don't bother anybody.

In order to enforce this rule, I make surprise visits to their classes at random intervals. I also ask their teachers to tell me if they miss class. This checking is inconvenient, but I only have to do it once in a while, unless a particular kid proves to be a slow learner.

Being There in Body

I encourage my reluctant teens to participate, but if they absolute-ly refuse, they may bring journals, scriptures, and inspirational mate-rial, like the *New Era* or the *Ensign* (no comic books, magazines, or novels). But, I repeat, they must not be disruptive.

This stance has been part of the family's code of conduct since my oldest son yelled, "Help! Bishop, help!" as I carried his kicking, scream-ing two-year-old body from the chapel. I've never had a kid complete-ly defy me. But I'm not saying one never will or that yours won't.

Try to keep a sense of humor and don't let the resistance and irri-tating antics make you mad. One of my fifteen-year-old daughters tested me almost beyond my endurance on the idea of what consti-tuted appropriate actions and materials for Church. She latched onto "journals are okay" and began bringing hers every Sunday. For a cou-ple of weeks, I watched her detail her weekly activities and pour over some sort of index on pages and dates. She became very engrossed. The journal-writing led to flipping open her checkbook and balanc-ing it between the bread and water service. When I told her to stop making rustling noises, she rolled her eyes and kept right on scribbling and rustling. I held myself back from ripping the notebook out of her hands and thumping her like a four-year-old.

I suppose she thought if she bothered me enough, I'd give up and let her stay home next time. But she failed. She finally progressed to jotting messages to me about whatever popped into her head. Then she actually started taking notes on some of the talks.

As of this writing, she no longer brings her journal to Church. She sits with her returned missionary husband and wrestles with her baby daughter.

Some people disagree strongly with my "must be in Church" approach, and it may not work for everybody. All I know is it works for me—and it's been put to the test time and time again. At about age ten or eleven, and no later than twelve, every child tried some variation of the "I'm too sick, tired, bored . . ." routine. But they gave it up after a while when it didn't work.

Keep the Spirit Intact

However, it's very important to remember the essence or intent of this compulsion to attend. Anger, shouts, and any kind of contention negate what you're trying to accomplish. Don't lose your temper or let that resistant, rebellious youth push your "mad" buttons. Make your actions a matter of prayer, contemplation, and study. If you set the example, talk about why you go, and explain what you get out of it, your children will be less inclined to resist.

You also need to think ahead. You can't suddenly get up in the morning and start arguing with a teen who's been out late the night before and wants to sleep through Sunday School.

When my kids go out with friends, I caution them to "be home before the Sabbath starts" (midnight) even if they're Late Teens with a 1:00 a.m. weekend or holiday curfew.

If they stay out too late and can't get up for Church, then they don't go out the next weekend at all! Ditto for "Don't feel good." If they felt well enough to go to a dance or party, they can make the sacrifice for the Lord that they made for their own pleasure.

All Together Now

Not only do I want my kids at Church, but I want them to sit with me. When they're off with their friends, very little worship takes place. The only exception I make is trading kids with another family.

My ward in San Luis Obispo, California, had an amazing number of missionaries go into the field between 1987 and 1992. I don't recall anything particularly different about that ward except the bishop's insistence that families sit together.

He dismissed the Aaronic Priesthood after they passed the sacrament to return to their families. Then he watched to be sure they followed his directions. If any slipped out the door or hunkered down on the back row, he often left the stand to retrieve them.

Perhaps there's no correlation, but his attitude and follow-through carried a clear message: "The meetings are important and your presence is important, and the best place for you is with your family."

Importance of Attending Youth Activities

Being in the right place includes Sunday School, priesthood, and Young Women classes as well as sacrament meeting. Too many people, including adults, think they've done their duty if they make it to sacrament meeting, without bothering with the rest of their meetings. If your kids don't want to attend their Sunday School and youth meetings, be sure you aren't chatting in the halls instead of going into Gospel Doctrine and Relief Society or priesthood meeting.

The Church recognizes the volatile episodes brought on by teenagers in the throes of "growing up." Young Men/Young Women activities were structured to channel all this loose energy. The programs are age- and gender-specific, with combined activities designed to allow boys and girls to socialize in a gospel-centered place. If your teen is your oldest and you are not familiar with the programs, be sure to ask for copies of the materials he or she is given on graduation from Primary. You should also attend "Priesthood Preview," "Standards Night," and other programs even if you've been to twenty years' worth of them.

The Scout program gives boys a chance to burn up a lot of hormones (and tennis shoes) through campouts and hikes. Each age group corresponds to a level in the Aaronic Priesthood: ages twelve and thirteen, Scouts (deacons); ages fourteen and fifteen, Varsity (teachers); and ages sixteen through eighteen, Explorer (priests).

These levels have detailed advancement procedures that can be a lot of fun and very enlightening. Unfortunately, I've found that unless a child wants to participate in a particular activity, no amount of parental prodding will have any effect. I watch in envy as my friends beam through Eagle and Silver Palm ceremonies.

Maybe the Lord wants me to relax a bit and accept my kids for the unique individuals they are. I need to be sure that whatever activity I urge my children toward appeals to their interest, not mine. Besides, there are plenty of opportunities for parent-teen conflict without making more.

However, please don't think I'm against Scouting. I'm not at all. I use every aspect of the program I possibly can. My kids have no choice about joining Scouts and being active in their priesthood quorums, but I don't require anything beyond their presence in those places.

I go by that old adage, "You can lead a horse to water, but you can't make it drink." But that horse may get mighty thirsty! Free agency doesn't eliminate the consequences of a choice. Some of my sons have been almost as embarrassed as I was when their friends wore Eagle bandanas while they barely qualified for Second-Class rank.

In an earlier chapter, I discussed how some of my friends made sure their sons earned Eagles before they were sixteen by making Eagle Scout rank a prerequisite for a driver's license. That's one idea. Progress through Scouting ranks can be encouraged in a variety of ways—just keep the emphasis on the positive. Remember that you have to come up with rewards and incentives that match what your child wants, rather than what you want. Always remember that the least amount of power lies with the person who wants something the most.

The Young Women's program is designed to do the same thing for girls as Scouts does for boys. The medallions earned in each class are equivalent to progressing through the ranks for the boys. The eight areas of focus in the Personal Progress Program relate very well to merit badges. And the Young Womanhood Award equals the Eagle rank in effort and achievement. At ages twelve and thirteen, girls are Beehives; at fourteen and fifteen, Mia Maids; and at sixteen and seventeen, Laurels.

Teenagers who resist going to Church need to know what the consequences are. If they refuse to participate in their Church activities, their testimonies will wither. And they will draw further away from the source of eternal happiness.

A wise bishop gave one of my wayward teens some profound advice. My son insisted, "It's my life—nobody can tell me what to do." The bishop agreed that he, indeed, had his free agency. In fact, he had his free agency to choose to climb up on the roof of the meetinghouse and jump off. However, he couldn't change his mind on the way to the ground. He would have to pay the consequences, no matter how much he wished he hadn't jumped.

Once a choice is made and an action taken, no amount of regret will change the results. Only Christ's atonement will wash away consequences.

TEACHING THEM ABOUT REVERENCE

When your kids attend Church and sit with you, you will be able to teach them reverence. Reverence is a quality that needs more attention from all of us.

Certain physical and mental actions have to take place before worship can be achieved and testimony can grow. A quiet body and calm mind produce reverence. Reverence brings the Lord's Spirit, and the Lord's Spirit nourishes testimony.

Noisy babies and restless children may come to mind when you think about the lack of reverence in our meetings, but I think that adults are the worst offenders because they should know better. All of us, including me, are guilty of either not setting an appropriate example or not insisting on correct behavior from our children.

Set an Appropriate Example and Follow Through

Adults who use a whining baby as an excuse to wander the halls give their children the example of cutting classes or leaving meetings if things get boring. Adults who doze, doodle, or daydream during sacrament meeting are also sending the wrong signals.

When my kids were young, I required a certain number of minutes on the couch after Church for every irreverent act during meetings. The offender had to sit, with arms folded, for the designated time. Moving off the spot, yelling, or some other disrespectful conduct doubled the penalty.

Now, when my teenagers behave like little kids in Church, they suffer the same punishment. I rarely need to do more to gain their cooperation than say, "Do I have to give you fifteen minutes on the couch practicing your reverence skills?" Only twice have I actually been forced to carry out my threat.

I also establish "rules of reverence" for the whole family:
During the sacrament service—
- Be quiet and respectful (no whispering, gum chewing, eating, or sleeping—and seeming to sleep is just as bad as actually sleeping).
- Concentrate on Christ (read scriptures, pray, or meditate in writing).

During any meeting—
- Stay in your seat. If an emergency occurs, leave between speakers.

- Look at the speaker.
- Bow your head, close your eyes, and say "amen" for prayers.
- Sing with the congregation.

During classes—

- Pay attention to the teacher.
- Volunteer to pray or answer a question once in a while.

If the meeting/teacher bores you, remember why you're there in the first place. You should continue to worship and respect your Heavenly Father. Consider your own ideas on the topic that is being discussed.

The Importance of Music

Another way to help teens develop reverence is through music. The Lord tells us that "the song of the righteous is a prayer unto me." Hymns set the tone and foster His presence.

My returned missionaries and their friends tell how humble people in foreign countries understand this principle. Their voices ring in praise to God. Everyone sitting in those gatherings instantly feels the Spirit. Unfortunately, in most of the meetings I go to, fewer than half the congregation actually join in the songs.

My kids know their dad's and my feelings about singing, so they usually at least move their lips. I think it's as rude not to sing hymns as it is to gaze around and ignore the "amen" during a prayer. But I don't growl and hiss at my kids when I see them sitting mute. The following example indicates how I handle reluctant singers:

I hugged my twelve-year-old when he scowled and slouched down in his seat. He was having a grumpy day and didn't want to be in Church. In fact, the half-hour before we left for Church almost unhinged me—he moaned about "Not feeling well," being "too tired," and "It's boring, anyway."

I whispered, "I love you almost as much as Jesus does! 'I Stand All Amazed' is one of my favorite sacrament hymns."

I ran my finger under the words "that He should die for me" and said, "Can you imagine loving anyone that much?"

My son's scowl diminished and he straightened up a little to lean against me. I put my arm around him and reminded him to focus his eyes on the words and form them in his mind as well as with his voice. By the end of the hymn, he was relaxed and attentive.

As in the description of my scowling twelve-year-old, most teenagers go through periods of inexplicable anger and touchiness that make them difficult to have around—especially at Church. You just have to be positive and ignore a lot.

Criticism rarely works. Instead of hissing "sit still and stop kicking the seat in front of you," try noticing when your kid is actually paying attention or sitting still. Give her a one-armed hug or a shoulder squeeze and say, "Good for you—I know Heavenly Father appreciates your effort and so do I."

I do lapse occasionally and insist strongly on certain behavior, however. It drives me crazy to see teenagers with their elbows on their knees and foreheads on the pew in front of them. To me, that posture is definitely *not* reverent. I want my kids to sit up and at least look like they're paying attention.

Partaking of the Sacrament

I try to use sacrament meeting to help my teenagers understand how to worship. Sitting reverently is only the beginning. Sacrament participation and worship takes prayer, contemplation, and study. Refer to the exercise "Preparing to Partake," which was adapted from Sunday School course manuals. It is located in the Appendices.

OBSERVING THE SABBATH DAY

During those times we're actually successful at keeping the Sabbath day holy, everyone's level of happiness and endurance increases immeasurably. At my house controversy surrounds just what constitutes appropriate activities, however.

My kids think "a day of rest" translates into four-hour naps and "zoning out" under a pair of headphones. They also give me a lot of grief over my "no TV or video/computer games on Sundays" rule.

Sit down with your family and decide what you will and will not do on Sunday. Keep in mind that the Sabbath was made for man—not man for the Sabbath. Sundays are a lovely gift to us from our Heavenly Father. All of our actions on that day should be directed toward worship.

Observing "mission rules" on Sundays is an excellent way to encourage reverence among teenagers. I didn't come up with this observation until after Sherri and G.W. returned from their missions, but I heartily recommend it. Mission rules serve a dual purpose: they result in reverence right now, and they inspire focus on eventual service in the mission field. A mission then becomes a process as well as a goal. For more information, check out "Suggested Mission Rules for Sundays" in the Appendices.

Also, see the chart "Evaluate Your Spiritual Level." I use that chart in private discussions with my kids—and so does Gary, especially during his Personal Progress interviews.

Number 12 on the "Evaluate Your Spiritual Level" chart reads, *As I learn more about Christ-like love, do I try to make it a real part of my life?* It is a frequent topic during scriptures and prayer or other more casual conversations. This is a subject I try to address at least once a day.

CHANGING A NEGATIVE ATTITUDE

We are told by our leaders and in the scriptures to "try it and see." The formula is the same for gaining a testimony or gaining a happy, productive life: Act as if you have a testimony or are happy, and you will be.

Elder Charles Didier's October 1992 general conference talk on building testimony gave five aspects for obtaining, maintaining, and sharing a testimony. He suggested that anyone who wants a testimony should:

1. Articulate what you want to know.
2. Open yourself to the power of the Holy Ghost.
3. Search the scriptures.
4. Pray and contemplate.
5. Stay in tune so you will know the answer when it comes.

Testimonies will die unless they are nurtured. A testimony today doesn't mean one will be there tomorrow. I try to teach my kids to spot the symptoms of a faltering testimony, just like I can spot when my house plants need water.

A beautiful burgundy, cream, and forest green coleus sat in my study when I lived in Tulsa, Oklahoma. I could tell immediately when I became lax about watering it. The plant shriveled and drooped, but a good soaking brought it around without apparent harm if I acted immediately at the first sign of a problem. Each time the plant came back, though, it was just a little less luxuriant. It finally died. Too much neglect and subsequent repair can be fatal to plants—and to a testimony.

I found two charts in one of my *Ensign* magazines several years ago that describe "When I Have the Spirit" and "When I Don't Have the Spirit." I keep them posted on the refrigerator to help my family evaluate their individual spirituality. Please see them in the Appendices.

When your teenager resists, refuses, and defies your authority, keep in mind that you can insist on Church and activity attendance. But remember that your demeanor is crucial—maintain a spirit of love, stay alert, and never give up.

CHAPTER 14

Forging Eternal Family Ties

"Which side do I come from? Yours or Dad's?" Seven-year-old Nathan puzzled about his place in the family line. He'd listened to hours of conversation between my brothers, sister, mother, and me while we planned the annual reunion of my father's children. By the end of that reunion, Nathan knew his position in a diverse family lineup.

Not only do I want my kids to get along with each other, but I want them to realize that they are part of a larger continuum. Forging eternal family ties comes through regular and consistent contact with their uncles, aunts, and cousins, as well as their grandparents.

When twelve-year-old Micah admired his Grandma Paxton's watercolors or shared an artist's perspective with his Aunt Celestia, he understood his own need to fill every blank piece of paper in the house with intricate drawings. When fourteen-year-old Linda giggled with her older cousin—an international model whose picture was on the cover of *Vogue*—about the big feet, long fingers, and slender waists they had in common, she no longer thought her height and skinniness were liabilities.

Family reunions are always successful when they're remembered, even if they seem like a flop at the time. Six-year-old cousins throwing sand in each other's faces, an elderly uncle who falls asleep in his plate, or the teenage nephew who mows down his aunt's prize rose bushes may exasperate or embarrass the group. But when time passes and the picture albums are opened, everybody shares a laugh and a sense of family.

But teens don't always see it that way. The words "family reunion" initially brought groans and sighs from my teenagers. "Do we have to go?" they moaned.

I spent a lot of time urging, pleading, and finally threatening to get their cooperation. My sister, who has twelve kids, suffered the same frustrations and embarrassment, as did both my brothers, who have nine and seven kids.

When we all lived near each other, we got together frequently. But any time we had a formal "reunion," things often deteriorated into Us against Them squabbles among the cousins—especially among the Early Teens.

I don't understand the psychological implications, but reasons probably stemmed from that age group's innate insecurities and the breaking away from the family that happens at this time. Whatever the reasons, I didn't want to put up with the results.

After attending and hosting several family reunions among my immediate family, as well as larger affairs involving second and third cousins, I've stumbled upon some insights. Certain things lessen the grumbling and contribute to shared memories that help my teenagers sense their place in their eternal family.

I've found that reunions are most successful if:
• They are planned but not rigidly detailed
• They have some kind of theme or unifying event
• All the participants communicate clearly

PLANNED BUT NOT RIGIDLY DETAILED

Planning must take place well ahead of time—how early depends on how widely scattered your family is. When my brothers, sister, and I lived in the same town and our families were small, we only needed a few days, and we often went out together with an hour's notice. However, now that we're at a day's drive apart and our numbers have grown, our reunions take months of planning and we're lucky if we see each other once a year.

Whose Turn Is It This Year?

Choosing the person to do the planning is as important as the planning itself. Most families find that one or two members are more interested in taking on the challenge than anyone else. When this is the case, the other members should recognize the good deal they have going and wholeheartedly support that person—both financially and emotionally.

My brothers and sister and their spouses take their turns, but I'm the oldest sibling and often end up in the position of "chief." Early in the planning stage, I talk to everyone and get their input.

I also write everything down, because nobody remembers a conversation the same way. The written word is my protection against "I thought we were going to . . . ," "Why don't we . . . ?" or "Why *didn't* you . . . ?" I keep my notes in folders in a special file, so I can find what I need quickly.

I've found that three or four days are good lengths for reunions. People start to burn out after four days, but they really don't get into the swing of things until the second day.

The last reunion that I planned very carefully took place in San Luis Obispo, California. Activities ranged from romping at the beach or park to a Sunday night fireside where my mother displayed a map while she told about my father's and her trip up the Alaskan Canadian highway in 1947. Then everyone was encouraged to stand up and say what the family meant to him or her and what might be fun to do next time. We also enjoyed a sand castle building contest, a road rally, a water balloon fight, and several impromptu soccer games.

Age-Appropriate Activities

As much fun as we had mixing it up together, some activities had to be geared strictly for adults, teens, or little kids in order to keep everybody sane.

My favorite event is the "Adults Night Out." We reserve a room at a medium-priced restaurant where we order off the menu. During dessert, each person reports on the past year and plans for the future. As the years go by, we've endured everything from foreclosure, bankruptcy, and brain aneurysms to promotions and major book sales, so the reports bring both tears and laughter.

While we are at dinner, the teenagers (including kids down to Merry Miss and Blazer Scout ages) enjoy a pizza and video party. The younger kids, under the care of non-family babysitters, do the same thing at another location.

Food Preparation and Consumption

Once a reunion's sequence of activities has been outlined, I've found that the next most difficult planning tasks are food and related clean-up. During the reunion discussed earlier, nobody had much money to spend, so motels were out, and I'd just moved into a new house that I wanted to keep in reasonable shape. Sixty people between the ages of two and eighty attended, with most of them between ten and twenty-one years old.

Feeding that ravenous horde during our four fun-filled days challenged my crowd control skills. Luckily, my house was very large, with tile floors and three patios. I set up tables outside for most of the meals. We set out the food on the kitchen "island," and everybody filed past it with their plates. Toddlers and preschoolers ate inside in the breakfast room. Older kids ate in the dining room or picnic-style on the lawn or patios. Adults and kids older than sixteen ate wherever they found a spot.

We used a lot of paper products and convenience foods, but we had to make some absolute rules about consumption. Certain six-foot-plus teenage boys were impossible to fill up. Even if I succeeded in providing enough food at a particular meal, they were ravenous within an hour after finishing.

Meals and snacks were served at set times, and nobody was allowed to raid the kitchen between those times. The only exception was one cupboard stocked with bread, crackers, peanut butter, jelly, apples, and oranges. Of course, anybody could go out and buy whatever they pleased, if they had the money.

The menus were heavy on salads, fresh fruits (cheap and abundant in August), pastas, and breads. We ate a lot of sandwiches, pancakes, and cereals. The Strawberry Sourdough Pancake Brunch on Saturday was a huge success, but I thought we'd never finish handing out pancakes and saying "two sausages and two strips of bacon per person." A variation on that chant was, "You may have another pancake with syrup, but only one scoop of strawberries and cream."

Keeping the Mess Under Control

The next planning challenge was assuring that everybody, especially the teenagers, refrained from their usual slovenly habits.

Kitchen, bathroom, and general clean-up duties rotated between age groups and families.

I drew up a "Duty Roster" ahead of time and posted it in several places. I also made a checklist for the bathrooms and kitchen, so everybody would know that flushed toilets, wiped sinks, and emptied garbage cans were necessities.

One of my more important "mess control" measures was the sign on the front door that announced, "Take Off Your Shoes." The four-foot pile of shoes became a bit laughable, but it kept a lot of sand and debris from the carpets.

Sometimes a particular family was in charge of setting up, supervising, and cleaning up an activity. The responsibility could be harrowing, but it was always fun. For example, the Beach Party at our California reunion was under my brother's family's direction. They had to stake out a part of the beach and some tables early enough to beat the crowds. Then they had to make sure the food was set up, served, and cleaned up. The fact that a 50 mph wind sandblasted anybody and anything over two inches tall wasn't their fault.

The fire pits were too small, and nobody could find hot-dog roasting sticks. Someone was assigned to bring hangers, but forgot. Another person was supposed to start the fires, but forgot to bring charcoal. Oddly enough, the beach party—wind, sunburns, and raw hot dogs aside—was a high point for most of us, especially the family members who came from 100-plus-degree temperatures in Arizona and Idaho. Everyone who wasn't blistered returned the next day during free time.

A UNIFYING THEME SIMPLIFIES PLANNING

Reunions can be planned around a holiday like Christmas, Easter, or the Fourth of July. These holidays focus the festivities and nobody needs to struggle with a theme for decorations or for a program.

I've attended or been involved with reunions during weddings, funerals, and baptisms or ordinations. A grandparent's eightieth birthday, a missionary's farewell, or a teenager's sixteenth birthday are all good opportunities for a party. Birthdays, weddings, and farewells have the added advantage of singling out family members for honor and recognition.

The Clermont Oborn branch of my family made a flag several years ago. Since there are four of us, we divided the flag into four sections, and each of us designed and produced a section that we thought represented who and what we had become with our spouses and children.

Gary's sister did a similar project for their folks' forty-seventh anniversary, but she put together a quilt that allowed greater diversity and more input from individuals. She sent both her brothers enough twelve-inch cloth squares for each member of the household, with a set of liquid paints. We were to complete the squares and mail them back to her in time for her to sew the blocks together.

I drew a cartoon of myself at my typewriter with several babies hanging on my arms and back. Gary drew himself in front of a cliff that had the forms of children all through it; below it, he wrote, "Gary mining at the mother lode." Twelve-year-old Dolly drew herself in a fur-trimmed parka, holding a fish and singing, while standing on an ice floe. Ten-year-old Sherri drew herself doing cartwheels. Six-year-old G.W. put himself in a race car. Five-year-old Roch drew a very determined muscle man in an airplane. Four-year-old Eric illustrated a story about a whale that ate an ocean liner, and three-year-old Linda drew herself in a tutu and "tappy" shoes. Micah was only a few months old, so his block contained scribbles I helped him make.

Gary's sister and his father died within a few months of each other only two years later, so that quilt is one of my mother-in-law's most prized possessions. The effort and love that went into its making still inspire everyone in his family.

I attended a reunion for my father's grandfather's family, and I'd only met about ten percent of the 110 who came. That reunion's organizer made up name tags that had a picture of the common ancestor for each group there. I was quickly able to sort out my first cousins and figure out just how others fit into the lineup.

At another reunion someone had prepared a huge genealogy sheet the length of a picnic table with several albums of old pictures near it. We took turns flipping through the albums and locating different faces on the genealogy sheet. My kids enjoyed finding themselves and visualizing just where they fit in.

Collecting favorite pictures and displaying them during the activities has always worked well with my family. Sometimes we make up a large bulletin board with notations under each snapshot. We also use slides and videos of past gatherings.

Skits work well in a family like mine that has more than its share of spotlight hogs. Each branch of the family takes ten minutes for an original (or slightly plagiarized) presentation that showcases particular talents. If you're stymied about what to do, contact your kids' Scoutmaster or camp director—these people have access to time-honored skits that have put thousands of groups at ease.

During a reunion about ten years ago, my brother Paxton's nine children rapped out their introductions. They ranged all the way from nineteen-year-old Tammy, who snapped her fingers behind the *Wall Street Journal*, to three-year-old Elizabeth, who forgot her lines but stayed in rhythm.

My youngest brother Chuck's wife and five kids came up with a melodrama spoof, complete with yellow yarn wig on his fourteen-year-old daughter and a choo-choo train powered by his four-year-old son.

A couple of my sister's boys rendered "Shorty," a messy, hilarious skit that has become a tradition with her twelve kids. We've seen some variation of it every year for the last eighteen years. Her thirteen-year-old daughter Angela stood behind a draped table and put a robe over her head with her arms through the sleeves. Angela's fourteen-year-old brother Jarom stood behind her, buttoned into the robe, with his head showing—his hands encased in a pair of slippers that peeked out beneath the hem of the robe like feet. Twelve-year-old Lesti stood out of sight and described Shorty's routine: brushing teeth, shaving, and so on.

Shorty's toothpaste-covered hair, wildly waving razor, and spraying shaving cream convulsed our most hardened "don't bug me with family stuff" teenagers. By the end of the show, we had to yank some of them off stage; they didn't want to quit.

ALL PARTICIPANTS COMMUNICATE CLEARLY

Besides connecting with extended family, my children learned a lot about cooperation and third-party responsibility during the big San Luis Obispo reunion. Nowhere were these attributes more obvious than during clean-up.

Clean-up worked when each person paid attention to the space around him or her and bigger people watched out for the littler ones.

My fourteen-year-old niece spotted a three-year-old cousin with a permanent marker in his hand and intervened before he decorated my beige carpet. Toddlers with dripping bottles and preschoolers with jam-covered fingers were intercepted on their way into the living room by watchful parents or siblings.

I had also indulged my penchant for charts by dividing up the responsibilities by day and family. I gave each family copies of who was supposed to do what when. I also posted charts about responsibilities in the bathrooms, so everybody knew that they were to keep the toilets flushed, the toothpaste wiped out of sinks, and their clothes picked up. The kitchen had a chart that told people what they could eat and basic standards for keeping the area clean.

When the dust cleared and the last van or station wagon full of waving, cheering bodies left my cul-de-sac, a great quiet settled over the house. And, oddly enough, a few hand smudges on the stairwell, three broken flower vases, a ripped canvas cot, and a mysterious symbol inked on one of the kitchen chairs were my only real damages.

Once again, although a few squabbles had arisen and towels and socks had disappeared, my family and my siblings' families reaped rewards and built memories.

We try to have some kind of reunion once a year now, because we are so scattered and have endured so much economic and personal bludgeoning. My kids still grumble about attending reunions before they happen, but they're gradually learning the importance of renewing their connections with uncles and aunts and cousins.

In conjunction with our reunions, we hold family council meetings and try to be as organized as possible. Some of my extended family has nonprofit status and formal charters. I'm not quite that formal, yet, but a discussion of running family council meetings is appropriate here. Note that the Player family has council meetings instead of family home evening when we need to cover important issues, like moves or job changes.

Family Council Meetings

Family council meetings are a little different from regular family home evening. They are more organized and have more in common with reunions. In fact, as stated earlier, family councils are sometimes held in conjunction with reunions.

During family councils we set goals for our mutual benefit and plan such things as how we are going to make the house payments, eat, and keep Micah on his mission. Councils are excellent times for bringing teenagers into active roles with household finances.

During some councils, Gary would sit down with the monthly bills, a calculator, and his paycheck. Then he would read aloud what needed to be paid and would deduct each amount. By the time he reached the end of the money and several bills still remained to be paid, he'd taught our spend-thrift teens some economic realities. Today, we have a business that seems to suck every resource, but we still try to show the kids where the money goes.

The following sample agenda is self-explanatory:

Player Family Agenda

1. Welcome, including opening song and prayer
2. Plans for our upcoming Family Home Evening Academy Awards
3. Plans for vacation at Red Fish Lake in July
4. Setting of family goals:
   • Supporting our missionaries
   • Preparing Brian and Nathan for serving
   • Assembling our family history
   • Helping Roch and Eric through college
5. Discussion of problems or concerns:
   • Ideas on convincing people to finish assigned chores
   • Kid X's attendance at seminary is slipping—what can we do?
   • Nobody wants to take responsibility for the dog—do we get rid of him?
6. Hugs and accolades for (whoever's turn it is to be spotlighted)
7. Keep On Keeping On—Hurrah for the Player Pack!
8. Closing prayer

Family council meetings, family reunions, and family home evenings could be the focus of an entire book. My purpose in bringing up the subject in this chapter is to stress the importance of such formalized activities. Reunions and family councils define relationships among our scattered, extended family, and help renew our optimism about life. Our children realize that they "come from both Mom's and Dad's side." With that realization comes an understanding of their identity.

And what we as adults need is an understanding of why so many of us chose to be parents.

HEAVENLY FATHER'S GREAT MYSTERY

Why do we have such a need to subject our psyches and strength to twenty-plus years of child-rearing? Maybe there's no explanation; perhaps the desire to nurture a child is ingrained in our humanity, an instinctive drive that propels us as strongly as the spawning instinct of silver salmon.

Maybe we're helpless against the desire to renew the world's hope through a child. As somebody has said, "Babies are God's way of telling us He's not yet discouraged with man." And babies invariably grow into teenagers, so I guess teenagers are also God's gift . . .

Despite all the mess and worry and expense, I agree. My baby's delighted smile when I stagger into her room at 2:00 a.m. is almost worth the sleep deprivation. My toddler's dimpled curves and "Me wuvs Mom" when I discover him bathing his teddy bear in the toilet earn my forgiveness.

My grade-schooler's Mother's Day poem, "In al the wurld there is no uther/ that can take the place of my own swete mother," is a most intelligent, profound piece of literature.

And my teenager who bathes the dog without being asked and packs his lunch so he can buy his little brother a coveted robot is entitled to sleep until noon once in a while.

Life's Best-Kept Secret

The last thirty years of struggling with kids between twelve and twenty have finally clicked on a light in my brain. I understand *The Plan*. I know why Heavenly Father suckers us into having babies and keeps the bewildering facts about teenagers a secret.

Babies test our physical strength while we're still growing emotionally and spiritually. Then teenagers test our emotional and spiritual endurance. *If we survive the tests, we get to have grandchildren— all of the fun and none of the exhaustion.* And we get to sit back and watch our children struggle with their own teenagers.

My advice to all you bewildered parents is: relax and enjoy the burden you have hoisted.

My years as a mother have taught me not to hurry this business of being a parent; I just "go with the flow." Sometimes the flow meanders through a sunlit goldfish pond; sometimes the flow gushes from a backed-up septic tank.

Remember, too, that the teenage years don't last anywhere as long as early childhood. That sense of eternity you feel stems from the absence of control—sort of like a roller coaster. The Matterhorn, Loop-D-Loop, and Twister are apt metaphors for the time any parent spends with a teenager. A key to enjoying the ride is to strap yourself in securely and accept the limited control; you may just find yourself having a bit of fun after all.

If this book has boosted your spirits and helped you understand your child/adult a bit better, it has accomplished its purpose.

I hope it has made you laugh in places. I also hope it has convinced you to either be thankful the numbers you face aren't quite as mind-boggling as mine, or to be confident that you can survive your herd of adolescents, too.

Trust me; there will come a time when memories of life with your teenagers will make you smile. You'll laugh with those grown-up children and share words of comfort as they repeat the cycle.

Afterword

My Nest Runneth Over

I find that I must plan carefully, or the days whip by without much being accomplished. My teenagers keep turning into young adults and leaving. This Afterword is included to remind both you and me why we started this whole process in the first place.

MY NEST RUNNETH OVER

People ask me, "How do you ever get them all out the door in the morning?" almost as often as they ask, "Are they all yours?" or, referring to our special-needs foster home for troubled teens, "Are you insane? Who in her right mind would *choose* a bunch of teenagers?"

I thought life would simplify as my nine children matured, but I was wrong. Life just became more complex. However, I was able to draw on the Spirit of the Lord and experiences that came along to keep from floundering.

One set of circumstances involved our family living in six different places. Sherri and Gary Willis left in June and July of 1989 to serve missions in Washington State and Brazil; Roch began Brigham Young University that August; in October Gary took Eric, Micah, and Nathan to our new home in Cedar City, Utah, and I kept Linda with me in San Luis Obispo while I finished my teaching contract at Cal Poly.

I also had a foster daughter with me for about six weeks while paperwork for her adoption by another family crept through bureaucratic mazes. We shared a room with our year-old grandson Cameron at Dolly and Roland's apartment.

Linda and I joined Gary and the boys just before Christmas. Then Roch came home from BYU to get ready for his service in the Oklahoma Tulsa Mission, and the state of Utah passed several teenagers in and out our doors.

Dolly gave birth to Nicholas a few months before she and Roland decided to leave California and go to school in Utah. The four of them lived with us for a couple of months while they scrounged an apartment in Cedar City's overcrowded housing market.

Gary Willis came home from his mission, and Eric prepared to leave for his in the Minneapolis Minnesota Mission. Through a series of circumstances that are too complicated to go into here, we lost our lease. Ten of us had to move into the only vacant rental in town—a three-bedroom, one-bath house we not-so-lovingly dubbed "The Slum."

We moved the five current boys into the master bedroom, the three girls into the next smaller bedroom, and Gary and me into the smallest room. I posted a shower schedule on the bathroom door, and we actually stayed relatively calm—even when the place flooded and the carpets became so damp a weed grew inside the front door.

How I get them all out the door in the morning changes, because where we live and the number of people in our household varies from year to year, and sometimes from month to month—or week to week. Since we were a special-needs foster home for many years, we sometimes had as many as fourteen kids littering the premises.

When I wrote the original draft of this book, we had two young adults, five teenagers, one grade-schooler, and two preschoolers living with us. A few weeks later one of the foster teenagers left to join Job Corps, and our social worker brought us a ten-month-old baby. Our license was increased by one, because another child had turned eighteen and graduated from high school.

When dealing with the disarray of living with teenagers, I've learned to close my eyes and take a deep breath. No matter what happens, I either laugh or count to ten. Becoming angry or irritated accomplishes nothing, escalates my frustration, and adds to the confusion.

YOU'VE GOT TO BE KIDDING

To illustrate my point, I'd like to share a morning in the fall of

1987. I choose that period of time because our living situation then was absurd—even for us.

The lack of an affordable large home in San Luis Obispo, California, had forced us to rent two three-bedroom condominiums. All eight original kids were still at home. (We hadn't adopted Brian, yet; he became number nine in 1994 as a fifteen-year-old.) Dolly and Roland had only been married a few months and were living with us to save up a deposit for their own place, so Roland had just joined the family.

The condos faced each other, which was handy, but their two sets of stairs wore me out. Whenever I wanted a kid (to answer the phone, do the dishes, explain a mysterious dent in my car), I had to guess which condo he or she was in. Most of the time I guessed wrong.

I'd trudge in the front door and up the stairs, only to find the object of my search had walked out the back patio doors to the "other side" yelling, "Mom? Mom? What do you want?"

(The four full bathrooms and two half baths were a luxury beyond compare, however. Later, when ten of us were stuffed into those three bedrooms and *one* bath, we remembered "the condos" wistfully.)

Pre-Dawn Beginning

The alarm blared at 5:20 a.m.—my time for breakfast before the rush. Gary immediately flopped to his back for some contented snoring without my elbowing him. Light from the bathroom illuminated my trip down the stairs. As I groped by the couch, the neighbor's cat meowed at me; somebody must have left the patio door open again.

Muttering under my breath about fleas, I lunged at the cat, but with a flick of its tail, it slipped out. I didn't turn on the dining room light while I poured my granola and sliced my banana, because I didn't want to wake up Micah and Nathan. They slept on a day bed in the living room, since Dolly and Roland occupied their bedroom. I made do with the night light that glowed over the stove.

I savored the cereal and the peace; I've found that this quiet time to myself has always been much more important than extra sleep. Just sitting in the stillness, as dawn lightens the sky, helps prepare me to face the day. I also use this time for my personal scripture studies.

But on this particular day I only managed a couple of verses; my eyes kept slipping closed. So as soon as I finished eating, I hurried back to bed.

The Wheels Start Rolling

When the alarm rang again at 6:15 a.m., it was my turn to flip over for a few minutes while Gary got up to take Eric, then fourteen, and Roch, then sixteen, to early-morning seminary.

Doors slammed and cries echoed through the walls: "Where's my lunch?" "Who left the ice cream out?" "We're out of milk!" "Shut up! Some people are still asleep!"

Pipes rattled as two or three showers started. I crammed my pillow over my head and clenched my eyes shut, but the floor shook as footsteps pounded up the stairs. Then my bedroom door crashed open.

The steps continued into my bathroom; clinks, thunks, and thuds followed.

"For Pete's sake, who's in here?!" I yelled.

Eric poked his dripping head around the corner and grinned at me. He waved my curling brush, his dad's razor, and a towel. "I can't find a comb." Water dribbled from his blonde bangs onto the carpet.

I sat up. "If you'd ever put anything away, your bathroom would be as well-stocked as mine; besides, *I* clean up after myself and never drip on somebody else's rug." (As you know from reading this book, I believe in using every possible teaching moment.)

The car honked outside and revved its engine; Eric grinned again, flipped his hair out of his eyes, blew me a kiss, and departed.

I pulled on sweat pants and a T-shirt, then yanked the bedspread and pillows into a somewhat orderly configuration. On my way downstairs, I rapped on the little boys' bedroom door. "Rise and shine, Dolly!" It was her turn to make breakfast and run two loads of wash before she left for the day.

Roland peered out of the bathroom. He shifted his toothbrush to the side of his mouth and said, "I'm letting Dolly sleep in. She had an awful stomachache last night."

I didn't say anything, but rolled my eyes (out of his sight, of course). I figured Dolly and Roland would eventually divide up adult responsibilities, and Dolly would tire of her extended vacation—about the time a couple of children arrived. (I was right.)

I entered the kitchen just in time to catch six-year-old Nathan, who had slipped while climbing up the cabinet drawers. In the process, he also kicked over a cooler (our extra refrigeration) and splashed water across the floor.

A broken bottle of mayonnaise lay in front of the refrigerator; a white blob oozed under the door near the hinges. Thirteen-year-old Linda opened a new quart and sliced some salami.

"Did you do this?" I glared at her and the spreading puddle.

"No, honest, Mom. It was there when I got up." Linda continued slathering mayonnaise on her bread.

Carrying her apron and shoes, twenty-year-old Sherri slid open the patio doors. "Has anybody seen my name tag? The health department guys are coming today, and I have to wear it."

Several "Nopes" and shrugs answered her. Ten-year-old Micah, naked except for underpants and a blanket slung around his shoulders, caught my attention by switching channels to another cartoon show.

I grabbed the remote control and blanked the set. "How many times do I have to tell you not to watch television in the morning? Now, get yourself dressed!" I pushed him toward the stairs.

I could have ignored him, just this once. But even though it's easier to overlook such infractions, I've discovered that consistency pays off. Micah's older siblings finally gave up the television fight; he would, too—eventually.

The Great Shoe Hunt Begins

Nathan flung sweaters, tennis rackets, and baseball gloves from the hall closet. "I can't find my strap shoes, so I guess I'll wear my soccer shoes."

"Oh no, you won't; the school doesn't allow cleats. Keep looking," I answered, as I picked up the pillows and folded the blankets he and Micah had slung over the table.

"Mom, can I have a dollar for milk?" Linda rolled her lunch bag shut and stuffed it into the top of her backpack.

"A *dollar?* I thought milk was twenty-five cents." I washed Nathan's lunch pail, which had been put away sticky. Then I rummaged through several drawers to find a dish towel. I settled on a terrycloth hot pad and turned back to her. "Well? Has the price gone up?"

"No, but I want some other stuff."

"Linda, we have plenty of food in the house. Take a pear or some grapes."

"Yuck. I want french fries. I can't pack french fries."

"Buy one of my soccer candy bars," suggested Nathan as he prepared to dump a cup of sugar onto his cereal.

I intercepted the sugar and kissed Gary, who had just walked in the door. "Give Linda a quarter, honey. And Micah needs thirty-five cents for juice because of his cold; milk makes him cough."

"I just gave them money yesterday. Here, take my last penny." Gary dramatically pulled his pocket inside out and handed coins to Linda and Micah.

Linda slipped hers into her purse, but Micah shook his head and put his hands behind his back.

"That's okay, Daddy, I can drink water. School has a water fountain."

"Quit giving the kids a hard time about milk money," I said. "Most of them know you're kidding, but Micah takes you seriously."

I re-aimed Micah upstairs and retrieved the sugar that Nathan had swiped when I turned to talk to his dad.

"Who dropped the mayonnaise?" Gary stooped to pick up the glass.

"Probably Roch. His lunch was behind it," said Roland, who appeared behind us.

Roland carried a plate with a few toast crumbs on it into the kitchen, stepping cautiously around the slimy lake. Then he started making his and Dolly's lunches.

"Is Dolly up yet?" I asked. "Somebody go wake up Gary Willis for prayers. Linda has to catch her bus in five minutes." When nobody acknowledged my question or request, I scooped up the laundry heaped by the television. "Never mind, I'll get him when I start the dryer."

My trek to the side that served as five kids' bedrooms, recreation room, and laundry room was invigorating. Coastal fog grayed the bush-lined walk, and rustling eucalyptus dripped on me.

I reflected on all the confusion—confusion that had been escalating over the past twenty years. I knew I was lucky; I could handle the constant uproar without cracking because of Gary's committed, active role in the family.

Gary was (and is) so much more than a nominal "priesthood" leader. In all our married life, he has never left the rearing of the kids to me. We've worked as a team—out of necessity. If either of us had left the job to the other, we'd never have survived. I couldn't have written this book, and you couldn't have read it!

Setting the Tone for the Day

Seventeen-year-old Gary Willis snored with his head under his pillow and his feet sticking out the end of his bed. Ironed shirts, rumpled pants, and dirty socks littered his floor. Crumpled love notes, a *Rolling Stone* magazine, and three hangers were the sole residents of his closet.

I nudged his bare toes. "Up and at 'em, Big Gair. We need you for morning prayers—*now*."

He grunted something which I took to mean, "Right away, Mom." So I left.

We Keep Trying—and Sometimes We Succeed

Everyone made the morning gathering, even Dolly, pale and clucked over by her husband. A less than spiritual atmosphere pervaded, however.

Gary Willis knelt with his head resting on the low table in front of the couch and failed to open his eyes after the "Amen." Linda muttered, "Hurry up. I'll miss my bus," under her breath. Nathan clicked and buzzed some robotic anthem, and Micah lounged in his underpants—he had put on a shirt, however.

As I've explained before, this moment to pause before the Lord as the day began was and is the single most important activity that welds us together as a family. Although on this particular morning the effort seemed futile, I remembered that sometimes the form must be maintained in order to build the substance.

When we first tried to establish the habit of morning and evening family prayer, reverence was minimal. In fact, I often found myself clamping a wiggly toddler in the crook of each arm and pinning an ornery five-year-old with my knee. Meanwhile, Gary glared from under lowered eyebrows at a pre-teenager who refused to close her eyes or acquiesce to his request that she get up on her knees.

Sometimes I felt like giving up or running away. But I hung in there, and we made progress—most of the time.

Roland jump-started his pickup and left in a roar of blue fumes. Dolly helped Sherri search for her name tag, which they finally found in the toy box. Then Dolly hurried back upstairs.

Linda ran for her bus in a beribboned flurry, shirttail flying, tripping over her untied shoelaces. She also left her lunch on the counter. Gary raced after her and delivered it just as the bus pulled away.

Gary Willis sneaked back to bed and was very indignant when I booted him out. He slouched down the stairs, grumbling under his breath about "never getting any rest" and "having to do everything."

Two neighbor kids who walked with Nathan and Micah arrived, but Nathan still couldn't find his shoes.

The Great Shoe Search Continues

"We'll be late!" Micah crammed books, notebook, and lunch into his backpack.

"I know where they are! They're over by Sherri's bed." Lugging his backpack, Nathan ran out the door in his stocking feet.

"Go on ahead, they'll catch up." I walked the neighbor kids through the house to the back door. "Micah, you need an undershirt or long sleeves. That fog is chilly."

"This is very warm, Mom. It's 100 percent cotton." Micah started tying his shoes.

"You don't have any socks on—get some socks." I sent him back to his room, where he kicked the door to alert his sister.

Nathan flung back into the room. "Oh, why can't I wear my soccer shoes?"

"You'll have to wear your Sunday shoes. Go up and get them. Give me that; you don't have your jacket on." I pulled his backpack from his shoulders and followed him up the stairs.

"I know where they are! They're over by Gary's bed." Nathan ran back down the stairs.

Micah wandered into the hall. "I've got everything, but you have to write me a note for why I was absent last week."

I sighed and leaned against the balcony that overlooked the living room. "Can't they figure it out? The office called me to come when you threw up all over."

Micah shrugged.

"Where's the mop?" Gary called from the kitchen. "I wiped all the mess, but the floor's still greasy."

"I need a towel!" Dolly's voice wailed from the bathroom.

"Sherri, get your sister a towel. I don't know, honey; Roch was chasing Eric with the mop the last time I saw it." I searched for something to write on and with. I finally found a used envelope and a piece of green crayon.

"We'll be late! Tell Nathan to run and catch us, or you can give him a ride." Micah zipped his backpack and yanked it over his arms; its weight threatened to tip him over backwards.

The Great Shoe Hunt Continues Some More

"You have to wait for me—you have to!" Nathan repeated the last three words several times as his voice grew fainter. I could hear him slamming doors on the "other side."

A few seconds later Nathan dashed past me. "I know where they are! They're in your bathroom over here."

"I think Nathan's almost found his shoes! You guys go on. We're coming!" Micah yelled out the window to his friends. Then he gave up trying to put on his backpack and dragged it down to the door.

Nathan raced by me again. "I know where they are! Maybe they're by Roch's bed!"

"Nathan," I said to his fleeing back, "you have to have your shoes. Your socks are getting dirty."

Micah left by the front door, just as Nathan ran back in the patio doors.

"I know where they are!" Nathan pounded up the stairs for the fourth time. A few moments of silence followed his shout of "Well, *okay* now!" Then he yelled, "You bad shoes! I couldn't find you."

Micah came in the patio doors. "Nathan wasn't over there. Where is he?"

Gary answered him, "Upstairs yelling at his shoes."

Nathan ran up to his father; his socks bagged around his ankles and his shoes were on the wrong feet. "I found them, but they're too small for me; they pinch my toes."

Gary smoothed out Nathan's socks and switched his shoes, then he drove both boys to school.

Parental Patience Sometimes Wears Thin

When Gary returned, he found Gary Willis back in bed. At this point fatherly forbearance vanished and Gary's faint but firm admonition reverberated through the walls: "If you don't get up and stay up this second, I'll sell your car and tear up your driver's license."

G.W. knew exactly how far he could push his dad, because he arrived in the kitchen, fully dressed, thirty seconds later.

Although Gary hasn't been quoted much in this book, he is very adept at handling teenagers. He rarely speaks in anger, keeps his "no's" to a minimum, and always follows through on any threats. He was the one who decided our errant teen should spend graduation night in his room when he wouldn't produce evidence that the "Party of the Year" was chaperoned and drug-free.

Sherri helped me finish degreasing the kitchen while Gary Willis unwound the cord to the vacuum cleaner. That chore accomplished, G. W. left the vacuum in the middle of the floor and yelled at Dolly, "Hurry up! We'll both be late."

Her job only a short walk away, Sherri skipped out the back while Gary Willis and Dolly left from the front.

Gary and I, arms around each other, walked upstairs to our home offices. We ran Tahoma Resources, a geological and technical writing/consulting business that almost supported the family. The silence was broken only by the dishwasher's rumble and the neighbor's cat meowing and scratching at the screen door.

THEY'RE FINALLY ALL GONE

We had about six hours before the outgoing flood reversed. As I sat down in front of my computer, Gary suggested, "Why don't you list everything that's gone on this morning? We might repress it all and not be able to remember when we're old and gray."

He had a good idea.

I can't imagine ever suffering from "empty nest syndrome," but I know the day will come when our food budget and car insurance bills no longer resemble the national debt.

Someday the blouses I starch and iron will await me in my closet instead of mysteriously evolving into rumpled piles on my daughters' beds. My shampoo and conditioner will cease evaporating at the speed of light, and I'll be able to fall asleep without setting my curfew alarm.

And life won't be half as much fun.

References

Most of my activities and ideas were developed from "hit and miss" experience during my thirty-two-plus years of being a parent and an active member of the Church. However, I have drawn on the formal training offered by the states of Alaska, Oklahoma, Texas, California, and Utah as part of my licensing as a special-needs foster home. Some of the resources that were used are listed below.

For secular information, I drew most extensively on the *Skills for Adolescence* curriculum that was developed by Quest International in conjunction with the Lions Club International and various nonprofit foundations. Two of my children participated in the year-long classes offered in the San Luis Obispo California School District, and I was on a parents' committee for those classes. I have also been part of an effort to get the classes offered in southern Utah schools, an effort that is ongoing.

The following books are some that I've read and used. The list is by no means exhaustive.

Bieler, Henry, M.D., *Food is Your Best Medicine.* Random House, New York, 1972.

Dinkmeyer, Don & Gary D. McKay, *Parenting Teenagers.* American Guidance Service, Minnesota, 1990.

For Kids' Sake, Inc. R.C. Law & Co. Fullerton, CA 92631.

Friedman, Barb & Cheri Brooks, *On BASE! (Behavioral Alternatives*

Through Self Esteem). BASE Systems Publishers, Missouri, 1990.

Johnson, Kenneth E., M.D., *Mormon Wisdom and Health* (formerly *Word of Wisdom Food Plan*). Cedar Ford, Inc., Springville, Utah, 1993.

Kimball, Spencer W., *The Miracle of Forgiveness*. Bookcraft Publishing, 44th Printing, Salt Lake City, Utah, 1997.

Latham, Glenn I., *What's a Parent to Do? Solving Family Problems in a Christlike Way*. Deseret Book, Salt Lake City, Utah, 1997.

Lindsay, Richard P., *The War to Save Our Kids*. Horizon Publishing, Bountiful, Utah, 1998.

Lions-Quest, *Skills for Adolescence*, Teacher's Resource Guide. Lions Club International and Quest International, W.K. Kellogg Foundation, 1992.

Nielson, Linda, *Adolescence: A Contemporary View*. Holt, Rinehart and Winston, Inc., 1991.

Resnik, Hank (editor), *Changes! Becoming the Best You Can Be*. Quest International, 1988.

Wilcox, Brad, and Barbara Barrington Jones, *Straight Talk for Parents: What Teenagers Wish They Could Tell You*. Deseret Book, Salt Lake City, Utah, 1994.

Appendices

Chore Charts

CHORE CHART AND CHECKLIST: COOK (REGULAR)

MAKE SURE YOU'VE ACCOMPLISHED EACH STEP
Remember, do each of these things for "outstanding" points!

___ 1. Plan menu with Mom or Dad. Be sure to look in the refrigerator, cupboards, and freezer for possibilities.
___ 2. Write down your menu. Get approval from Mom or Dad.
___ 3. Shop for any necessary ingredients.
___ 4. Assemble everything you need at least two hours before dinner time.
___ 5. Be sure you know how to prepare items.
___ 6. Cook.
___ 7. Soak pans, dishes, measuring cups, and anything else you use in the sink as you finish with them.
___ 8. Put away ingredients as you use them.
___ 9. Throw away wrappings, egg shells, and any other garbage you generate. Separate items for recycling and composting.
___ 10. Wash everything in the sink.

CHORE CHART AND CHECKLIST
LIVING ROOM, PLAY ROOM, FAMILY ROOM

CHECK AND BE SURE YOU'VE ACCOMPLISHED EACH STEP
Remember, do each of these things for "outstanding" points!

___ 1. Pick up trash, toys, games, clutter of all kinds. Use a box or a basket to save steps.
___ 2. Put away and/or dispose of everything that doesn't belong in the living room.
___ 3. Assemble furniture polish, cleaning rags, paper towels, broom, and vacuum cleaner.
___ 4. Clean furniture surfaces, including chair and table legs and pedestals.
___ 5. Wipe off picture frames, books, the VCR, and other non-furniture surfaces.
___ 6. Vacuum and/or sweep. Use the hose along the base of the carpet. Move small items of furniture.
___ 7. Dust baseboards; wipe off woodwork.
___ 8. Wash and dry doorknobs and inside of windows.
___ 9. Once a week: move the couch and vacuum under it. Vacuum under the couch cushions (and any chair cushions).
___ 10. Look at your work. Is it attractive and neat? Don't use the excuse, "I cleaned, but somebody messed it up . . ."

CHORE CHART AND CHECKLIST:
BATHROOMS

CHECK AND BE SURE YOU'VE ACCOMPLISHED EACH STEP
Remember, do each of these things for "outstanding" points!

___ 1. Pick up trash, towels, and anything else that is out of place.
___ 2. Put away and/or dispose of everything that doesn't belong in the bathroom.
___ 3. Assemble cleanser, Windex, cleaning rags, paper towels, and the toilet bowl brush.
___ 4. Sprinkle/pour cleanser into the toilet bowl, tub, and sink (use

a gentle cleanser for plastic or marble surfaces).

___ 5. Wipe out the sink: get behind faucets and around splash boards. Wipe the front and sides of the cabinet. Rinse if necessary and dry with paper towels.

___ 6. Wipe out the tub/shower. Scrub shower base; wipe around faucets. **Go over all surfaces, even if they "look clean" to you.**

___ 7. Scrub the toilet bowl with the brush. Wipe under the seat and next to the tank. Wipe around the base of the toilet.

___ 8. **Wash, rinse, and dry all surfaces on the toilet, even if they "look clean" to you.** Germs don't show up very well, but they're persistent little devils.

___ 9. Sweep the floor. Wipe the floor with the rag you used on the toilet; get the corners and behind the door.

___ 10. Polish the mirror; hang clean towels and replenish the toilet paper roll (if necessary) or put an extra roll on the tank.

LAUNDRY TIPS

If you want your clothes to look good and last longer, follow these rules:

1. ALWAYS sort everything before you load. Consider the color as well as the type of fabric. Sort by the following:

COLOR
Whites only
Light colors and medium colors with white patterns
Medium colors
Dark colors
Blacks only

TYPE
Cotton and cotton-blend fabrics
Lightweight fabrics like nylon
Heavy fabrics like jeans and corduroy
Terrycloth, towels, and bedspreads
Wool, silk, and other fabrices requiring special care

2. Empty pockets, then load the clothes LOOSELY into the washer; do not pack them in.

3. Use warm wash and cold rinse settings unless you have special-

care fabrics that require a cold wash.

4. Measure the detergent. Remember, we have soft water, so 1/4 cup is plenty. If you forget and use too much soap, run the clothes through an extra rinse.

5. Check labels before you throw things in the dryer. When in doubt, hang it up instead.

6. Take clothes out of the dryer promptly, hang or fold them, and put them away. If you forget, don't ask me to iron your shirt!

SAMPLE RESTRICTIVE CONTRACT

Note: This contract was developed for use with foster kids who were in the Youth in Custody program. All of those kids were in counseling and had brushes with the law, including truancy, running away, under-age smoking, and shoplifting. Modify it for individual needs.

DATE:
GOALS:

1. _____'s growth and maturity; ability to enjoy relationships, and become a happy person.

2. _____'s ability to support him/herself at age eighteen or end of schooling (*this depends on the particular kid's situation*).

MAIN AREAS OF CONCERN:

1. Attitude and personal appearance
2. School performance and attendance
3. Home chores, responsibilities, and relationships

METHODS FOR ACHIEVING SUCCESS IN THESE THREE AREAS:

1. Attitude and Personal Appearance
   - Express feelings and ideas in a neutral tone of voice without accusing or blaming.
   - Accept parental and teacher direction without objecting and/or becoming defensive and defiant
   - Cooperate in counseling and psychiatric care. Admit the need for such help. Remember appointments (write them down) and

try to follow the counselor's suggestions.
- Keep clothing and hair clean and neat—no holes, excessive ragging, or other sloppy dressing. No "punking" or extreme attire.

2. School Performance and Attendance
   - Maintain or improve all grades to a C- level or above.
   - Leave for school no earlier than 7:40 and no later than 7:45. Return at 2:50 p.m. on regular days; on shortened schedule or assembly days, return no later than 15 minutes after dismissal.
   - Do not leave school grounds for any reason during school hours without specific parental permission. Be on time for all classes.
   - Any after-school activities must be approved by Mom or Dad and accompanied by a note from teacher or administrator.
   - Study one hour immediately after returning from school. No radio or television during study time. No television on school nights without specific permission.

3. Home Chores, Responsibilities, and Relationships
   - Eliminate contact with_____ and any other person who encouraged or aided sluffing and/or running away. A full list of off-limit friends will be developed by your social worker, principal, and parents.
   - Approach and attempt to form friendships with boys/girls like_____.
   - Check chore chart daily and accomplish assignments without being nagged. Finish and follow through as appropriate; refer to specific guidelines for various chores.
   - Save spending money for necessities. Discuss special purchases with Mom or Dad (savings account money cannot be used except by permission).
   - Attend church and family activities.
   - When visiting with relatives, remain with them. Do not leave relative's residence for any reason, except on relative's instruction or request.
   - Maintain possessions and clothing in neat and orderly manner. Ask for help if needed.
   - Do not trade clothing or accessories with anyone other than family members.

I WILL ABIDE BY THIS CONTRACT AND ACCEPT THE PENALTIES FOR ANY VIOLATIONS:

_____

Signature

PARENTS' STATEMENT

If these conditions are agreed to and met, the Player family will continue providing a caring, structured home for_____.

_____ can count on nourishing, pleasing food, adequate clothing, comfortable sleeping space, thoughtful discipline, and frequent pleasurable family outings.

_____ will be listened to and directed in a spirit of love and concern.

AFTER FOUR WEEKS, MORE RESTRICTIVE TERMS OF THIS CONTRACT WILL BE REVIEWED AND EVALUATED ON THE BASIS OF _____'S BEHAVIOR.

_____   _____

Gary Farnsworth Player   Corrie Lynne Player

BRAINSTORMING DIRECTIONS

Brainstorming with your teenager will help both of you come up with areas where your child excels or is accomplished. The rules for successful brainstorming are:

1. **Set a time limit.** If you don't, you'll be distracted by watching the clock.

2. **Write everything down.** If you don't, you'll sabotage yourself before you start.

3. Write everything that occurs to you; **the principal behind brainstorming is to let your mind run free.** As soon as you start saying to yourself, "Naw, that's a dumb comment," or "I really can't do that," you inhibit the creative process or eliminate it altogether.

Try the following "I'M GOOD AT . . ." exercise:

1. Give your child a pen and blank sheet of paper, then set some kind of timer, such as an alarm or the timer on the oven.

2. Tell her to write "I'm good at" at the top of the paper. Explain that you're going to do some brainstorming. When you give the signal, she should start writing; she should not stop until the timer goes off.

3. Participate by writing as many things as you can think of about your child; you'll gain some insights, and your son or daughter will realize how important he or she is in your life.

You may have to go through the exercise several times before your teen understands exactly how brainstorming operates.

CONSEQUENCES:
SITUATION/RESPONSE ROLE-PLAYING

SITUATION: A friend says, "Let's go to WalMart for lunch."

YOUR CHOICES:(a) Go, (b) Stay, or (c) Go with reservations.
Consequences of Choice A —
* Friend will think I'm cool, unafraid.
* I might get caught and suspended for truancy.
Consequences of Choice B —
* Friend will call me a "dweeb," "chicken," or worse.
* I would get to class on time.
Consequences of Choice C —
* Friend might call me "chicken" or say that I worry too much.
* I might get to class on time, but I probably wouldn't, because WalMart is too far away for a thirty-minute lunch break.

POSSIBLE RESPONSES TO THE SITUATION:
- "Go ahead if you want to, but I'm not taking the chance of another tardy. I don't want to be suspended."
- "I can't—my mom (or dad) would kill me, and I don't want to be grounded. I want to go to Homecoming."
- "I'd just worry the whole time, so count me out."

SITUATION: Friend says, "Let's invite the guys over—just to talk and hang out."

YOUR CHOICES:
a. "Okay, but they'll have to leave by curfew."
b. "We'd better not; my mom doesn't let me have boys over when she's not home."
c. "I'll call my folks and check it out."

Consequences of Choice A—
- Friend will think I'm cool, unafraid.
- My parents would be disappointed and probably punish me.

Consequences of Choice B—
- Friend might call me a "dweeb," "chicken," or worse.
- Not only would my family be glad I remembered the house rules, but Church leaders will be reassured and my conscience will be clear.

Consequences of Choice C—
- My folks would know I'm trying and they'll be more likely to let me stay out later or do something that requires self-discipline.
- Friend might call me "chicken" or say that I worry too much.

POSSIBLE RESPONSES TO THE SITUATION:
- "If my mom finds out, she'll ground me for the rest of my life."
- "My folks will be glad I remembered the house rules."
- "My folks will probably say no, but they'll appreciate my effort, and I'll better my chances for having my curfew extended the next time I want it."

LOVE VS. LUST (INFATUATION): IS IT LOVE?

Over the years, I've borrowed many ideas from my kids' Church meetings. I really like the following discussion of how to tell the difference between love and infatuation, which I got from a Sunday School Course 17 manual.

INFATUATION:

- Leaps quickly into bloom and can die just as fast.
- Stems from a desire for self-gratification.
- Can cause loss of appetite and make it difficult to concentrate or study.
- Can make you irritable and short-tempered with members of your family.
- Involves a lot of sexual excitement.
- Lacks confidence and breeds jealousy.
- Makes you miserable when your partner is away. You worry about his or her heart turning to someone else.
- Causes disagreements and impatience with the partner's point of view.
- Brings the feeling that you must marry right away. You can't wait—you don't want to take the chance of losing him or her.

LOVE:

- Takes root slowly and grows with time.
- Brings a deep concern for the welfare of the loved one.
- Is constant, even in the face of misfortune that may take away the loved one's status or popularity.
- Enables you to be sensible about diet and rest. You study or work harder because you want to do and be your best.
- Makes you realize that sex is only a part of love. Your partner doesn't ask you to be immoral or to do something that would bring serious consequences.
- Enables you to have fun together without relying on sexual excitement.
- Occurs when you are good friends before you are "in love."
- Means trust. You are calm, secure and unthreatened, even when the person is away.
- Enables you to wait and plan; miles don't separate you.

- Brings a willingness to compromise and hear your partner's point of view.
- Helps you realize that though you might prefer to marry at once, you can wait until the time for marriage is appropriate.
- Lets you plan your future with confidence.

SACRAMENT: PREPARE TO PARTAKE

Read each passage of scripture and follow the instructions. Keep this sheet where you can refer to it before sacrament meeting each week.
  1. 2 Corinthians 13:5: "Examine yourselves . . ."
      a. Make a list of your most serious sins and temptations.
      b. Rank the things on your list in order of seriousness, difficulty, or effect on your spiritual development.
      c. Start working to correct the most serious ones first.
  2. 3 Nephi 12:23 - 24: "Repent" and "be reconciled . . ."
      a. Decide if there are some things on your list that you need to discuss with an offended person or with your bishop.
      b. Repent of sins and wrongdoings, and seek forgiveness from Heavenly Father.
  3. D&C 31:12: "Pray always. . . ."
Commit yourself to morning and evening prayers; ask for help for the day during your morning prayer, and report on your progress during your evening prayer.
  4. D&C 59:9: "Offer up thy sacraments on my holy day."
      a. Protect yourself spiritually by participating regularly in the sacrament service. Covenant to obey the Lord's commandments.
      b. Receive the companionship of the Holy Ghost for strength to help you overcome weaknesses and wrongdoings.

SUGGESTED "MISSION RULES" FOR SUNDAYS
These ideas are adapted from a Course 15 manual.

WORSHIPFUL DOS
- Read scriptures, Church magazines, and uplifting literature.
- Pray and listen to classical or religious music.

• Visit with loved ones and/or those who need comfort.
• Write a letter to a missionary or write in your journal.
• Prepare talks or Sunday School lessons.

WORSHIPFUL DON'TS
• Don't play heavy metal or rock music.
• Don't watch television or videos.
• Don't play video games (especially violent ones).
• Don't quarrel with brothers or sisters.
• Don't spend the majority of the day sleeping.

ALWAYS ASK YOURSELF:
Of all the things you could do today, which ones do you think are right?

WHEN YOU HAVE THE SPIRIT
1. You feel happy, calm, and clear-minded.
2. You feel generous.
3. Nobody can offend you.
4. You wouldn't mind everybody seeing what you're doing.
5. You are eager to be with people and want to make them happy.
6. You are glad when others succeed.
7. You are glad to attend your meetings and participate in church activities.
8. You feel like praying.
9. You wish you could keep all the Lord's commandments.
10. You feel "in control." You don't overeat or sleep too much. You don't feel uncontrollably drawn to sensational entertainment, lose your temper, or feel uncontrollable passions or desires.
11. You think about the Savior often, and you want to know Him better.
12. You feel confident and are glad to be alive.
(Adapted from an *Ensign* magazine article.)

WHEN YOU DON'T HAVE THE SPIRIT
1. You feel unhappy, depressed, confused, and frustrated.
2. You feel possessive, self-centered, or resentful of demands made on you.

3. You are easily offended.
4. You become secretive and evasive.
5. You avoid people, especially members of your family, and you are critical of family members and Church authorities.
6. You envy or resent the successes of others.
7. You don't want to go to church, go home teaching, or take the sacrament. You wish you had another church job or no job at all.
8. You find the commandments bothersome, restricting, or senseless.
9. You don't want to pray.
10. You feel emotions and appetites so strongly that you fear you cannot control them; these include hate, jealousy, anger, lust, hunger, and fatigue.
11. You rarely think of the Savior. He seems irrelevant to your life—or, worse, part of a confusing system that seems to work against you.
12. You get discouraged easily and wonder if life is really worth it.

(Adapted from an *Ensign* magazine article.)

10 TIPS FOR TALKING TO TEENS

1. Stay open to the Spirit.
2. Don't take anything personally; maintain a positive attitude.
3. Set a good example.
4. Tune in, not out.
5. Use "I Feel" statements.
6. Watch tone and pitch of voice.
7. Keep body language optimistic.
8. Work wonders with hugs.
9. Insist on respect for everyone in the family.
10. Use a specific, concrete method like the Point System.

EVALUATE YOUR SPIRITUALITY LEVEL

Keep this chart in a private place. Set some goals and reevaluate yourself every few days.

1. Do I do things for others on my own, or do I have to be asked?

2. Does my main gospel instruction happen only at church? Do I read and study regularly on my own?

3. Do I pray in private, as well as with family and in church meetings?

4. Do I talk sincerely, without rushing, to my Heavenly Father?

5. Am I friendly with others, especially those who may be "different"?

6. Do I treat my family with love, courtesy, and respect?

7. Do I represent gospel standards at all times and in all places? Or do I have to be pressured by friends or parents?

8. Do I make decisions based on counsel from my Church leaders and parents and confirmed by the Lord in prayer?

9. Do I want to go on a mission for myself, or am I going because it's "expected"?

10. Do I see marriage as an escape from my present frustrations, or do I regard it as an important part of my eternal progress, requiring mature preparation and commitment?

11. Do I follow the counsel of the living prophet as it is given in general conference, through local Church leaders, and in Church publications?

12. As I learn more about Christ-like love, do I try to make it a real part of my life?

SATAN'S STRATEGIES

Adopted from a Sunday School manual.

IF YOU WANT THE POWER TO RESIST SATAN'S TEMPTATIONS, YOU MUST:

1. Be resolute.

2. Stand in holy places.

3. Avoid all appearance (kinds) of evil.

4. Pray.

5. Live the gospel.

6. Seek the Spirit of Christ, the priesthood, the gift of the Holy Ghost, and the gift of discernment.

SATAN HITS US IN OUR WEAKEST PLACES. HIS TOOL AND TACTICS INCLUDE:

ANGER (2 Nephi 28:20): "For behold, at that day shall he rage in the hearts of the children of men, and stir them up to anger against that which is good."

CARNAL-MINDEDNESS (2 Nephi 28:21): "And others will he pacify and lull them away into carnal security, that they will say: All is well in Zion; yea, Zion prospereth, all is well—and thus the devil cheateth their souls, and leadeth them away carefully down to hell."

DECEPTION AND LIES (D&C 10:25): "Yea, he saith unto them: Deceive and lie in wait to catch, that ye may destroy; behold, this is no harm. And thus he flattereth them, and telleth them that it is no sin to lie that they may catch a man in a lie, that they may destroy him."

FLATTERY (2 Nephi 28:22): "And behold, others he flattereth away, and telleth them there is no hell; and he saith unto them: I am no devil, for there is none—and thus he whispereth in their ears, until he grasps them with his awful chains, from whence there is no deliverance."

PRIDE (D&C 23:1): "Behold, thou art blessed, and art under no condemnation. But beware of pride, lest thou shouldst enter into temptation."

SPIRIT OF CONTENTION (3 Nephi 11:29): "For verily, verily I say unto you, he that hath the spirit of contention is not of me, but is of the devil, who is the father of contention, and he stirreth up the hearts of men to contend with anger, one with another."

"BUT IT'S NOT MY FAULT"

The single most difficult task I've had as a parent is to convince my kids that they are in control, that they (and only they) make choices which determine the course of their lives.

Teenagers must understand that they have control over their emotions *and* their lives. Agency isn't just some nebulous idea that sounds good—it's NATURAL LAW.

Nobody—not a mother, a father, a boyfriend, or a girlfriend—can make anyone else happy. I've often told my glowering offspring, "*You are the only one who can cheer you up. By the same token, you are the only one who can make you mad.*"

I learned this fact of life several years ago, and it has made all the difference to my peace of mind, as well as my parenting skills.

Gary came up with a phrase that summarizes this point nicely, "Life is a test—to react positively to negative situations."

Those words are deceptively simple. Like Naman, the man Ezekiel told to cure himself of leprosy by washing seven times in the River Jordan, most of us have a hard time believing something simple can solve complex problems.

One of my foster daughters continually fought with her teachers at school. She'd come home furious about the way she'd been treated. She cried and stomped around the house and clearly expected sympathy, if not irate parental action (such as our demanding to have the teacher fired).

Obviously, she wasn't doing very well in her classes. She had a .03 grade-point average and was suspended several times.

Nothing changed for her until she changed her attitude. I convinced her that she didn't have to react with anger if a teacher unfairly singled her out for talking or wouldn't let her go to the bathroom or to fetch her misplaced homework from her locker.

She finally understood that she *chose* her reaction. She couldn't control what the teacher (or other kids or friends) said or did; she could only control how she responded.

My daughter's hysterics, anger, and righteous indignation only brought her suspension and failing grades. When she began to "react positively to the negative situation," her grades rose, her appearance changed, and she felt better about herself.

QUALITIES OF CHARITY

Read Moroni 7:45-46 for the Lord's definition of charity. Discuss the scripture with your teenager to come up with terms that fit the following definitions:

_____   1.   Is not jealous, discontented, or envious.

_____ 2. Is clean in thought and action.

_____ 3. Always looks for good in others; is not suspicious or hateful.

_____ 4. Is trusting and believing, exhibits confidence in others.

_____ 5. Forgives, forgets, and tries again. Does not judge or hold grudges.

_____ 6. Is kind, thoughtful and concerned for others; is patient, even under adversity.

_____ 7. Studies and lives the gospel; speaks the truth and searches for the truth; improves talents, disposition, and relationship with others.

_____ 8. Does not lose temper, is not overly sensitive; returns good for evil.

_____ 9. Bears injustice with dignity; endures misfortune with fortitude.

_____ 10. Sets high goals and has faith in the ability to reach them; is optimistic and develops an attitude of happiness.

_____ 11. Is humble—not self-righteous, conceited or proud.

_____ 12. Seeks only uplifting entertainment, does not (even secretly) rejoice over others' trials or wrongdoing; does not gossip or criticize.

_____ 13. Is not self-centered or selfish; is thoughtful of the feelings, desires, and needs of others; expresses appreciation.

_____ 14. Reacts to disappointments, sorrows, and trials with dignity; keeps the channel of communication open with Heavenly Father.

_____ 15. Sets the celestial kingdom as a goal.

(Adapted from Course 15 manual.)

FOOD FOR THOUGHT

"I got two A's," the small boy said.
His voice was filled with glee.
His father very bluntly asked,
"Why didn't you get three?"

"Mom, I've got the dishes done."
The girl called from the door.
Her mother very calmly said,
"Did you sweep the floor?"

The children in the house next door
Seemed happy and content.
The same things happened over there,
But this is how it went:

"I got two A's," the small boy said.
His voice was filled with glee.
His father proudly said,
"That's great! I'm glad you belong to me."

"Mom, I've got the dishes done."
The girl called from the door.
Her mother smiled and softly said,
"Each day I love you more."

Children deserve a little praise
For tasks they're asked to do,
If they are to lead a happy life,
So much depends on you.

Author Unknown

266

ABOUT THE AUTHOR

Corrie Lynne Player holds bachelor's and master's degrees from
Stanford University. A recognized writer educated in child care and
family-related issues, she has published numerous articles in *Family
Circle, Woman's Day, Parents, McCall's, Ladies Home Journal, American
Baby,* and other magazines. She has written about, consulted with, and
helped organize such programs as Tough Love, Adoption Advocates,
and Families Anonymous. She has also served as one of Utah's delegates
at two National Foster Parents Association conferences.

Corrie Lynne is currently President and CEO of Tahoma
Companies, a geotechnical and environmental engineering firm. She
also has a growing part-time business in individual and family counseling. She and her husband, Gary, frequently speak to community and
school groups about problems confronting teenagers. They also work
together to provide marriage counseling for dysfunctional families.

Corrie Lynne and Gary, who make their home in Cedar City,
Utah, are the parents of nine children and grandparents of twelve. Their
special needs foster home has sheltered more than forty children over
the past thirty years, during which they have also cared for and healed
disturbed adolescents. They credit Christ-centered principles for their
success in handling troubled children.